Class Act

Class Act

Readings for Canadian Writers

Gary Webb   Donna Kerrigan

HARCOURT
BRACE
CANADA

HARCOURT BRACE & COMPANY, CANADA
Toronto   Montreal   Fort Worth   New York   Orlando
Philadelphia   San Diego   London   Sydney   Tokyo

Requests for permission to make copies of any part of the work should be mailed to: Permissions, College Division, Harcourt Brace & Company, Canada, 55 Horner Avenue, Toronto, Ontario M8Z 4X6.

Every reasonable effort has been made to acquire permission for copyright material used in this text, and to acknowledge all such indebtedness accurately. Any errors and omissions called to the publisher's attention will be corrected in future printings.

Canadian Cataloguing in Publication Data

Kerrigan, Donna, 1952–
  Class act: Readings for Canadian writers

Includes bibliographical references and index.
ISBN 0–7747–3556–2

1. Readers (Secondary). 2. College readers.
3. Readers – Essays. 4. Canadian essays (English).*
5. English language – Rhetoric. I. Webb, Gary.
II. Title

PE1417.K47 1996   808.4   C96–930972–4

Director of Product Development: *Heather McWhinney*
Acquisitions Editor: *Kelly V. Cochrane*
Projects Manager: *Liz Radojkovic*
Developmental Editor: *Su Mei Ku*
Director of Publishing Services: *Jean Davies*
Editorial Manager: *Marcel Chiera*
Supervising Editor: *Semareh Al-Hillal*
Production Editor: *Louisa Schulz*
Production Manager: *Sue-Ann Becker*
Production Co-ordinator: *Sheila Barry*
Copy Editor: *Gail Marsden*
Cover Design: *Steve Eby Production and Design*
Typesetting and Assembly: *Matthew Beck & Sharon Moroney*
Printing and Binding: *Best Book Manufacturers*

Cover Image: Christiane Pflug, *Kitchen Door with Ursula*, 1966, oil on canvas, 164.8 x 193.2 cm. Ernest Mayer, Winnipeg Art Gallery; purchased with the assistance of The Women's Committee and The Winnipeg Foundation (Accession #G-66-89). Reproduced with permission.

This book was printed in Canada.
1 2 3 4 5   01 00 99 98 97

Preface

Class Act: Readings for Canadian Writers carries on in the tradition of the previous text, *Who's Going to Read This Anyway?* This new edition preserves the concept that a writer's most important concern is to communicate effectively with a real (though perhaps unseen) reader. *Who's* posed a challenge; *Class Act* suggests a style.

The act of writing is essentially an act of generosity. To communicate effectively, the writer must look beyond a self-centred urge to transmit his or her message and look instead into the mind of the reader. This is not to say that the writer's message is unimportant — without it, nothing gets communicated at all — but classy writing doesn't just stand on a soap box. Instead, it carefully articulates an invitation to the reader to follow a line of thought, and to make such an invitation the writer must give painstaking consideration to the reader's needs, biases, and ability to understand. The only type of writing that doesn't demand this type of reflection is journaling, the recording of one's own thoughts strictly for private purposes.

Any other writing necessitates a willingness to see things from the reader's point of view. The serious writer asks, "How can I convince the Minister of Justice to change the government's position on parole?" Or, "What tone must I take in this letter to show the employer I would be a careful and diligent worker?" Or, "How can I show the professor that the extensive research I have done proves my point without annoying her with a string of quotations from various sources?" Generous writers work hard to find the best answers to such questions, in contrast to the dogmatic or self-centred ones, who never bother to ask.

Many of the writing experiences in this text designate peers as the intended audience, so writers have instant readership, sitting right in the next desk. Since most writing is an attempt to reach out to others, the classroom is really an ideal place to test the product, because there fellow students may find companionship in their struggle to find a style that works for the reader. This text encourages novice writers to give their ideas a dry run by sharing them verbally or in draft form with others. But a word of caution is in order: classmates should agree from the very beginning to hear each other out and give honest appraisals, since nothing is worse than bravely showing forth one's efforts and gaining nothing from the experience. Students sometimes make the mistake of believing they should all praise one another, and thus they conspire to applaud each offering, no matter how feeble it is or how likely to suffer at the hands of real critics. Likely these are misguided efforts toward friendship, but they contribute nothing toward writing that will be judged a real "class act."

We would not feel honest if we didn't say that really good writing is hard work. It's difficult enough for the writer to think of what he or she wants to say; even more so to consider how to make those ideas acceptable or understandable to a reader. To guide writers through the process (and we emphasize that it *is* a process, not a simple one-shot deal) *Class Act* provides a variety of essays on a wide range of topics to meet as many interests as possible. The "Style and Structure" part of each chapter allows students to analyze the reading critically by discussing its component parts and evaluating how effectively they work together to achieve the writer's purpose. There are no brownie points for being agreeable here, so if students feel a writer hasn't made a point clearly enough they should be encouraged to share their opinions. In doing so, students can promote greater awareness of what appeals to readers — and what doesn't.

The "Warm-up" section is provided in recognition that most of us need a sort of intellectual kick-start to our writing, just as athletes need stretches to help them limber up before a race. Generally, these exercises are intended to take just a few minutes to stimulate thought and action as a prelude to the real work at hand. Properly done, these exercises should help energize the writer and sustain him or her through the longer process that follows.

The final section of each chapter, "Thinking and Writing," offers a choice of assignments and generally designates an audience to keep in mind. Writers should understand that they may quote from the essay studied in the chapter to support their ideas, or they may prepare ahead of time by interviewing, researching in the print or electronic media, or discussing with peers in a group setting. Once again, viewing all writing as an act of generosity means the writer can almost always be open to what others think or have written on the subject. Including the contributions of others in an original work has traditionally given students difficulty, so a new section entitled "Fair Usage" (page 220) has been included as well.

Finally, a section at the back of the book has been devoted to an outline of the process of writing and the components of an essay, plus an investigation of the more common grammar and word selection problems. Words appearing throughout the text in **bold face** can be found with explanation and examples in this section.

On a more personal note, we would like to mention that this book is the product of many years of teaching and writing on a professional level, and, on the home front, of guiding our kids through the joys and frustrations of writing during their school years. Many of the difficulties they encountered as students have inspired passages of this text. So this book is written particularly for them, especially the ones who aren't finished their education yet.

We know we never will be.

The Instructor's Manual for *Class Act* supplements the text so teachers can be flexible in adapting it quickly to their individual classroom needs. It provides structural analyses to complement the "Style and Structure" sections and detailed writing exercises leading to the essay topics in the "Thinking and Writing" sections. Other features of the Instructor's Manual include

- A bank of alternate essay topics for various organizational structures
- masters for overheads to teach organizational structures
- formats for debates
- proofreading and editing exercises

Acknowledgements

This book is a product of wide consultation and discussion. We are indebted to those who responded to our survey, especially to the teachers at Cambrian College. Their wise comments and suggestions have greatly enhanced the book.

For kind permission to reprint the selections in this text, acknowledgement is hereby made to the following:

David Suzuki, "Monster Threatening Earth Is Us." Reprinted with permission of the author.

Neil Sandell, "Roller Coaster Heaven," *Canadian Heritage*, Fall 1988. Reprinted with permission of the author.

Elaine Carey, "Crime Rate's Down, Our Fears Are Up," *The Toronto Star*, 20 August 1995, A1, A12. Reprinted with permission of The Toronto Star Syndicate. Figures 1–4 accompanying Carey article were provided by the authors, G. Webb and D. Kerrigan. Information was taken from Statistics Canada. Readers wishing further information on data provided through the co-operation of Statistics Canada may obtain copies of related publications by mail from: Publications Sales, Statistics Canada, Ottawa, Ontario, K1A 0T6, by calling 1-613-951-7277 or toll-free 1-800-267-6677. Readers may also facsimilie their order by dialing 1-613-951-1584 Figure 5 was taken from research done by The Fraser Institute.

Jennifer Hunter, "Baby, It's Yours," *The Globe and Mail*.

Brenda Yablon, "Repeat Performances," *Homemaker's Magazine*, May/June 1988. Reprinted with permission of the author.

Charles Gordon, "How Dumbed-Down Can Things Get?" *Maclean's*, 12 February 1996, 9. Reprinted with permission of the author. Charles Gordon is a columnist for *The Ottawa Citizen* and *Maclean's*.

Greg Heaton, Lori Cohen, and Patrick McManus, "An Alternative to Incarceration," *Alberta Report*. Reprinted with permission of Alberta Report. (Alberta Report is also called Western Report.)

Rona Maynard, "Why Men Are Mad as Hell," *Chatelaine*, December 1988. Reprinted with permission of the author.

John Colapinto, "Crowd Control," *Saturday Night*. Reprinted with permission of the author. John Colapinto is a contributing editor at *Rolling Stone Magazine*.

Adapted from Stevie Cameron, "Saying Goodbye," *On the Take: Crime, Corruption and Greed in the Mulroney Years* (Toronto: Macfarlane, Walter & Ross, 1994), 1–2. Reprinted with permission of the publisher.

Mayo Mohs, "The Making of a Wasteland." © 1984 Discover Magazine. Reprinted with permission of Discover Syndication.

Excerpts from Guy Saddy, "Do Computers Change How We Think?" *Equinox*, May/June 1996, 54, 56, 57, & 63. Reprinted with permission of author.

A Note from the Publisher

Thank you for selecting *Class Act: Readings for Canadian Writers* by Gary Webb and Donna Kerrigan. The authors and publisher have devoted considerable time and care to the development of this book. We appreciate your recognition of this effort and accomplishment.

We want to hear what you think about *Class Act*. Please take a few minutes to fill in the stamped reply card at the back of the book. Your comments and suggestions will be valuable to us as we prepare new editions and other books.

Contents

Thematic Table of Contents

Monster Threatening Earth Is Us

by David Suzuki

Science-fiction writers have long recognized that an invader from outer space   1
could unite all earthlings in a battle against a common enemy.

Imagine that as that alien runs across the planet, it crushes an acre of forest   2
with each step, scrapes a wide swath of topsoil, blows noxious carbon com-
pounds into the upper atmosphere, and sprays toxic chemicals into the air,
water, and land. We would instantly declare a global crisis endangering all life
on Earth and marshal all of our forces to do battle with the threat. Today, we are
facing precisely those dangers, yet we are doing little to counter them.

That's because the monster is us. Consider the straight facts, the ones   3
about which there is no controversy.

We are overrunning the planet like an out-of-control malignancy. There are   4
far more of us than any other large mammal on the planet, and we keep adding
to our numbers by 90 million every year.

We are destroying our soils. Twenty-five billion tons of agricultural topsoil   5
are swept away annually. That's seven percent of the globe's good growing land
every decade. As well, vast areas are being degraded by poor land use. A report
by Senator Herbert Sparrow in June 1984 concluded that Canadian farms are
mining our soil, degrading it by failing to replace the organic content of farm-
land. Consequently, since 1984, global food production has declined each year.
And this is precisely at the time that human population is exploding.

The devastation is unrelenting. Every five minutes around the clock,   6
365 days a year, a major shipment of chemicals crosses an international border to be disposed of somewhere, somehow; no place on this planet is free of
the toxic debris of technology. Every minute, 50 to 100 acres of tropical
forests are destroyed, and the rate of destruction is accelerating. Every year,
at least 20 000 species disappear forever, and the rate of extinction is speeding up. Every year, in spite of two decades of research and contention, acid
rain sterilizes thousands of lakes and kills whole forests.

In addition, greenhouse heating of the planet is being caused by human   7
beings through our use of fossil fuels (which release carbon dioxide), our farming
of cattle (which produce methane), and our production of chemicals (such as
CFCs). Warming is already under way, and the agricultural and ecological
consequences over the next decades will be totally unprecedented and unpre-
dictable. Even after CFCs are completely eliminated, ozone thinning will continue
for years as CFCs already in use escape into the air.

8   The 1978 UN-sponsored Brundtland Commission on world environment and development documented the obscene disparity between the industrialized nations and the Third World. Making up only twenty percent of the world's population, industrialized countries consume 80 percent of the planet's resources and generate most of its industrial toxins and wastes. Any attempt by the Third World to achieve a level of affluence comparable to ours will be suicidal.

9   The challenge, then, is clear. We in the industrialized world must abandon immediately the notion that we must have continued growth, greater consumption, and more material goods. We are already using an immoral amount and we, not the Third World, are the major cause of the current environmental crises.

10   At the same time, we have to help the developing countries raise their standard of education and living in order to reduce their birth rate and avoid exploiting environmentally destructive technologies such as dams, coal burning, CFC refrigerators, etc. Out of pure self-interest, we have to pay to ensure a higher standard of living and more efficient and ecologically benign development in developing countries. We share this finite world with all other people and can no longer treat the disadvantaged of the earth as recklessly as we have in the past.

11   Stanford University's Paul Ehrlich points out that people can make major changes swiftly. After Pearl Harbor, we sacrificed, we cut back, we changed our lifestyle, and we fought for survival. Today, "we face a million ecological Pearl Harbors at once," Ehrlich says, "and that's the scale of public response that's needed now."

12   We are now in a war to save this planet. Small groups all over the country are drawing their own battle lines, but federal muscle is essential. There is money and personnel — military defence should be redirected to environmental defence while our soldiers can fight oil spills and PCB fires or help to reforest and rehabilitate damaged ecosystems. The war metaphor is appropriate — we are battling to keep the planet livable for our children.

13   In the science-fiction stories, human ingenuity and courage usually win out over the aliens from outer space, but this isn't make-believe — it's real and the monster is here.

Style and Structure

1.   Write a one-paragraph description of this essay's intended reader. Support your conclusions with specific references to the text.

2. (a) Write a short summary of Dr. Suzuki's **thesis**.

  (b) Identify the sentence in the introduction that presents this **thesis** to the reader.

3. (a) Explain three advantages Dr. Suzuki gains by using the science fiction analogy in his introduction.

  (b) Why would Dr. Suzuki not reveal the identity of the alien invader until the third paragraph?

  (c) Given the intended reader, why is his use of this science fiction analogy appropriate? For what kinds of readers do you think this analogy might be less effective? Why?

4. (a) Write a point-form summary of the topic dealt with in each paragraph in the body of the essay (paragraphs 4 to 12).

  (b) Does each of these topics relate to the **thesis** announced in the introduction? Does the essay have unity?

  (c) These topics are grouped together into two sections, each of which presents one aspect of the **thesis**. What aspect is dealt with in each section? Why might Dr. Suzuki have chosen to present these sections in the order that he has?

5. In what ways does paragraph 13 act as an effective **conclusion** for this essay?

6. Dr. Suzuki uses a number of techniques to gain the reader's acceptance of his ideas.

  (a) Identify two examples of Dr. Suzuki's use of the following types of supporting arguments:

   (i) citing an authority;

   (ii) statistics.

   For each, explain the reasons for its effectiveness in convincing the reader.

  (b) Choose any paragraph in the first section of the body. How many facts does Dr. Suzuki provide concerning the topic dealt with in that paragraph? What is the effect of providing so many specific details in each paragraph? How does this quantity of detail affect the reader's acceptance of the suggestions in the second half of the essay? Why?

  (c) Identify four examples of the subtle use of emotionally charged words (e.g., "malignancy") to develop the reader's almost unconscious agreement with the essay's ideas. Explain the effect achieved by each.

  (d) What special technique does Dr. Suzuki use in paragraph 6 to drive home the urgency of the situation? How well does it work? Why?

(e) What is the effect of his using the first person plural ("we," "our," and "ours") throughout the essay?

(f) How do his references to Pearl Harbor in paragraph 11 affect the reader?

Warm-up

Together with three or four others from your class, use the library to research measures that are being taken (or could be taken) to overcome one of the ecological problems mentioned by Dr. Suzuki.

Working on your own, write a short report of your findings. Then, with the others in your group, use your reports as the basis for a five to ten minute group presentation to the class.

Thinking and Writing

1. Sometimes when we read essays like this one we feel helpless in the face of such global problems. Yet, as Dr. Suzuki points out, if we are going to avoid ecological disaster, each and every one of us is going to have to make changes in our way of life.

    Write an essay that suggests one action that everyone in your community could practise to help in this war. Try to convince your reader to implement your idea.

    Audience: the average person living in your community.

    When you have completed your final draft, share it with several others in the class; see how many of their suggestions you can adopt into the way you live.

2. Write an essay outlining a program that could be implemented by the municipal, provincial, or federal government to fight one of the environmental problems described by Dr. Suzuki.

    Audience: a politician in a position to influence government policy.

    Send a copy of the final draft to your local representative at the appropriate level of government and ask for comments on your suggestions.

Roller Coaster Heaven

by Neil Sandell

It lasts 114 seconds. A white-knuckle, heart-in-your-mouth, dizzying, tizzying,   1
scream-at-the-top-of-your-lungs 114 seconds. By Terror Standard Time, it's an
eternity. I stagger off hoping the bloom will return to my ashen cheeks, perhaps
by next month. My guide, Tim Sykes, doesn't budge from his seat. Grinning
from ear to ear, he waits for one more ride. At least one more.

Tim is a roller coaster aficionado. The objects of his affection are the coasters   2
at Crystal Beach Park in Ontario's Niagara peninsula. With the Giant, the second-
oldest roller coaster in North America, and the Comet, a middle-aged but feisty 42-
year-old, Crystal Beach comes as close to roller coaster heaven as you can get.

Heaven, and the pursuit thereof, was the whole idea at Crystal Beach   3
from the beginning. One hundred years ago, the site attracted revival camp
meetings. Over the then-sparkling waters of Lake Erie, the faithful travelled
by excursion steamship from nearby Buffalo, New York, for a day of religion
and recreation. This early version of R&R soon gave way to worship of an
earthier variety. By the 1890s, Crystal Beach had turned into a full-fledged
amusement park complete with sideshows. A ferris wheel was built, along
with a scenic railway, and finally, in 1916, the wooden-trestled Giant roller
coaster.

Today, the Giant is venerated by coaster buffs from around the world. A   4
plaque from American coaster enthusiasts commemorates its seventieth birthday. But the Giant almost didn't make it that far. In 1982, Crystal Beach Park
was caught in the interest rate squeeze and fell into receivership. Devotees
despaired. They flocked to Crystal Beach for one last ride on their cherished
coasters. They filmed the Giant and the Comet for posterity.

Then, a trio of businessmen plucked Crystal Beach from the brink. The   5
coasters were saved. Now, if anything, they're more secure. In 1986, atten-
dance at the park soared by 54 percent, and in 1987 by another 28 percent. By
the end of summer 1988, between 325 thousand and 350 thousand people had
visited Crystal Beach.

The Giant is like an old friend to Tim Sykes. He figures he has ridden it at   6
least 100 times. It's what is called a side friction coaster. Coaster connoisseurs
care about such things. Simply put, the trains aren't bolted to the rails. The
sheer weight of the cars keeps the coaster on track. Unlike the banked curves
of a modern coaster, the corners are flat. Sykes says the Giant is like a big
comfy sofa. It's slow and smooth, and its charm is nostalgic.

7   But the Comet is Sykes' first love. Sykes got hooked on roller coasters nine years ago. He had read about the Crystal Beach Comet in a *Weekend Magazine* article listing "100 Best Things About Canada." One thrilling ride, and he was smitten.

8   Since then, the 31-year-old dental technician from Cambridge, Ontario, has travelled to Nashville, San Diego, Coney Island, and Myrtle Beach, South Carolina, in pursuit of his hobby. The Crystal Beach coasters stand up to the best. The Comet is "fast from start to finish. They run it flat out, and that is one of the joys."

9   The Comet is routinely rated among the top ten coasters in the world. At 35 metres, its highest arch affords a spectacular, if brief, *reconnoitre* of the countryside. Its first big drop plunges the equivalent of ten storeys. The coaster reaches a heart-stopping 100 kilometres per hour. You feel as though you're plummeting into Lake Erie. If you have your eyes open.

10   Sykes says there's a technique to riding a coaster like the Comet. "You have to ride with the ride. If you fight it, hold your head down, or close your eyes, you'll end up getting bumped pretty good. What you have to do is look for the hills. If they're going down, you just kind of float."

11   Float indeed.

12   It's hard to imagine, but the Comet was built to replace a more terrifying coaster, the legendary Cyclone. It was dismantled after only twenty years. According to folklore, the Cyclone was so frightening that the park employed a nurse to attend to woozy passengers.

13   Tim Sykes says he relishes the legend surrounding the ghost coaster. It lives in his imagination, kindled by memories passed on by his father. In his collection of coaster memorabilia, Sykes prizes the ageing postcards of the Cyclone. As Sykes waits patiently for another spin on the Cyclone's "tame" successor, he laments the fact that he was born too late to ride the original as his father did.

14   It's a pity, I agree. Chances are, Tim Sykes wouldn't have needed the nurse.

Style and Structure

1. (a) Sandell begins his essay with the words "It lasts 114 seconds." What is "It"? Where do you discover this information?

   (b) What is your immediate reaction to the first paragraph? Is the writer successful in grabbing your interest? If so, how has he managed it?

2.   What is the role of paragraphs 2 through 5? How different would the tone of the essay have been if the writer had begun with paragraph 2, instead of with the introduction he devised?

3. (a) Write out paragraph 6, sentence by sentence. What is the unifying factor that holds these sentences together?

  (b) Can you suggest ways in which the unity of the paragraph might be improved? Rewrite the paragraph, illustrating your suggestions.

4. (a) Throughout the essay, the writer gives a fair amount of technical information about the functioning of roller coasters, particularly the Comet. Do you think readers interested in roller coasters want this sort of information? Explain your opinion.

  (b) How successful do you think the writer has been in presenting this technical information in a readable fashion? Why?

5. Very likely, Sandell could have written his essay without employing the figure of Tim Sykes at all. Yet Tim plays an important role. In one well-developed paragraph, examine the role of Tim Sykes, using specific references to the essay.

6. (a) Examine the **topic sentence** of each paragraph as a means of determining what that paragraph is about. Then, devise an outline of the essay, one such as Sandell might have used if he had been working from an outline. Into how many sections do you find the essay divided?

  (b) Make a list of the **transitional devices** Sandell uses throughout his essay. Comment on the effectiveness of these devices in helping the reader to follow the thread of meaning from section to section.

Warm-up

Discover some of the techniques that good writers use to convey heightened emotions to their readers. Find a sample of writing that contains very emotional passages and answer the following questions about it.

  (i) What emotion does the passage attempt to evoke?

  (ii) How many strong action verbs can you identify in the passage? (Write a list.)

  (iii) How many colourful adjectives? (Write a list.)

  (iv) How are sentences structured to suit the action?

  (v) How are paragraphs structured to suit the action?

  (vi) Roughly, on a scale of one to ten, with ten being "most successful," how would you rate the writer's success in conveying the emotion in (i) to the reader?

Read aloud to the class the passage you have chosen. Then, after all passages are read, hold a class discussion, focussing on comparing your answers to questions (i) through (vi) above.

Thinking and Writing

1. Even very good writers acknowledge the challenge of describing an emotion-filled experience in such a way that the reader is not put off — either by the personal nature of the experience or by the lavishness of the language used to describe it. The trick is to write so that the readers share the experience, even if they have never had the opportunity themselves.

    List some "white-knuckle" experiences you have had and choose one. In a small group, relate the experience aloud so that your listeners get some insight into the emotions the experience stimulated for you. You may wish to jot down a few notes beforehand, concentrating on how you can introduce the subject so that your listeners are brought into the experience itself.

    Write your descriptive essay, following Sandell's example of providing some nonemotional information about the subject as well. Be sure that your reader is informed, not just emotionally affected, by your writing.

    Audience: people who may not have had the experience themselves.

2. In his essay, Sandell mentions an article that appeared in *Weekend Magazine*, entitled "100 Best Things About Canada." Draw up your own list of five "best things" — specific attractions either in Canada or in your immediate area. Using your list as the basis for an outline, write an essay developing each of the five examples.

    Throughout the essay, keep in mind the value of drawing the reader into the experience of the attractions. Be careful to provide an appropriate introduction, so that your readers know what unifying principle ties the examples together. You might consider developing your essay as a list, numbering each example.

    Audience: someone who is not familiar with these attractions.

    Send your final essay to a local tourism board.

Crime Rate's Down, Our Fears Are Up

by Elaine Carey

It just doesn't add up. 1

The average citizen — fueled by politicians, the police and the media — 2
firmly believes that young people are out of control, guns and drugs are everywhere and murderers and rapists plague our streets.

Fear of crime is the public's fastest growing concern, rising relentlessly 3
over the past decade; yet the crime rate for every kind of offence has gone
down just as steadily for the third year in a row.

Consider the following: 4

- Almost half the public believes violent crime is on the increase yet violent
  crime fell 3 per cent last year, the biggest drop since 1982, according to
  Statistics Canada. Murder is at a 25-year low.

- In his law and order campaign, Ontario's Premier Mike Harris pledged to 5
  set up boot camps for young offenders to whip them back into shape. Yet
  the youth crime rate went down 6 per cent last year and has declined
  steadily for three years.

- The federal Liberals passed a controversial gun control law in June, 1995, 6
  to deal with a perceived growing problem; yet only 6 per cent of violent
  crimes involve firearms, a rate that has stayed stable for the past 10 years.

- Burglar alarm sales are going through the roof — one former police 7
  chief is even on the radio urging homeowners to buy a particular brand
  — yet break and enters went down 6 per cent last year for the third year
  in a row. In Toronto, for instance, Metro police handled 75,985 alarm
  calls last year and only 3,166 were valid, costing the taxpayers a whopping $12 million.

- A growing number of women report carrying a weapon, buying a dog, tak- 8
  ing self-defence courses and staying home in the evening to protect themselves. Yet across Canada, nine women were killed by strangers last year
  (down from 30 in 1980), while 97 were killed by their spouses.

- Parents are taking all kinds of measures to protect their children from 9
  strangers, from fingerprinting them to refusing to let them out of the house
  alone. Yet abductions account for less than 1 per cent of all violent crime,
  a rate that has stayed the same for a decade, and six in 10 are abducted by
  one of their own parents.

10 • The highest murder rate for any age group is among babies under a year old and almost all were killed by a parent.

11 This list goes on and on. But perception has become reality to the point where reality can't get in the way. So when Statistics Canada's Centre for Justice Statistics released its annual report on crime rates in August, 1995, Reform Party critic Diane Ablonczy simply refused to acknowledge them. "I would tend to say, to put more belief, more credibility, more credence in what people are telling me than what Statistics Canada might come out with in a particular report," she said.

12 The statistics are compiled from reports submitted by Canada's police departments, but even the police disagree on their significance. "Statistics are not really totally accurate in painting the picture," said Toronto Police Sergeant Nigel Fontaine. "It's probably improper to even use statistics to measure the whole mix of society and whether it's violent or not. I think the public should be afraid of crime and they should put more pressure on politicians to give more money to the police."

Figure 1: CRIME BY COUNTRY

Country	Number homicides	Rate per 100,000	Number property crimes	Rate per 100,000	Number sex assault*	Rate per 100,000
Canada (1994)	596	2.0	1,524,931	5,213.8	31,690	108.3
US (1994)	23,305	9.0	12,100,000	4,658.0	102,096	77 per 100,000 females
Denmark (1992)	237	6.0	295,039	6,873.0	556	13.0
New Zealand (6/91–6/92)	53	1.5	100,604	287.0	1,193	34.0

* US law refers to "forcible rape"; Canadian statistics distinguish between "sexual assault" and "other sexual offences" (not included here). Statistics from Denmark and New Zealand refer to "rape."

SOURCES: Statistics Canada, *The Daily*, August 02 1995; Federal Bureau of Investigation (US), November 19 1995; *World Factbook of Criminal Justice Systems*.

Figure 2: CRIME RATES FOR SELECTED CITIES
(RATES PER 100,000 POPULATION)

	Violent crime rate (1994)	% change (1993 to 1994)	Property crime rate (1994)	% change (1993 to 1994)	Total crime (1994)	% change (1993 to 1994)
Halifax	1,762	2.0	7,761	−13.0	13,739	−9.3
Montreal	1,359	−0.1	6,703	−9.4	10,278	−7.4
Ottawa	1,524	−14.8	9,859	−2.0	16,019	−4.5
Toronto	1,252	−6.4	5,515	−8.5	9,579	−7.0
Winnipeg	1,371	1.8	7,877	3.7	12,254	0.7
Regina	1,091	−1.1	9,333	3.3	13,643	0.2
Calgary	858	3.1	6,271	−14.7	8,871	−13.7
Edmonton	1,097	−20.7	6,618	−17.8	10,223	−19.0
Vancouver	1,636	−4.8	13,440	4.5	19,260	1.4

SOURCE: Statistics Canada, *The Daily*, August 02 1995

Figure 3: POLICE-REPORTED INCIDENTS OF VIOLENT CRIME 1994

	Number	Rate per 100,000	% change in rate from 1993	Youths aged 12–17 as % of persons charged
Total	303,398	1,037.3	−3.2	15
Homicide	596	2.0	−6.4	11
Attempted murder	918	3.1	−7.7	15
Assaults	236,364	808.1	−1.9	13
Sexual assaults	31,690	108.3	−9.8	15
Other sex offences	3,812	13.0	−9.6	16
Abduction	1,130	3.9	−7.1	6
Robbery	28,888	98.8	−4.6	31

SOURCE: Statistics Canada, *The Daily*, August 02 1995

13   So what's going on here?

14   The simple explanation is the aging population, the experts say. The crime rate is down because the big mass of the population, the baby boomers, are now in their 30s and 40s and crime is largely committed by youth aged 15 to 24. University of Toronto demographer David Foot explains that the typical crime of a 19-year-old is a break and enter, with no physical contact. But a 29-year-old moves up to robbery with a gun.

15   The peak of the baby boom, born in 1960, reached 19 in 1979 so through the '60s and '70s, the largest number of crimes were those relatively minor break-ins committed by teenagers, he said. By the early '80s, the crime rate flattened out. But when the peak of the baby boom hit 29 in the late '80s, there was a corresponding increase in violent crimes, peaking in 1990, "That's why people are more fearful because the crimes are more violent," Foot said.

16   At the same time, as you get older "your tolerance for crime goes down and your fear of crime goes up, even though your actual risk of being a victim is lower," said U of T sociologist Rosemary Gartner. "That creates this odd variance between the reality of the crime rate and the perception." And everyone in the world wants to feed that perception. The media use it to sell their products, politicians to get votes, and police forces to increase their budgets.

17   "You get politicians and police — people who should know better — talking about crime going up as though it were an undisputed fact," said Anthony Doob, a U of T criminologist. "I don't blame somebody on the street for not

Figure 4: ACCUSED OF BREAKING AND ENTERING

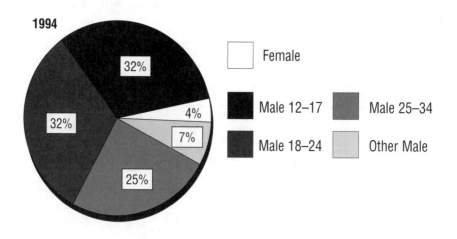

SOURCE: Statistics Canada, *The Daily*, September 25 1995

knowing, but you hope a politician would. You think they would be informed enough to tell people the truth."

Yet when Ontario's Mike Harris announced his sweeping budget cuts after the election, the only two departments spared were health and the police. And he promised to "take the cuffs off the police and put them back on criminals" by reinvesting all the money saved from streamlining the courts into putting more cops on the street. 18

That decision was based on two false assumptions, Doob says, that there's a serious, growing crime problem and having more police is going to solve it. "It's just pandering to the public's concern about crime," he said. "No politician I know of says 'now we can cut the justice budgets because crime is down and we don't need all these jails.' Nobody's saying that." 19

The media are another major culprit in all of this. "If you look at newsrooms and how many more bodies they throw at crime than anything else, it's a good indication," said John Miller, head of the school of journalism at Ryerson Polytechnic University. "Violent crime is played up for all it's worth. There's a perception that crime news sells papers and makes good pictures on TV. And it's easy to get and cheap to cover." 20

A study by Vancouver's Fraser Institute found that, while the murder rate dropped 8 per cent between 1993 and 1994, reports of murders nearly doubled that year on the CBC and CTV evening news. "By providing people with the sights and sounds, they experience the events much more graphically than if they were to read or hear about it," the export says. "That inflated experience has made people more afraid than they've ever been before. Television news has been extremely successful in presenting a reality that does not exist except in the minds of its viewers and those who produce the programs." 21

Random murders by strangers accounted for a constant 13 to 18 per cent of all murders in the past decade, yet they made up between 75 and 98 per cent of the murders reported on the nightly national newscasts, the report says. 22

"That's totally in opposition to what's really going on out there," the report's author, Lydia Miljan, said in an interview. Television news has become much more entertainment driven," she said. "And a lot of it is to do with news having to compete with tabloid shows in the U.S. 23

"And they have to keep viewers tied to the continuing saga," she said, pointing out that every report from the (Paul) Bernardo trial ended with a rundown of what was coming up the next day. "I argue it's selling murder," she concluded. 24

The problem is the same in the U.S. where the crime rate fell 4 per cent last year but nine in 10 people believe it's on the rise, according to a Gallup poll. High-profile crime creates sensational news coverage and the greater the 25

Figure 5: MEDIA HYPE ON MURDER

The number of television stories on murder has more than doubled in the last six years, although the murder rate in Canada has dropped.

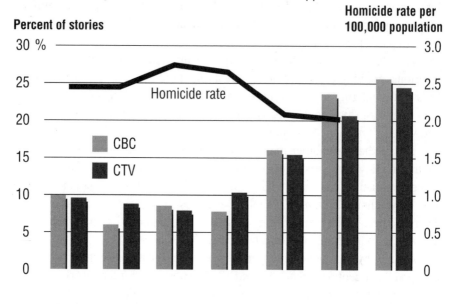

SOURCE: The Fraser Institute

news coverage, the larger the proportion of Americans who cite crime as the most important problem facing the country, according to an analysis by Jeffrey Alderman, director of polling for ABC News.

26   In a once-a-year survey of social trends and attitudes in Canada, Environics Research found fear of violence was the only one of 75 trends that has progressively increased over the past decade.

27   "You see it across a range of areas," said Environics vice-president Donna Dasko. "They're fearful when they walk at night. They don't think sentencing or enforcement or the laws themselves are tough enough. There's a feeling not enough is being done," she said. "It's a concern of the majority in all age groups and every region of the country. You name it, it's all gone up."

28   The high-profile crimes of the last few years, like the random killing of Georgina "Vivi" Leimonis at Just Desserts, a middle-class downtown restaurant, and the sensational Bernardo murder trial really grab the public's attention and inflate its concern about crime, she said. Seventy-nine per cent of Canadians think courts are not harsh enough on criminals, up from 43 per cent in 1966, according to Gallup Canada, and 70 per cent think the federal government isn't doing enough.

Quick facts

- 63% of all homicides occur in one of 12 metropolitan areas, which include 61% of the population.
- 40% of violent incidents against children involve some type of sexual offence; 16% of violence against teens and just 4% against adults involves sex.
- As children and teens, males and females are equally likely to be victims of violent crime. Girls are more likely to be victims of sexual crime; boys, robbery.
- Youths aged 12 to 19, who represent 11% of the population, make up 20% of victims of violent crime. Children, who make up 16% of the population, are victims 6% of the time; adults, 73% of the population, are victims in about the same proportion.
- One in five violent incidents against children and youths accurred at the hands of family members; parents were implicated in half the cases.
- During the 1990s, infants under the age of one year had the highest risk of homicide at a rate of 5.6 per 100,000 population; children had a rate of 1.1; teens, 1.8; adults, 2.7. Parents were accused in two-thirds of child killings.
- The crime rate in Canada dropped 5% in 1994, the third consecutive year of decline, while violent crime dropped 3%, the largest decrease since data collection began in 1962. Reported homicides in 1994 were at their lowest rate in 25 years.

SOURCE: Statistics Canada, *The Daily*, August 02 1995, September 25 1995, December 19 1995

"The sensational stories tend to grip people with concern about their own personal situation," said Gary Edwards, Gallup's managing research director. He added, "People aren't as tied to one place any more. They're more transient. They don't know their community as well. They've lost that sense of stability, that you know everyone on your block. All those things affect people's sense of security." 29

The economy is also a factor, Edwards said. "As people have more personal anxieties around their job and their family, they look for scapegoats. Immigration is one," he added. "And it all gets linked to crime statistics." 30

The public may want tougher sentences, "but tough sentences don't do anything about crime," said Doob. Punishment is a different issue, and people 31 need retribution. "But that's separate from whether it's going to have any impact on how safe we are," he said. "Increasing the number of people we lock up won't do anything about crime.

32   Ironically, a federal justice committee, headed by Bob Horner, a former Mountie and Conservative MP, concluded just that after a four-month study in 1993. "Members of the committee are convinced that threats to the safety and security of Canadians will not be abated by hiring more police officers and building more prisons," said the report.

33   Instead, the committee said the key to ending crime lies in improving the quality of life and rehabilitating those that have gone wrong. And Horner says the time he spent on the committee, hearing testimony from experts, victims, police and community groups, dramatically changed his perspective. "If anyone had told me when I became an MP nine years ago that I'd be looking at the social causes of crime, I'd have told them they were nuts," Horner said at the time. "I'd have said, 'Lock them up for life and throw away the key.' Not any more."

34   The committee's report led to the formation of a national crime prevention council, made up of prominent local citizens, "but that's not sexy, that's not Mike Harris's boot camp that purports to solve the problem," Doob said. "So it doesn't get attention."

35   Foot predicts there's another crime wave on the way, this time in bank and credit card frauds, as the peak of the baby boomers, who can't run as fast as they used to, turn from robberies to less active crimes. And, there's a new wave of break and enters on the horizon as their children, the baby boom echo, hit the teenage years.

36   The fear is not apt to go away.

Style and Structure

1. (a) This essay, which studies violence in Canada and some of our beliefs about the extent of the problem, begins with a very short paragraph: "It just doesn't add up." What is the tone of this paragraph and how might it affect readers?

   (b) Locate the other short single-sentence paragraphs in the essay. What function do they perform?

2.   Identify the **thesis statement** in this essay. How does it set the tone and outline the content of the entire piece?

3.   Evaluate the effectiveness of Carey's opening strategy (Paragraphs 1 through 3). Note that she could have begun with a grabber involving a real-life crime story such as that of Paul Bernardo, mentioned later (Paragraphs 24 and 28). Why do you suppose she chose not to begin with this type of narrative technique?

4. Paragraphs 4 through 10 are marked with bullets and highlight our perceptions of crime.

  (a) As a reader, what is your reaction to the statistics shown in these paragraphs?

  (b) Do you see a progression in the aspects of crime as Carey moves down the list of issues she asks readers to consider?

  (c) Why might she have arranged her material in this way?

5. In Paragraph 11 politician Diane Ablonczy gives her opinion of a report by Statistics Canada on crime rates. How is the reader likely to react to her words, given Carey's discussion in Paragraphs 4 to 10? How might Anthony Doob's comments in Paragraph 17 further influence the reader's reaction?

6. Identify, both by name and by occupation, the experts who give opinions throughout this essay. What institutions have also contributed information? For an essay of this length, how effective do you think Carey's research is? Be ready to explain your appraisal.

7.(a) The major part of this essay deals with why people generally believe crime is on the increase. Which part deals with the causes of our fear and what main causes are highlighted?

  (b) Given all the causes Carey identifies, how successful do you think her essay would be in convincing the general public that their fear of crime is not entirely well founded — that in fact, "it just doesn't add up"?

8. The concluding paragraphs speak of what we are likely to see in the future. How does the tone here compare with that of the introductory paragraphs? What would you say is the writer's outlook on the future?

Warm-up

Canadians are known around the world as a culture that loves to count. In fact, we may be justifiably proud of one institution, Statistics Canada, which is renowned as one of the most dependable — that is, thorough and unbiased — research agencies in the world. Many of us are suspicious of statistics, however. As this essay points out, we tend to discount anything that doesn't support our own preconceived opinions. (See Paragraph 11.) Perhaps the problem is that we don't know how to question the information presented to us.

Take any one of the tables that accompany this essay. In a group or individually, generate as many questions about the content as you possibly can in a short period of time, perhaps 15 or 20 minutes. Discuss your questions with the class and see how satisfied the group is with the completeness of the data and effectiveness of the presentation. As a class, suggest tips for displaying statistical information in your essays.

(You may wish to ask an instructor from the accounting or math departments to give their advice on how to provide convincing data.)

Thinking and Writing

1.   Many experts believe that violent crime gets more coverage in the media than it should, given the relatively small percentage of such crimes committed. For instance, Carey points out that although random murders account for only about 13 to 18 per cent of all murders, they make up between 75 and 98 per cent of murders reported on newscasts (Paragraph 22). With figures like that, it is easy to understand how the average television viewer might misinterpret the severity of the problem.

But do newscasts really give a false impression of the situation? And are certain channels more likely to emphasize the blood-guts-and-gore type of crime than others do? Gather information on the topic yourself by designating certain members of your group or class to watch TV evening newscasts for one specific week. During that time keep a detailed record of reports, the percentage that deal with violent crime, and the length of time given to footage of victims and their injuries, the scenes of the crimes, or re-enactments. Compare results of each student's study and decide which newscasts offer the most distinct contrast in their perspective on crime, from most to least violent. Keep in mind that while TV viewers do not necessarily live in the city where the broadcast originates, they may nonetheless use that station's reports to form their impressions about how dangerous our society is.

Write a compare-contrast essay offering the results of your research and showing which newscast projects the more violent impression of society. Present the findings of your study in tables such as those modelled here. Refer to the warm-up exercise above and give your data in such a way as to avoid any of the criticisms expressed. Finally, conclude by speculating on what effect such news reports have on viewers.

Audience: people who are likely to believe that the evening news shown on TV is the whole truth about our society.

2.   One of the experts whose opinions are cited in this essay, Rosemary Gartner, suggests that as you age "your tolerance for crime goes down

and your fear of crime goes up" (Paragraph 16). Discuss among class-mates and decide on a target age when you would most likely see the variance between reality and perception of crime that Gartner identifies.

Do some research to identify what people of the target age and older think about crime and punishment in Canada. You might like to question a number of individuals about their reaction to some of the facts outlined in Carey's essay, perhaps in a true-or-false quiz. (For example: "True or False? The violent crime rate dropped 3 per cent between 1993 and 1995." Or "True or False? The highest murder rate for any age group is among babies under a year old.")

Compile your results and add documentation from research articles on how the aging process affects social attitudes; if possible, prefer Canadian sources. Then write a descriptive essay in which you offer a profile of the typical citizen of the target age, and his or her opinions on crime and punishment.

Audience: members of the target age group who may be unaware of how their attitudes may have changed over the years.

Select the best essays in the class and send them to a local newspaper for publication.

Baby, It's Yours

by Jennifer Hunter

1   Simone Robin Hunter Cruickshank is a very privileged little girl. A West Coast baby, she has acquired a taste for smoked salmon and salmon caviar sushi. Her cupboard and drawers are stuffed with adorable clothes that carry trendy labels such as Bravo, Esprit, Roots, and Beaver Canoe. Many were bestowed by wealthy great-aunts too young to be grandmothers. For Simone's third birthday last June, her mother (me) and father bought her a $25 green dinosaur cake and a Fisher-Price kitchen for $100. The thirteen pint-sized party guests left with $4 loot bags and appetites sated by Häagen-Dazs ice cream. By the time my husband and I realized what had happened we'd blown at least $200 on the birthday bash. Okay, so I felt several twinges of guilt when I looked at the bills. But since I have the income, I told myself, why not give my only child the best? Besides, my mania for buying her things isn't unique.

2   Thousands of other working women and men, affluent children of the prosperous 1950s and 1960s, are lavishing extraordinary amounts on their offspring. Says one mother, whose basement is filled with Little Tikes toys: "You get the same kind of jollies buying luxuries for your child as you do for yourself." Indeed, retailers have stocked their shelves with so many entrancing items for youngsters that parents almost feel guilty not buying. One father sighs: "It's tough to go out for a walk and avoid the stores."

3   Businesses catering to the under-twelve group are burgeoning; designer clothing boutiques, bookstores, video outlets, and toy shops have sprung up to serve this strategic consumer segment. Retail marketing expert Len Kubas estimates the children's market has grown to a $3.5-billion-a-year phenomenon in Canada.

4   Split families are one reason why we are buying so much for our kids. A third of Canadian marriages end in divorce, and dual households for kids demand dual toy boxes. In families where Mom and Dad remain a unit, it's Mom who does most of the buying, and guilt is often a motive. Three out of five women who have preschool children are in the work force and feel torn between double duties as mothers and career women. They shop to relieve the stress of their inner conflict. "Last week I spent $30 on a train for James," says Alison Pickard, 30. "He wasn't feeling well and I sent him to school. I felt guilty." Sandra Ross-Dixon, 40-year-old mother of two, says: "I try to make up for not being there. So I'll buy things like Speak & Spell or other educational toys so they'll have something stimulating to do when I'm not at home."

Many first-time moms are older, often in their 30s, before their children are born, which means that they are discovering the bliss of motherhood after having established their careers. Not only do they have a lot of disposable income by then, they also have fewer children than their parents did — an average of 1.7 per family. The children become that much more precious. Take the example of Tory Dickinson, a charming, sunny two-year-old. The treasured first-born of working parents, she spends her days in OshKosh overalls and Weebok sneakers. One of her favourite toys is a plastic child-sized shopping cart. "You work hard and you convince yourself the only reason you're working so hard is for the money, so you can spend it on your child," says her mother, securities lawyer Sheila Murray, 32. "When I was growing up you'd go out shopping once or twice a year. You'd get one pair of shoes and one pair of jeans. You'd get gifts on your birthday and at Christmas. With Tory, Dave and I very often go out on the weekend and get her shoes or clothes. She is more indulged."

Another mother, a university professor, confesses that when she goes out shopping for her eight-year-old and three-and-a-half-year-old she can easily spend up to $200. "I have a bag in my cupboard with four unopened toys and six new books. It's like I have this garrison mentality. My mother-in-law has a house full of food, just in case. I have a house full of toys, just in case." Her own mother has splurged on the children, too, buying an elephant slide and chipping in for a $240 Little Tikes playhouse.

Grandparents have become a big factor in boosting retail spending on the under-twelve set. Canadians over the age of 45 are the most prosperous group in the country, with money to burn. They have fewer grandchildren to indulge than their parents did and have had to wait longer for them. Simone's maternal grandmother was 57 when her first grandchild arrived. Mine was just 48 when I arrived on the scene. Grandparents hanker after the opportunity to bestow upon these long-awaited grandchildren the material benefits they could never afford to give their own kids. Ede Ross, 70, has eleven grandchildren, all under the age of ten. She recalls that when her four children were young, they had three sets of clothing. "One on, one in the laundry, and one that was clean." Now her grandchildren are outfitted in designer clothes, many of which were bought by Mrs. Ross herself. "I don't need to buy a lot of things for myself. And I love to see my grandchildren nicely dressed."

Practically every weekday, the enormous shopping mall in the Toronto suburb of Mississauga, Square One, is filled with jeans-clad mothers pushing strollers, and relaxed-looking grandparents browsing through the stores. One area of the mall, Kid's Place, is devoted strictly to children. It has twelve shops selling toys, shoes, clothing, and baby furniture. In the window of a store called Mom & Me is a corduroy jump suit (size two) with a Pierre Cardin label. It's

$73. "When parents need something unique for their children they don't mind spending the money," says Sophie Dawod, the store manager. Naturally, the spending boom has been like manna from heaven for retailers and manufacturers. Even though there were fewer kids between the ages of five and twelve in 1986 than in 1980, retail spending on those kids steadily increased by twelve percent a year, says Glenn Asano of Micromedia Ltd. His company has recently completed a study aimed at companies who want to capture a greater chunk of the children's market. "Children are big business today," the study notes. "The 1980s mini-boom created a huge new demand for trendy, expensive baby and children's clothes, accessories and toys that didn't exist in the 1970s."

9   What's more, kids are demanding, picky, and ruthlessly status-conscious. The study goes on to say: "Children aged nine to twelve have a high level of awareness of the status associated with brands and brand names. This is largely attributable to the pressure they feel from their peers to wear fashionable clothing. When children are actually buying, or are influencing the purchase, they are more likely to choose a quality, brand-name product. Hence, it is important for marketers to plant the first seeds of brand loyalty at an early age." The advice would seem insidious if it were not based on the plain truth. Marlee Ross-Bakker, a Vancouver mother, comments, "I have a niece who is thirteen who will only wear Esprit and Benetton. You don't want to be the only mother who is not letting her kids wear that."

10   Kids, of course, start picking up brand and status consciousness in the cradle, from their parents. There are, for instance, right baby strollers and wrong baby strollers, and the right ones cost $350. Perego stroller salesman Doug Ineson says he is no longer selling utilitarian pushcarts for babies; he is "selling fashion."

11   Parents have extended their generosity to hairdos, books, records, birthday parties, and other forms of entertainment. Derek London, a Vancouver hair-salon owner, opened a children's salon called Headz at the back of a trendy children's boutique two years ago. Boys and girls can watch Pee Wee Herman on video while they get their hair cut by London's stylists. Some little girls even get perms. "It's the only business I've ever opened that's paid for itself in a year," he says. He charges between $15 and $25 for a cut and shampoo and his 600 clients allow him to bring in roughly $5000 a month. Some of the more style-conscious moms are allowing their public-schoolers to get their hair streaked. London says, "If mother is blonder than daughter, she wants her child to look more like her." One Toronto mother says her husband was aghast to learn that she planned to spend $25 on her three-and-a-half-year-old daughter's haircut. "But I know if you have a horrible haircut you look horrible," the mother says. "I want my daughter to look wonderful."

Kids' show biz has become a big item, too, and singers such as Raffi and 12 Sharon, Lois, and Bram are hounded like rock stars for autographs and a pat on the head. The Vancouver Children's Festival, a week-long feast of songs and fun, has been mimicked by fifteen other such festivals in North America. Sales of children's cassette tapes have become so lucrative that the Children's Book Store in Toronto will soon open a second store specializing in cassettes and videos. Raffi's latest album has even been released on CD. Meanwhile, the store sells $2 million worth of kids' books a year. Fourteen years ago it was the only store of its kind in Canada. Now there are 55 others, and Coles Book Stores Ltd. is opening a chain just for children called Active Minds. There are no Canadian statistics on children's book sales, but in the United States, sales grew 160 percent from 1982 to 1987. The boom, say the booksellers, started only about five years ago.

A huge demand has developed for clowns and musicians at birthday par- 13 ties ($75 to $90 a party), for parent–tot gym classes, which teach parents how to play with their kids ($80 for ten sessions), and for educational toys. Creative Kids, which sells toys à la Tupperware in mothers' homes, is projecting sales of $4.5 million this year. Last year, sales were $2.5 million. "Our best party was $2500 in one evening," says Ivana Kuttas, the company's public relations manager. "I do know consultants who said they were surprised at some of the people who spent money. But I guess when it comes to your children, you're not as rational as you are in other areas of your life."

What is this spending spree doing to our kids? Plenty, say children's 14 experts Lynne Williams, Henry Berman, and Louisa Rose. In their book *The Too Precious Child*, they see overspending as a symptom of something more. Having waited longer than previous generations to have children, many cou- ples throw themselves into parenthood with heightened expectations. They hold an ideal of parenthood that resembles Glinda the Good Witch in *The Wiz- ard of Oz*, who grants a child's every wish with a wave of her wand. But in return for giving their children so much, they expect perfect children. This places a burden on the child that may be intolerable for some. "Excess pro- duces excess," the trio writes. "Excessive involvement may lead to a surplus of guilt; excessive adoration may result in the extreme self-absorption of nar- cissism. And this thesis is borne out empirically every day in psychiatrists' offices around the country, where victims of too-intense parenting attempt to examine their insatiable need for achievement, their unreasoning feelings of failure, or their difficulties in sustaining relationships."

Are we creating a generation of overindulged juvenile basket cases? When 15 I watch Simone heedlessly splashing paint on her Roots sweat pants, I don't really see a *too* precious child. Most of the time — usually when she gets a good nap — she is a co-operative three-and-a-half-year-old, loving, sensitive, and self-assured. Maybe the child experts have a point. But maybe, if we can instill our children with a sense of balance, a social conscience, and respect for others, all our spending may not do them too much harm. In any case, steering clear of the stores may prove far too difficult for a generation of baby boomers born to shop.

Style and Structure

1. (a) How would you describe the opening strategy Hunter uses in her essay?

   (b) What is your immediate reaction to "Simone Robin Hunter Cruickshank"? How do you think the writer intends you to feel? How might you have felt if the child had been introduced simply as "Simone"?

   (c) Judging by your own reactions, to what sort of readership do you suppose the writer means to appeal?

   (d) In using her own case as a starting point, Hunter sets up certain expectations in the reader. Discuss the effectiveness of this technique under the following criteria:

      (i) credibility;

      (ii) objectivity;

      (iii) stimulation of interest.

2. Throughout the essay, the writer refers to a number of resources, quoting frequently from both named and unnamed sources. Count the number of sources that she cites. What effect do you believe this technique has on the reader?

3. (a) Hunter gives several reasons why the children's market has grown so rapidly in Canada in recent years. Identify what these reasons are and in what paragraphs they are found.

   (b) How do the **topic sentences** of these paragraphs help you to identify the information in (a)? Comment on the usefulness of each.

4. (a) This essay takes a cause-and-effect approach to the subject of parents' spending on their offspring. Determine which parts of the essay are devoted to the investigation of causes and which to effects.

   (b) Would you say that the development is consistent?

   (c) Discuss what improvements, if any, you would like to see in the development of causes or of effects.

5. Throughout the essay, the writer provides a great many figures to indicate costs, ages, numbers of clients, and so on. What is the overall effect of these figures? What is your personal reaction to the numbers cited?

6. (a) Examine the last paragraph of the essay. Jot down in your notebook a list of the issues covered, sentence by sentence. What is your opinion of the **unity** and **coherence** of this paragraph? (See pp. 211 and 212).

   (b) Rewrite the body of the paragraph, using three or four sentences while retaining the original **topic** and **concluding sentences**. Compare your paragraph with the one in the essay and discuss which you prefer and why.

Warm-up

Preliminary research can help a writer to confirm personal suspicions and get "a fix" on what is actually happening in the world. One method of preliminary research involves checking newspapers and advertisements. In preparation for the following essay, check to see what is selling, and at what prices, in children's clothing and services.

Imagine a typical middle-class child of a certain age. Make a list of the new clothes, toys, furnishings, and/or services that this child might require during a month. Next, consult advertisements, newspaper articles, and consumer reports to list what products will best satisfy those hypothetical needs. If possible, indicate the range of prices; for instance, haircuts for children may be advertised at $5 to $25. From your lists, write a paragraph summary indicating trends in kid-consumerism.

Thinking and Writing

1. The writer asks us a leading question: "Since I have the income, why not give my only child the best?" The best, in this case, was a $200 birthday party for a three-year-old.

   Many people, including experts, feel that overindulging children, regardless of family income, is a bad idea. The writer suggests a few of the undesirable results throughout her essay. Review the points that she makes and compose a list of four reasons why you believe that extreme generosity to one's children may be a mistake.

   With your list as a guide, develop an outline for an essay in which you argue that giving the best is not always the wisest choice. Use four paragraphs for the body of your essay, one for each of the reasons on your list. Try to provide as many real-life examples as possible to illustrate your ideas.

Audience: affluent parents who are unaware of the possible results of their spending habits.

Send a copy of your final draft to an instructor of family life studies or sociology for in-class discussion.

2.   Every generation seems to feel that its youngest members are the worst examples humanity has ever seen. To some people, the suggestion that kids today are "demanding, picky, and ruthlessly status-conscious" has a certain ring of validity. Others are quick to point out that all children, whatever age they are born into, are self-centred and out merely to please themselves — that this is what childhood is all about. Are children of the 1990s any more demanding than children of any other age?

To answer this question, visit a shopping mall and speak to several store managers about children's fashions and accessories. Find out about trends and prices, and the influence children have on their parents' purchasing decisions. Ask if the managers have found appreciable differences in buying behaviour for children in the last five years. Also, be careful to note the behaviour of shoppers as a clue to the answers you are seeking.

With the results of your investigation, develop a descriptive essay to answer the question of whether or not children are now more demanding.

Variation: Write a compare/contrast essay, in which you use examples of your own and your friends' spending habits when you were pre-teenagers, showing how these habits were different from or similar to those you see in pre-teens today. Be as objective as possible, giving plenty of examples to demonstrate your ideas and showing the opinion of your parents as well.

Audience: people in your own age group who are wondering about the future of today's children.

Repeat Performances

by Brenda Rabkin

For many of us, getting married is the ultimate sign that we have attained independence from our families. We are now free to make choices and take on responsibilities based on our own wishes. Yet the pattern of our marital relationships will likely bear a strong resemblance to the one we observed between our parents, even when we consciously wish to change it. Why should this be so?

There are two major familial influences that will have shaped us by the time we declare ourselves ready to marry: the relationship between our parents, and the way we came to view ourselves as a result of having grown up in a particular family. "How we see ourselves gets translated into what we want, expect, and demand of our partners," says Francine Klagsbrun, author of *Married People: Staying Together in the Age of Divorce* (Bantam, 1985). Were we constantly criticized and put down, leading us to believe that we were unworthy of being loved? Or were we so indulged and overprotected that we could not possibly see ourselves as strong and independent? How did we work out a way to win approval for ourselves?

By providing the opportunity for intense closeness, marriage often simulates and reawakens the relationship we had with our parents. In many ways, it is as though we have never left home. So much of what has gone into making us who we are is buried under the thick overlay of family heritage that we are often unaware of these formative components and how they have affected us. The ghosts of our family's past will not only determine our choice of partners, but will also play a significant role in influencing the dynamics of the relationship. In other words, marriage is a perfect stage on which the ghosts can emerge and dance.

In *Intimate Partners* (Random House, 1987), a book about how love relationships are formed and how they change during marriage, author Maggie Scarf notes that a couple will often conspire — albeit unconsciously — to restage some version of a family drama that has special meaning for each of them. "It's as if family dilemmas that had never found their satisfactory resolutions needed to be resurrected in the real world, so that different individuals could work on those problems once again."

What Scarf found so astonishing is that these resurrected dramas emerge with a decided inevitability, even when the couple makes a deliberate choice not to repeat them. She cites the example of a woman whose father was never able to find secure employment. Her mother had to work hard as a secretary to

27

support the family, and the daughter vowed to do better for herself. She married a professional who was committed to climbing the corporate ladder. But in mid-life, her husband became disenchanted and opted for the challenge of running his own business. The venture was a failure, and the woman was forced to accept a low-paying job in order to make ends meet.

6   The strong connection between generations is nowhere seen as clearly as in the choices we make in intimate partners and how we behave in relation to those partners. We are all familiar with the expressions "He married his mother" and "She married her father." Although there may be some folk wisdom here, we seldom marry duplicates of the opposite-sex parent. What is perhaps more accurate, according to Robin Norwood, author of *Women Who Love Too Much* (Pocket Books, 1985), is that through our choice of partner, "we are able to replicate the atmosphere of childhood already so well known to us, and use the same manoeuvres in which we are already so practised. This is what for most of us constitutes love." As adults we involve ourselves in relationships where we can re-create the challenges we faced as children, this time in an attempt to master them.

7   Norwood believes that until we realize what we are doing and work on changing ourselves, the struggle to re-create and triumph over painful family experiences is one we are doomed to lose and repeat. It also explains why so many people seem to develop a pattern of entering unhealthy relationships with unloving partners. This is especially obvious in the case of women who grew up with an alcoholic parent. Feeling unloved and unworthy because they didn't get the nurturing they needed, these women often choose emotionally remote men upon whom they can lavish unlimited attention and resources in the hope that they will be appreciated and loved.

8   Norwood based her findings on counselling work she did with women who came from dysfunctional homes. A "dysfunctional" home, by her definition, is host to one or more of the following: drug or alcohol addiction, physical or emotional abuse, and seemingly benign behaviour including compulsive eating or cleaning. Other homes that qualify as dysfunctional are ones in which the parents are competitive with each other or with their children, or there is one parent who cannot relate to others in the family. Extreme rigidity about money, religion, or use of time, and minimal displays of affection are other symptoms. The environments in these homes don't promote the expression of honest feelings and intimacy. Consequently, children from such homes "are to some extent damaged in their ability to feel and relate."

9   But who among us is not? To one degree or another, we all bear the scars of imperfect parenting, of hurts and disappointments never assuaged, never healed. We may succeed in covering them up through our attempts at denial or

control, but in situations where we feel vulnerable or defenceless, they will surely be exposed. A case study will help to illustrate the problem.

Catherine grew up in a family that was dominated by her mother, a strong, intelligent, capable but highly critical woman who cowed her family into submission through excessive displays of emotion, especially anger. Her father was a kindly man, gentle and soft-spoken, who appeared to adore his wife, but who hardly related to his daughter at all. He always seemed to be away at work.

From her mother, Catherine learned what it meant to be a woman, and she modelled herself after her. A gifted child, she distinguished herself in school and earned praise for her accomplishments. She became strong, outgoing, ambitious, and independent. When she was 24 she met Hugh, who at 26 was in the process of carving out a brilliant career as a lawyer. Though emotionally withdrawn and quiet (qualities that reminded Catherine of her father and so made her feel safe because she was choosing what was familiar), he adored Catherine for her intelligence and energy. Hugh's mother was somewhat shrewish and his father was easygoing. He and Catherine had so much in common. They fell madly in love and were married a year later.

Catherine had no difficulty in assuming the major responsibility for the efficient running of their household, while at the same time excelling in her demanding job as a teacher. When two children came along and added to the load, she simply pedalled harder.

But Catherine seethed with resentment and expressed it with the only emotion she knew well — anger — at everyone and everything. She came to believe that there was something fundamentally wrong with her. Why, in such enviable circumstances, could she not feel happy? If she could just accept things without complaint, then maybe her situation would improve. Nevertheless, no matter how much she accomplished or how hard she worked, her anger would not disappear. Hugh became quieter and more withdrawn, which served only to fuel her rage. Finally one day Catherine asked him for a divorce.

How could a union that began with so much hope and love end in such pain and bitterness? Sadly, what happened to Catherine and Hugh is very common among couples in conflict. "It is a fact of marital reality, well known to experts in the field, that those qualities cited by intimate partners as having first attracted them to each other are usually *the same ones that are identified as sources of conflict later on in the relationship*," says Maggie Scarf.

Perhaps because of the anger that Hugh saw his mother unleash toward his father, who shrank in its wake, he was determined to detach himself from Catherine's anger, so that he would not be victimized by it. It was easy for him to be gentle and quiet, because he never saw himself as angry — just like his father, who was the only role model he had of how a husband should act with an emotionally overbearing wife, which was now his view of Catherine.

16   For her part, Catherine could never see herself as soft and kindly, because she would then be vulnerable to her mother's wrath. Her mother in turn was behaving the only way she knew in the presence of an emotionally absent husband, which was now what Catherine perceived Hugh to be. They had both unwittingly re-created the most negative aspects of their parents' marriages.

17   To save their marriage from the painful deadlock of feelings they had created by means of these trade-offs, both Hugh and Catherine would have to realize that they'd done this — no easy task, admittedly. They then would have to take responsibility for the particular behaviours they had renounced and given over to the other for expression. They would have to learn to recognize the good and the bad in each other, and in themselves, rather than the either/or situation regarding anger and control that they had devised.

18   "When it becomes possible for partners to take on the unfinished work of childhood and to re-own parts of the self that once had to be disavowed and discarded," says Scarf, "then marriage becomes a therapeutic relationship in the best, most gratifying sense of that word. It becomes a place in which old wounds can be healed."

19   While it is true that we are shaped by our family histories, we are not doomed to repeat them. If we are comfortable with them and function well and happily, then we have no reason to change them. But if the ghosts of our past diminish our lives, then that pain can and should serve as the signal for change. And change is frightening, because it involves departing from what is familiar, even if familiarity means hell. Nor are there any guarantees that change will necessarily create an improvement. But if the pain is great enough, to change or not to change is no longer the issue. Survival is.

20   How do people depart from their hurtful family histories? "They stop fooling themselves by denying that they have problems," says Francine Klagsbrun. "Then they look for the sources of their pain. . . . Although for some people expert treatment is necessary, I believe people can look at themselves and say, 'Hey, what's happening? Why am I doing this?' I believe people can recognize, if they want to, the ways in which they repeat early family behaviours."

21   One way of recognizing these behaviours is simply to be on the lookout for them. What counterproductive family patterns are we emulating? For example, whenever Sarah got into an argument with her husband she would withdraw, wounded and sulking, and wait for him to make the overtures of reconciliation, which he inevitably did. In the early years of their marriage, it gave her a small sense of triumph and reassurance when he approached her, but after

ten years of marriage she began to feel frustrated and victimized, and found herself looking for subversive ways to express her power. Overspending on their joint charge accounts became her favourite method.

"One day it just hit me," says Sarah. "I was behaving exactly like my mother, who was a very passive and manipulative woman. My father indulged her and treated her like a child. I swore I'd never be like her, and here I was, my mother all over again. I knew that if I wanted power and respect in my marriage, I was going to have to act like an adult. I started to stand up to John when we had disagreements and to say what I really wanted, or what I was feeling. And boy did he listen! It's made things a lot easier for him too."

People can also change the perceptions they have of their family histories by acknowledging their more positive aspects. For example, in her marriage to Hugh, Catherine re-enacted her mother's unbridled anger and her own fear of expressing gentler emotions. But what she ignored was her mother's ability to be compassionate, loving, and supportive of her father, and her skill at being expressive and feminine with him. He was unfailingly understanding of her and respectful toward her. To her own surprise, Catherine saw that her parents actually had a successful marriage, one she did want to emulate.

Today Hugh and Catherine are struggling to revise the destructive, polarized patterns they established early on in their marriage. "If not for therapy, we wouldn't be here today," says Catherine. "We had hit rock bottom in our marriage. We were both so immobilized by pain that all we could do was blame each other." Therapy helped them identify the issues that needed work, and to understand how they had originated. The rest was up to them. "I believe that therapy can only take you so far," explains Catherine. "There comes a point where you have to translate what you've learned into action. It was a big step for me to say to Hugh, 'I'm frightened and I need your help.' And for him to say to me, 'I get really mad when you get bossy, but I don't know how to deal with it.' But it's a relief to both of us to know that we can express those feelings."

It can be very reassuring to know that there are positive features in one's family background to choose from as an alternative to replaying old, hurtful scripts. But what if they're not there, no matter how hard one tries to find them, because the negatives are so overwhelming?

"In a situation like that at least we can learn that we know what we *don't* want to be," says Marcia Jacobs, who practises psychotherapy in Vancouver. "And that requires risk because then we are stepping out into the void, into the unknown. But it's only when we're there that we can allow space for positive changes to take place. That is what creating our own lives is all about. People can learn to play roles other than the ones they were raised with. And once they do and find greater satisfaction, they also come to see that they don't have to be victimized by old family scripts. They can write their own."

27   A large part of coming to terms with family ghosts is understanding that they may never completely disappear. They will always be lurking in the wings, waiting for that angry word, that cold glance, that helpless expression, to make their reappearance. But we can choose not to give them centre stage by recognizing that within each of us are strengths and weaknesses for which we alone are ultimately responsible.

Style and Structure

1.   Rabkin's essay deals with relationships between men and women. Primarily for whom do you feel the essay was written? Give at least three reasons for your answer.

2.   Identify the **thesis statement** in this essay. Where does it occur? How helpful do you think its placement is for the reader?

3. (a) Make note of the number of questions Rabkin uses throughout her essay. Where do they occur?

   (b) Consider the value of a question by suggesting why the writer might have chosen to use this technique.

   (c) Occasionally, instructors of writing will insist, "Don't ask me; *tell* me." In other words, do not use questions unless you are quoting a research source. To what extent would you agree with this advice?

4. (a) The essay includes a number of case studies as examples. Discuss the effectiveness of this technique in terms of the following:

   (i) credibility;

   (ii) reader interest;

   (iii) clarity;

   (iv) general appeal.

   (b) Count the instances where Rabkin shows research regarding marriage problems. How many individual sources does she cite? How often does she refer to each? Using the same four considerations as above, discuss the effect of using multiple sources of supporting research.

5. (a) Discuss what a **concluding sentence** should do for a paragraph. Point out which of the **concluding sentences** in this essay are particularly effective, referring to them by paragraph number, and outline reasons for your choices.

   (b) An old philosophy of paragraph writing (which can also apply to essay writing) is that first you tell your readers what you will tell them, then you tell them, then you tell them what you told them. Comment on the effectiveness of this model.

6. In paragraph 3, Rabkin introduces a "ghost" metaphor, which she repeats in paragraph 19 and then again in the **conclusion** of the essay, paragraph 27.

   (a) How does the "ghost" metaphor help the reader to understand the text? Besides helping the reader to understand, what other effect might the use of this metaphor have?

   (b) How does the use of this metaphor in the **concluding paragraph** affect the reader?

Warm-up

Do you make an effort to use concluding sentences in your own writing, or do you generally rely on the material presented in the paragraph to carry its own meaning? Reading over a recent essay, count up the number of paragraphs in which you used concluding sentences. Devise conclusions for those paragraphs that you believe could be improved in this way. When you are finished, give both your first and your revised copy to a classmate and ask for comments on the effectiveness of your improvements.

Thinking and Writing

1. *For many of us, getting married is the ultimate sign that we have attained independence from our families.* (paragraph 1)

   "Ultimate," however, does not mean "only." Usually, we see the process of declaring independence from one's family as having several stages and as being achieved (if ever) only over a number of years.

   Draw up a list of milestones — those occasions that you see as important in the process of becoming independent. Consider those events that you believe are more or less common throughout your social circle. Using an outline drawn from your list, write a process-analysis essay in which you demonstrate that "leaving home" is a slow process. (You may wish to make this a personal essay, using your own experiences as examples, but be sure to show the process as being one largely familiar to most within your social circle.)

   Audience: members of a junior high-school health or family life class.

2.   Many of us have had the opportunity to see marriages within a family, marriages in which the partners act in patterns that seem to be almost pre-determined. As this essay points out, familiar marital dramas may "emerge with a decided inevitability, even when the couple makes a deliberate choice not to repeat them." (See paragraph 5.)

    If you have seen a case of "repeat performance," write a compare/ contrast essay in which you outline the major similarities, as well as differences, between the marriages. For this essay, do some research on the phenomenon of repeated marital behaviours, perhaps using the sources mentioned in this essay (if they are available to you), as well as this essay itself. Use at least three quotations, properly documented, in which you show how research predicts your observations.

Audience: those wanting to marry in the near future. Note, however, that these may be the people most difficult to convince, usually because they tend to have plans and expectations that may not be entirely realistic.

How Dumbed-Down Can Things Get?

by Charles Gordon

Too much has been made of the glowing puck episode on Fox TV. But that's no reason to stop talking about it. The network's decision to lend visual enhancement to the puck during the national Hockey League's all-star game can be seen as yet one more example of a growing trend in North American society — the dumbing-down of just about everything. 1

The overall concept of dumbing-down is not a new one, but the notion that sports could be dumbed-down any further takes a bit of getting used to. We have already seen sports journalism begin to concentrate less on how athletes perform, which takes some thought, to how much money they make, which takes none. Now, a purple electronic haze is put around the puck so that television viewers know where it is and a flashing red tail is added to it so that those viewers can follow it as it is shot at the net. 2

In this country, at least, the experiment received almost universally negative reviews, probably because people were aware that seeing the puck was not really the issue. Understanding the game was. Canadians have no difficulty finding the puck because they understand, by watching what the players are doing, where the puck is. Many fans, in complaining about the experiment, made the intriguing point that the purple haze forced their eyes to the puck, and away from the game. In other words, there is more to the game than the puck. 3

Something good could come of this, some small rebellion. Perhaps fans, when they ponder the purple puck, will come to a sharper realization of the many ways they have been treated as if they were dumb. From the designated hitter to the slam dunk competition to the scoreboard that tells them when to cheer, fans have had to endure one assault after another on their intelligence, one indication after another that the sports gods — and particularly the television gods — thought they were incapable of appreciating the game on its own merits, of understanding what was going on. And if the sports fans rebel, can rebellion in other dumbed-down areas of society be far behind? 4

Let's not even talk about advertising, which has been treating people like morons for more than half a century, and turn to political discourse, which has gradually been reduced to the most simplistic level. 5

This trend is most evident in the news media's reliance on the reaction story, the coverage of any development converted to the coverage of those who feel one 6 way or another about it. If there is a complicated piece of legislation, for example, the coverage of it will consist of asking different affected individuals and interest groups what they think and reporting their reactions. Watch the reporting of the next federal or provincial budget to see the practice in action. It is a far easier thing to do than report the ramifications and impact, not to mention the contents, of the budget. And it is all being done in the name of the voter/reader/reviewer, who is considered insufficiently clever to handle the straight goods.

7   In public life, the dumbing-down has many forms. The television debate is another, based on the ludicrous idea that how a politician looks in an artificial environment under the television lights for two hours has anything at all to do with the politician's ability to govern the country. Yet the event is treated with extraordinary gravity by the news media, whose creation it is, and by the politicians themselves. Even here, in a climate of oversimplification, further oversimplification takes place, in the search for the so-called knockout punch, the 20-second sound bite that is better than the opponent's 20-second sound bite and therefore qualifies the one to be a better president or prime minister than the other. Watch, next time, to see an electronic red flame follow the words out of the winner's mouth.

8   The latest and most influential bit of political dumbing-down began as what was thought to be an exercise in intelligence around the mid-1980s. Politicians were making too many irresponsible promises, with no regard for their consequences. So it seemed a natural and logical thing to ask the question: what will it cost? Politicians asked the question of other politicians. Journalists asked it. Suddenly, North American politics became cost-conscious.

9   To an extreme, as it turned out. In political discourse today, "what will it cost?" is the only question asked and the answer to it the only one required. Yet it is a dumb question producing a meaningless answer. The components of cost change, interest rates change, weather causes delays, unforeseen circumstance develop — so that a politician saying that a program will run for five years with a cost of $514.5 million really has not the foggiest idea what he is saying and not the remotest chance of being correct. Yet the question continues to be asked and continues to be answered. It has led to the current obsession with the deficit, with every public policy idea discussed and assessed only in terms of whether it will make the deficit go up or down, as if anyone really knows. The deficit obsession is the ultimate dumbing-down of political life.

10   To be sure, the question of cost is not without legitimacy: even an estimate of cost is better than no idea at all. But it should not be the only question, or even the most important. The most important questions are: what will it do? whom will it help? will it work? Similarly, in abolishing or cutting back a program, the important question is not what will it save but whom will it hurt. The numbers, like the puck, are not the only things worth watching.

Obviously, these are more difficult questions to answer, requiring more 11
understanding and more study. But the people are capable of understanding the
answers if the politicians and the reporters are capable of coming up with them.
Our leaders, with the memory of Meech Lake and Charlottetown clearly in
mind, should be only too conscious of what happens when the people are
treated as if their intelligence can't be trusted.

Style and Structure

1. Underline the writer's thesis. Why would he choose to present it in such
   a complex sentence?
2. In paragraphs 2 to 4, how does the way Gordon presents the example of
   the electronic puck lead the reader through a thinking process? Why is it
   important for him to establish this pattern in the opening paragraphs of
   the body?
3. What functions are served by paragraph 5? Examine Gordon's word
   choice in this paragraph carefully: how does it affect the reader's acceptance of the general argument he makes in the rest of the article?
4. What examples of dumbing-down does Gordon offer in paragraphs 6 to
   10? Why does he present them in the order he does? How does his presentation of each compare to his presentation of the electronic puck in
   paragraphs 2 to 4?
5. What role does paragraph 10 play in the development of Gordon's argument? How does his reference to the electronic puck at the end of this
   paragraph drive home his point?
6. What is the function of paragraph 11? What purpose does the last sentence of paragraph 11 serve?

Warm-up

1. Write a one paragraph definition of dumbing-down. Use the following
   formula: a topic sentence, one or two explanatory sentences, an example,
   and a concluding sentence. Exchange your paragraph with two other
   people in a workshop setting. Ask them to evaluate, with concrete reasons for their statements, how clearly you have defined the term and how
   well you have followed the formula.
2. Gordon's article implies that dumbing-down is found everywhere in our
   society, not just in the examples he cites. Some who agree with him

would cite, for example, how common it is to hear someone use the words "stupid" or "dumb" to win an argument, dismiss a serious question, or defuse a situation that poses a challenge. Make a short list of situations you have encountered lately in which someone has dumbed-down. Choose one of these situations and write a paragraph that explains what the person did, why it was done, and what effect it had.

Exchange paragraphs with others in a workshop setting. What different kinds of situations did your group find? (While they are looking at your work, ask them to find places where you might clarify your explanation.)

Thinking and Writing

1. Gordon seems particularly concerned about the way dumbing-down has become part of the way we make decisions.

    Wherever people work, play or live in community, they must make decisions together. Take a few moments to review a personal experience, yours or someone else's, in one of the following situations to see if you have encountered dumbing-down as part of the decision-making process:

    (a) a sports team   (d) a family

    (b) a workplace   (e) an intimate relationship

    (c) a social group

    Write an essay examining one way dumbing-down is commonly used in the chosen situation and its effect on the relationships involved, comparing and contrasting with more constructive techniques. (If you use specific examples from personal experience, be careful not to embarrass yourself or your reader.)

    Audience: people involved in such a situation so they can judge whether dumbing-down is affecting their relationships.

2. In paragraphs 8 to 10, Gordon presents a general argument about the way political decision-making has been dumbed-down, but he does not cite specific examples. Examine a political decision under discussion (or recently made) to see if people's approach to it supports or refutes his argument. Explore, as thoroughly and as objectively as possible, both sides' arguments. Then write an essay which argues that the discussion leading to the decision does (or does not) illustrate a general process of dumbing-down.

As you write, be careful not to let your own prejudices about the decision influence your stand.

Audience: a politician arguing a position on the decision that is opposed to yours.

Send a copy of your finished essay to a politician involved in making the decision.

An Alternative to Incarceration

by Greg Heaton, Lori Cohen, and Patrick McManus

1   Indians comprise 10 percent of the 12 500 inmates in Canada's penitentiaries but only 2 percent of the country's population. On the Prairies, Indians make up about 5 percent of the population but 32 percent of inmates. According to one study, a Saskatchewan treaty Indian boy turning sixteen in 1976 had a 70 percent chance of at least one trip to prison by the age of 25. The startling disproportions are blamed on alcoholism, poverty, welfare, and the failure of North American Indians to assimilate into white European society. The problems are obvious. The solutions, unfortunately, are not.

2   In August 1988, however, a nine-member committee of the Canadian Bar Association released a study that proposes an extraordinary solution. The gist of the report, written by University of British Columbia law professor Michael Jackson, is that traditional western notions of crime, justice, and punishment are incompatible with aboriginal culture and values, and must be replaced by a parallel justice system largely controlled by Indians.

3   Professor Jackson argues that Indians are the victims of three centuries of social, economic, and political dispossession and deprivation. The European colonization of North America not only usurped native ownership of the land, he suggests, but also undermined their culture and imposed a foreign criminal justice system. Poverty, alcoholism, and crime are not the only results. Infant mortality rates are 60 percent higher than the national average. Violent death rates are three times the national average. The suicide rate among natives is six times the national rate. Professor Jackson concludes that native self-government is vital to native survival, and that a justice system run by natives can be accommodated as part of the process of self-determination.

4   The system proposed by Professor Jackson would borrow from Indian traditions where practical and would be implemented by natives as much as possible. He concedes that serious offences — murder, for instance — and cases involving non-native victims must remain within the purview of mainstream courts. But many crimes that take place on reserves could be handled by the community. The mechanisms should reflect the diversity of tribal traditions. In some cases, native justices of the peace, in concert with band elders, could arbitrate disputes, dispense justice, and mete out punishment. In the Dene and Inuit cultures, where egalitarian social values reject awarding decision-making authority to individuals, community consensus would serve as judge.

Punishment would also reflect native values. Jail, says Professor Jackson, does not have the same stigma for natives as it does for whites. So "creative solutions" such as banishment or community service are necessary. For those natives who do end up in jail, the report recommends separate native-run correctional facilities.

Winona Stevenson, associate professor of native studies at the University of Saskatchewan, explains the principles of conciliatory justice as practised by the Plains Cree before the arrival of white settlers. In the case of a murder, for example, the killer and the victim's family would meet with a communally chosen moderator. In the village's Great Lodge — a giant structure that served as a kind of community centre, church, and court — the parties would pray, negotiate, and smoke the revered tribal pipe. "In the presence of such a sacred object," says Professor Stevenson, "anger had to be dropped." Retribution for a murdered son was usually two or three horses.

Professor Jackson's report is welcomed by Henry Quinney, an elder at the Saddle Lake Reserve, 80 miles northeast of Edmonton, who has been trying to establish an on-reserve, traditional disputes-settlement system. The 2500-member band, two-thirds of whom are under 25, is plagued with alcohol-related crime. "When our people go to court," says Mr. Quinney, "there's always a reason behind it. But with the adversarial system you have to have a lawyer and you can't really talk for yourself." He thinks native offenders should be judged by tribal elders. They would insist on alcohol counselling, if necessary, and seek reconciliation between the offender and his victim. Punishment, if any, would likely include some form of community work, often in the service of the injured party.

In a number of recent trials involving natives, courts have been asked to consider traditional, community-based justice systems in rendering judgments. In 1986, in the Northwest Territories community of Arctic Bay, a 21-year-old Inuit man was found guilty of raping his fourteen-year-old cousin. At sentencing, territorial court judge Bourassa heard that the "inumarit," or council of elders, could "rehabilitate the offender and reconcile the offender, the victim, and the community." Thus, he imposed a minimal sentence. But Judge Bourassa's decision was later overturned by the Alberta Court of Appeal, and the man was sentenced to eighteen months' imprisonment. A majority of the Appeal Court found that Arctic Bay is in most respects a modern community profoundly influenced by modern technology and culture. Thus, the inumarit is not "a remnant of ancient culture," capable of enforcing "traditional ultimate sanction on the offender. [The inumarit's] counselling service [cannot] replace the sentence of imprisonment which is required in virtually all cases of major sexual assault."

9   While the Appeal Court questioned the legitimacy of traditional native justice systems, other observers worry that self-government and an independent native justice system are socially divisive — tantamount to the creation of a nation within a nation. Others argue that special judicial treatment for Indians will invite other ethnic minorities, for instance, communal sects such as Hutterites and Doukhobors, to seek similar consideration.

10   Nonetheless, Professor Jackson remains optimistic that a parallel justice system can and will work, in concert with the development of Indian self-government. "Colonialism has run its course," he says. "The mindset of this country has been toward assimilation as a historical process, not only inevitable but desirable. This has to change. Eventually, Indians will not be a disadvantaged group, but they will always be a distinct society."

Style and Structure

1.   All of the other "Style and Structure" sections in this book present questions we developed. For this essay, *you* will develop the questions.

2.   Divide into three or four groups of approximately the same size. Each group will develop a series of ten questions. These questions should guide others through

 (a) the essay's organization (the introduction, the sections of the body, the conclusion, and paragraph structure), stressing any unique or striking things the authors have done,

 (b) specific strategies used to give impact to the ideas (statistics, citing authorities, examples, etc.), and

 (c) specific writing techniques used to communicate the ideas effectively (transitions, variations in sentence length, word choice, etc.).

3.   Use the following questions as a guideline as you decide which features of the essay to highlight: What strategies employed in this essay would our readers find beneficial in their own writing? How can we word our question to help them appreciate the strategies we have selected? (You might also find it helpful to review some of the questions we used in the "Style and Structure" sections for other essays.)

4.   Working together as a group, examine the questions developed by each of the other groups. Evaluate each according to the following marking scheme:

	Weak	Good	Very Good
Examination of Overall Structure	1	2	3
Examination of Paragraphing	1	2	3
Examination of Style, Word Choice, and Special Features	1	2	3
Examination of Adaptation to Reader	1	2	3
Usefulness of Features Highlighted	1	2	3

Final Grade ___ /15

Submit the list of questions your group has produced to your instructor.

Warm-up

1. In groups of three, act out a conciliatory meeting such as that described in paragraph 6. One person will be the victim (or victim's parent), the second will be the criminal, and the third will be the moderator. Assume that the criminal has either stolen (and spent) the victim's life savings or murdered a child. Try to negotiate a mutually satisfactory solution.

2. Write a paragraph in which you describe the advantages or disadvantages of this type of conciliatory justice.
   Audience: someone who has never heard of this approach to justice.

   Let the others in your role-playing group read your first draft before you revise it. Ask them for specific comments on strong and weak areas they find in your presentation of the ideas. (Do not be satisfied with "It's okay, I guess." Ask for specific comments.)

Thinking and Writing

1. Professor Jackson argues that Indians are the victims of three centuries of social, economic, and political dispossession and deprivation. The European colonization of North America not only usurped native ownership of the land, he suggests, but also undermined their culture and imposed a foreign criminal justice system. (paragraph 3)

   Most Canadians, however, have been taught to think of the settling of Canada in terms of European immigrants coming to an empty land. We seldom hear of the highly developed societies that existed all across the country thousands of years before the arrival of Cartier and Cabot.

Write an essay that explains the impact of European settlement from the point of view of the native people. Do not worry about including specific historical events. Concentrate, instead, on the general impact of *one* of the following: possession of land; religious and cultural beliefs; education of children in ways their parents desire; or the self-image that comes from being part of an independent culture.

Audience: an average non-native Canadian who thinks of the history of Canada as beginning with the arrival of Cartier or Cabot.

2. In the last paragraph of the essay, Professor Jackson is quoted as saying, "The mindset of this country has been toward assimilation i.e., incorporating the native people into white society as a historical process, not only inevitable but desirable. This has to change. Eventually, Indians will not be a disadvantaged group, but they will always be a distinct society." A separate justice system run by native people is part of this change.

Write an essay that answers the question, "Can a separate system of justice for native people, run by native people, be achieved in Canada?"

Audience: someone who is not aware of the problems faced by the native people.

Send a copy of your final draft to the public relations office of the Department of Indian Affairs in Ottawa or to the public relations officer at your local Indian Friendship Centre.

Why Men Are Mad as Hell

by Rona Maynard

The Toronto aircraft technician was feeling burned. His Canadian Auto Workers' local was sponsoring a course in Wen-Do, a self-defence technique designed for women. His dues had helped to fund the event, which would be held at his union hall. But men would not be welcome.

When the women gathered for the course on September 12, 1987, the aircraft technician asked to join them and was turned away by the female instructor. He asked to observe the class and again was refused. But he was ready for a long battle. He had In Search of Justice (ISOJ), a militant men's-rights organization, in his corner, and the group has taken his cause to the Ontario Human Rights Commission. The complaint: sex discrimination against men.

Nonsense, retorts Marilyn Walsh, a director of Wen-Do Women's Self-Defence. She points out that both the Canadian Human Rights Act and the Charter of Rights and Freedoms permit special programs for disadvantaged groups — and that women ought to qualify when it comes to street-fighting skills. "Most rapes happen to women," says Walsh. "Most spousal abuse happens to women. Yet, women in general don't participate in contact sports, don't learn to defend themselves." She adds that men can choose from literally dozens of other martial-arts courses.

So what? demands Ross Virgin, founder and president of ISOJ. He compares Wen-Do to an employer who refuses to hire blacks or Jews on the grounds that thousands of others would be glad to do so. If ISOJ wins its case against Wen-Do, its next target will be the luxurious all-female McGill Club, where Toronto's elite businesswomen meet for saunas and white-wine spritzers.

Only yesterday, gender bias was a women's issue. But after nearly two decades of government-funded efforts to advance women's status, an outspoken new breed of male activist claims that women now get all the breaks. Men are calling themselves the oppressed group. And they charge that women's drive for equality has become a selfish vendetta against men. "It's okay for women to force their way into men's clubs," says Virgin. "It's okay for women to join men's teams. But God help you if you reverse the genders."

Across North America, hundreds of groups campaign for men's rights. Most pursue a single goal: a better deal for divorcing fathers who want a chance to raise their kids and a break from alimony payments. Such men account for roughly 80 percent of ISOJ's 2100 recruits nation-wide. But Virgin, a 42-year-old health-care worker who has never been married, expects them to fight a mightier foe than any ex-wife — the National Action Committee on the Status of Women (NAC).

7   He plans the crusade from a spartan command post in a suburban Toronto industrial mall. The decor consists of men's-rights slogans ("Alimony should not be a lifetime sentence") and a colour blowup of a man permanently scarred when his wife threw a pot of boiling water at him. Unlike NAC, which this year boasts $611 211 from the federal purse, ISOJ has made do with donations from members ever since its inaugural meeting back in 1972. But tough odds don't daunt Virgin, who is betting that most of the four million people NAC claims to represent have little use for its official pronouncements.

8   He could be right, to judge from the response to his own agenda. Twenty percent of ISOJ's incoming phone calls are from supportive women — the mothers and partners of put-upon men. Meanwhile, legislators, politicians, and talk-show hosts pay increasing attention to his attacks on every plank of the feminist platform.

9   • **Rape** Feminists insist that a victim's sexual history has no place in the courtroom. Men counter that it may be essential to a fair trial for the accused. At trials for any other crime, defence lawyers routinely grill witnesses about past experiences that might cast doubt on their testimony. According to Virgin, a history of one-night stands suggests that a woman who says she has been raped has in fact "enticed" the defendant.

10   • **Sexual abuse** Conventional wisdom holds that kids never lie about abuse. Virgin claims that they often do, destroying the reputations of innocent people — most of whom are male. His group will help prepare a defence for any man accused of molesting a child, no questions asked. And his ideas are clearly spreading. Last summer, the 22 000-member Ontario Public School Teachers' Federation announced that it would take legal action on an accused teacher's behalf, once he is cleared in court.

11   • **Sexual harassment** Men's rightists say that they are sexually victimized at work. As they tell it, most sexual harassment complaints come from office temptresses who told co-workers "no" while signalling "yes." ISOJ argues that a woman's written "no," delivered to the alleged harasser, should be a condition for a human-rights investigation. The proposal appals feminists, who say that women going public with complaints need protection from retaliation by their harassers.

12   • **Wife assault** One million Canadian men beat their wives, says a study published last year by the Canadian Advisory Council on the Status of Women. Virgin, who accuses anti-male researchers of jumping to conclusions, guesses that the actual number is about 2000. He wants more attention paid to the battered husbands whose stories are dismissed by incredulous police

officers, and he is currently helping three ISOJ members to lay charges against violent wives.

- **Alimony** Now that more than half of Canadian women hold jobs, few 13 divorced women have the right to financial support from their ex — or so the men's movement contends. Dismissing feminist concerns about unskilled homemakers catapulted into the job market, its leaders say that alimony discourages women from working and shortchanges second wives. And judges are listening. Increasingly, they limit spousal support to three years, even for longtime homemakers.

- **Pay equity** If women want equality at work, say men's rightists, they 14 should accept the same deal that men do. That means no affirmative action, no paid maternity leave, and, above all, no government programs to fatten women's paycheques. Fumes Virgin: "Any pay based on your genital organs is sex pay, the same as prostitution."

Whenever activists like Virgin condemn the women's movement, one 15 issue is bound to surface — male-bashing. Feminists, they say, portray all men either as violent, lecherous exploiters of helpless women or as cold, selfish lovers. U.S. author Shere Hite, whose latest 922-page study consisted mainly of women's gripes about their partners, has men's tempers boiling over. "Feminists are realizing that cranking the male-as-monster myth pays terrific dividends," says Brian Demaine, a Montreal teacher and prominent men's activist. "Male hate explains why women aren't equally represented in the better-paying professions, in politics, in the arts, in sports — you name it. Male hate is the answer to every perceived failure."

Men are not alone in charging that feminism has gone too far. After all, 16 Hite's critics include female scholars who accuse her of biassed research techniques. Paid maternity leave, which Canadian feminists would like to see lengthened, strikes many female lawyers in the United States as discriminatory — and ultimately dangerous to women because it may discourage employers from hiring them.

Meanwhile, an emerging female elite is negating the feminist image of 17 oppressed womanhood. If a woman has the right degrees and the drive to make them work, she has options undreamed of by men. Like it or not, many employers expect less commitment from a woman than they do from a man — especially when she becomes a mother. The female lawyer who reduces her hours to nurture a baby must give up her hopes for partnership but not for society's approval. A male colleague who takes the same step will be viewed as a wimp. Amid growing evidence that neither sex truly has it all, some mothers are deciding, as one female MBA sums up, that they "wouldn't be a man for anything."

18   Does the men's movement have a legitimate case? Are feminists demanding more than just equality? It might seem so at first. But whatever men's rightists may say, equality is not their goal. Their arguments are based not on reason or fairness, but on corrosive anger at women.

19   Pat Marshall is not easily shaken. As head of Toronto's Metro Action Committee on Public Violence Against Women and Children, she knows how to keep cool under fire. But she admits to being frightened in May 1988, when she spoke at a public forum on sexual assault. ISOJ sent a delegation of about twenty men, one of whom shouted "Bull!" throughout a rape victim's account of her ordeal. The same man interrupted Marshall's own remarks with screams of "Nazi! Nazi! You're Gestapo!"; it took five men to restrain him. The mood turned so ugly that the organizers nearly cancelled the forum, and the women in the audience did not dare walk to the washroom alone. "It was an assaultive experience for all the women taking part," recalls Marshall.

20   That night, Virgin took the microphone to cite two of his favourite statistics: 60 percent of sexual-assault charges result in acquittals, compared to sixteen percent of other criminal charges. Virgin uses these figures, which he says he was given by the U.S. Federal Bureau of Investigation (FBI), as proof that lying women drag hundreds of innocent men into court. But the FBI denies any knowledge of the figures, and no comparable Canadian data are available. While most feminists admit that sexual-assault cases have an unusually high acquittal rate, they offer another explanation: the courts' reluctance to believe the victims.

21   Stacy Michener, a counsellor at the Toronto Rape Crisis Centre, points out that the courts expect more supporting evidence in a sexual-assault case than they do for almost any other crime. "But there's seldom any corroborating evidence, because men pick and choose places where there are no witnesses. So it's his word against hers. The courts look at the way she dresses and her lifestyle, and decide she's not the kind of woman they should put him away for."

22   Rightly so, if you ask Virgin. He took heart from the dismaying news, reported last spring by Rhode Island researchers, that 50 percent of junior high-school students believe that a woman who walks alone at night in "seductive" clothing is asking to be raped. "Thank God for the wisdom of young children," writes Virgin in an unpublished manuscript entitled *Rape: Fact or Fiction?* He overlooks the fact that men ought to be able to control their libidos. But that's hardly surprising given his belief that unsatisfied male lust constitutes a "medical problem" warranting free government-run prostitution.

23   When men's rightists do have a point, they swathe it in distortion. For instance, ISOJ's complaint against Wen-Do cites a 1985 U.S. survey showing that women are as likely as men to use violence against their partners. The

study purportedly proves that abused women have no need for all-female courses in martial arts.

Tell that to Jan Stets, a sociologist at Washington State University and an expert on violent relationships. She and fellow sociologist Murray Straus, a co-author of the very survey quoted by ISOJ, have recently found that marital and cohabitational violence seems to have a greater impact on women than on men. Women spend more time in bed and report more stress and depression. "Research [on violent women] is being used to cut off funds for women's shelters, ignoring the fact that women are being battered," worries Stets, who adds that existing studies raise more questions than they answer. Are women at last rejecting the taboo against female aggression? Are they only defending themselves against men who strike the first blow? Are abused men downplaying their pain in an effort to appear manly? So far, researchers have proved just one point: abused men need attention and support.

The irrational rage of men's rightists is nowhere more evident than in their own publications. *Equality*, a now-defunct Montreal newsletter, once parodied the 23rd Psalm as a divorced woman's hymn of praise to her alimony cheques: "My Cadillac tank runneth over." But divorced women splurging on Cadillacs are the exception. More than half of divorced and separated mothers raise their kids in poverty.

What does the men's movement really want? A return to the 1950s, suggests an essay in *Equilibrium*, another defunct Montreal newsletter. It blames employed mothers for most of society's ills: drug abuse, divorce, youth suicide, teen runaways, and street crime. The problem, it says, is that women have forsaken their rightful job: "making life worth living."

If women don't work, they will be hard pressed to support themselves in the event of a divorce. But consistency is not the movement's strong point. Virgin, who thinks that day care hurts children, nevertheless considers it the perfect career for displaced homemakers. "If there's so much demand for day care, these women can open up centres in their homes and set their own price." What this approach to child care would mean to kids and women does not trouble him. "Icicles hang from each chamber of my heart," he smiles.

It is tempting to dismiss men's rightists as a sick joke. But what they reveal about relations between men and women is no longer a laughing matter. Only a few years ago, when "androgyny" and "commitment" became media buzzwords, men and women seemed close to a truce in the sexual battles that followed feminism's rise in the 1960s. Now, hostility runs higher than ever. Until men and women understand the feelings that divide them, "equality" will remain a rhetorical device for extremists of both sexes.

At most, ten percent of men give women's quest for independence their whole-hearted support, concludes U.S. journalist Anthony Astrachan in his

1986 book *How Men Feel*. When Astrachan factored in all the men backing the feminist dream for pragmatic reasons, he still came up with a modest total of about 35 percent. What holds men back is fear: of exposing their own weakness, of losing other men's support, and of humiliation by women.

30   Feminists have long chastised men for refusing to share power. But while men still dominate political parties and corporate boards by a huge margin, the average guy has no power to share. He needs to view women as his inferiors, and the more heated their demands for a shot at the top, the more painful his awareness of his status on the bottom. The result, says Astrachan, is rage, denial, and "compulsive fantasies of power" that may erupt in wife beating at home or in sexual harassment on the shop floor. A male metalworker admitted to Astrachan, after a few beers, that he liked to harass women at work — and that sexual attraction had nothing to do with his advances. "Especially if she's the kind who works extra hard and talks like she wants extra credit for it, I don't mind showing her who's really stronger."

31   Women's assault on male job bastions threatens men on two fronts. History has shown that any job loses status when large numbers of women move in (time was when the public looked up to clerks). And men feel constrained by women's presence, especially blue-collar workers. They may not be less enlightened about women than managers and professionals, but they have traditionally been less inhibited about expressing sexual attitudes through off-colour jokes and crotch shots on walls. Man after man lamented to Astrachan: "With a woman on the job, I can't talk the way I want to."

32   The macho bond derives its force from men's shared distrust of women, which is based on biology and entrenched by cultural patterns. Ever since primitive people made female idols with swollen bellies, women's power to bear children has filled men with awe. And women's time-honoured responsibility for rearing children has pitted the sexes against each other.

33   U.S. psychologists Dorothy Dinnerstein and Nancy Chodorow unravelled the process during the late 1970s. Simply put, mother is the first source of comfort and of prohibition for sons and daughters alike. She inspires passionate devotion and searing resentment in children of both sexes. But sons, unlike daughters, must forsake her for a more appropriate role model — the father.

34   A boy's rebellion against his mother, whom he loves and fears more than anything or anyone else, unleashes a maelstrom of loss and betrayal. Alarmed by his own emotions, he shuts them away. But in his adult relationships with women, he unconsciously re-enacts his childhood tragedy again and again. He may demand too much from his partner, or withdraw from an argument into angry silence.

This is the behaviour that Hite's latest book describes in some 900 pages. 35
And even if she exaggerates its extent, what it means is clear enough. Women
and men will not be loving equals until children have two active nurturers.

Almost a decade has passed since Betty Friedan, in *The Second Stage*, 36
urged feminists to stop measuring their progress in terms of equality with men.
She pointed to a more urgent challenge — the restructuring of social institutions — and she predicted that men would be essential to the task. So far, neither sex has answered the call. The women's movement, perhaps understand-
ably, has focussed less on shared parenting than on expanded day-care services
to promote women's participation in the workplace. The men's movement,
sadly, has encouraged men to seek custody after divorce, but not to be active
fathers during marriage.

Surely women and men can fare better as a team. Here's to the day when 37
none of us need worry about defending ourselves from the opposite sex.

Style and Structure

1. (a) Write down the number of the paragraph that contains the **thesis state-
     ment** of this essay.

   (b) What effects do the paragraphs preceding the **thesis statement** have on
     the reader? What reasons might the writer have for placing them ahead
     of her **thesis statement**? What does her choice of this order of presenta-
     tion tell you about the attitudes she believes her readers will bring to her
     thesis? Is this strategy an effective way of dealing with the intended
     reader? Give reasons for your answer.

   (c) List the kinds of writing and the kinds of intended readers for which this
     type of introduction would be *appropriate.*

   (d) List the kinds of writing and the kinds of intended readers for which this
     type of introduction might be *inappropriate.*

2. In paragraphs 1 to 17, identify three ways Maynard presents her information to show objectivity toward male activists. Give one example
   from the essay for each. How does this objectivity affect the reader?
   How does it affect the impact of the attack contained in the second half
   of the essay?

3. Paragraph 18 acts as a **transition**.

   (a) What change in approach to the subject takes place in this paragraph?

   (b) What reasons might Maynard have for starting the paragraph with two
     questions?

(c) How does the wording of the third sentence prepare for the coming change?

(d) How does the development of the ideas in this paragraph reflect the development of the ideas in the essay as a whole?

4. Identify three techniques that Maynard uses in paragraphs 19 and following to convince her reader that "their arguments are based not on reason or fairness, but on corrosive anger at women" (paragraph 18). Give one example from the essay for each.

5. Identify ten words or phrases that Maynard uses in paragraphs 19 and following to influence her reader against the arguments of male activists (e.g., "dismaying news" in paragraph 22). How effective is this subtle use of diction? Why?

6. Maynard's **conclusion** is not a simple summary of the essay or restatement of her **thesis**. What does she do in her **conclusion**? Is it an appropriate way to conclude this essay? Is it effective in conveying her overall message to the reader? Give reasons for your answers.

7. Nowhere in the essay does Maynard use the word "I." Yet her opinion of the male activists' movement is obvious.

(a) What effect does keeping her arguments in the third person ("he," "she," and "they") have upon the reader? Would her arguments have been more effective or less effective if she had written them in terms such as "I think . . . ," "I believe . . . ," or "I know of men who . . ."? Why?

(b) Under what circumstances would it be better to use the subjective "I" approach in your own writing? When would the objective approach be more effective?

Warm-up

1. This essay ends with the statement, "Surely women and men can fare better as a team." Working with the entire class, make a list of specific ways and specific situations in which women and men could fare better if they improved their teamwork. Select one item from the list and write a paragraph that explains how the teamwork could be improved. **Audience**: your classmates.

Give a copy of your paragraph to a group of five or six people in your class. Lead them in a five- to ten-minute discussion of your suggestions.

Make any revisions to your paragraph that might be necessary to clarify your suggestions. Distribute copies of the final draft to the group members so they can create small booklets that will be circulated through the class.

2. In groups of five or six people, create a short questionnaire that will allow you to judge the attitudes of men and women in your community toward Virgin's ideas. Have eight or nine people answer the questionnaire; try to get a cross section of different people. When you have finished, compile the survey results gathered by everyone in your group.

Write a short report of your findings aimed at the other people in your class.

Make overhead projections of the report that best summarize the results of your group's survey. Use these overheads as the basis for a short oral presentation to the class. (Make notes on the presentations made by the other groups so you can use the results in the "Thinking and Writing" section. Ask questions about any points that may not be clear to you.)

Thinking and Writing

1. One of Maynard's sources, Anthony Astrachan, estimates that 35 percent of men, at most, support women's quest for independence. Even some women would seem not to support it, since 20 percent of the calls Ross Virgin receives are from women.

Based on your own experiences with the people you know, write an essay in which you examine the support given by men and women to the search for women's equality and independence. Take into consideration factors that might affect people's support, such as education and age.
Audience: someone involved with the women's movement.

2. Maynard suggests that "what holds men back is fear: of exposing their own weakness, of losing other men's support, and of humiliation by women."

Write an essay in which you explain the role these factors and any others you can identify play in keeping men from supporting the search for women's equality and independence.
Audience: someone involved directly on one side or the other of this debate.

Send a copy of your final draft to someone in your school or community who is involved with the ISOJ or the National Action Committee on the Status of Women. Ask for a response.

Power and Control: Why Men Dominate Women

by Rick Goodwin

1   As a counsellor in a re-education program for abusive men, I recently worked with a man who was convicted of assault causing bodily harm. The charges stemmed from an incident where he beat his wife severely on Christmas Day with their children present. Asked to explain his actions, he told the court he was upset that morning because his wife allowed the children to open their presents before he got out of bed.

2   Before we pass judgment on this man and look for the psychological rationale for his behaviour, let us examine the greater social context in which this man and his family live. Their world is one in which women are half the population, perform two-thirds of the work, receive one-tenth of the world's income, and own only one-hundredth of the world's property. This assault was not the only injustice this woman has ever faced — simply because she was a woman.

3   The unjust treatment of women should not be news, nor the fact that this man's abuse and the relative privileges bestowed on men in society are intertwined. If we search for reasons why this disparity exists between the sexes in the first place, we must understand why men maintain their position of power over women.

4   At least ten percent of all women are victims of physical assault inflicted by their husbands or common-law partners. In Canada, this translates to close to a million women. In response to the unmet need for intervention with the batterers, I co-founded New Directions, a counselling service for abusive men. In addition to working directly with the abusers, we conduct many workshops on the issue of men's violence. The question I am most frequently asked by social workers, community groups, and even abused women themselves, is, simply, "Why do the men do it?"

5   It is not an easy question to answer because we still do not fully understand all the causes of wife battering. In our work with close to 300 abusive men, however, one factor has emerged as one root cause of men's violence against women. For men who batter, their purpose is simple: to gain power and control.

6   Every month, my colleague and I offer an information session for prospective clients. One of the things we do in this two-and-a-half hour workshop is to ask the men outright what causes their violence. They are usually quick to respond: "She provoked me," "I was drunk at the time," "I lost control," "My

psychiatrist told me I was insecure," "I was abused as a kid," "She was making a fool out of me." But when we ask them what they gain from their abusive behaviour, the group is usually silent, or may insist they don't get anything from it. This begs our response: "If you don't get anything from it, why do you do it?" Silence.

After attending the information session and an individual interview, the men may begin a 24-week program of group counselling based on a preset curriculum. In these sessions, we present various psycho-educational exercises designed to examine the components of both physical and emotional abuse. Throughout the program, we must always steer the group back to the heart of the issue — that men don't need to be abusive, that they *choose* to be because violence as a means of control works. We let them know that accepting this fundamental truth and abandoning their excuses is the first essential for them to stop their violence. 7

This isn't easy. While batterers may experience some negative and painful consequences of their actions, they have much to gain. For example, the men benefit from the forced acquiescence and subservience of their mates. The abuse affirms their own sense of superiority. The acts of violence can also protect men from dealing directly with their insecurities about themselves and their relationships. Abusive behaviour, of any type, is often used by men to reinforce their "male privilege" in the relationship. The attitude that a man is "king of the castle" is still very much with us. 8

This work has made me grapple with some disturbing truths. Abusive men are not much different from most men. Contrary to popular belief, they are not sick, pathological, or psychotic. They have been socialized in the same male-dominated society as the rest of us. While men who batter certainly differ as to the extent and expression of their need for power in relationships, it would be folly to think that the rest of us are immune to this need. Just as we all need to critically examine issues of discrimination because we live in a racist society, all men need to come to terms with issues of power as they relate to the women in their lives. 9

Some may find this surprising. Yet, much of our culture is characterized by relationships of domination and subordination, not only of men over women, but of industrialized countries over Third World nations, of lighter skins over dark, of rich over poor. In the age of Rambo, we implicitly believe we can obtain what we want by supremacy and force. As part of this process, we spend a lot of energy classifying individual perpetrators of injustice as "deviants" or "criminals." Their behaviour, however, is simply a concrete manifestation of the destructive and darker aspects of the human psyche. 10

This theme of domination is endemic to our society, particularly in the area of male–female relationships. The imperialism over women engulfs both marital 11 relationships and gender politics. Much like the issue of wife battering, the analysis of this power differential has emerged from the feminist movement. As a result, we now know that masculinity and femininity are socially constructed entities, and that tendencies toward domination are an integral component of the male "social" identity. Before we can diagnose the origins of male dominance, however, it is imperative that we examine the psychology of men.

12　　Noted feminist writer Susan Griffin employs the term "chauvinist thinking" to describe men's perception of women. Men all too often regard their own masculine attributes as superior when compared to traditional feminine qualities. This allows men to oppress and exploit women as beings who are inherently "inferior." Griffin refers to this cognitive polarity as a "delusion" that men desperately need to hold on to. The blinders of this ideology distort the perception not only of women's lives, but of men's lives as well. By denigrating "feminine" qualities and projecting them exclusively onto women, men reject important aspects of their own psyches, since expressions of "female" emotions and qualities do not conform with notions of traditional hypermasculinity. We see this clearly in the way boys insult each other. They use put-downs like "sissy," "girl," "wimp," and "fag" to call one another's masculinity into question. The ultimate insult for a male is to suggest that he is not a male!

13　　Patriarchal culture dictates that men must live with this strict and confining definition of heterosexual masculinity. Any substantial variance will not be tolerated. The feminine "other" symbolizes the inadequacies, fears, and aversions of this macho ideal. For men to hold true to traditional masculinity they must not only reject this "dark side" of themselves, but condemn it as well. Only by purging any "female" qualities can the purity of masculine identity be upheld and unquestioned. Women are not the only ones maligned by this process. Gay men and "effeminate" men also fall victim to this masculine imperialism.

14　　For oppression to work, the "other" must be objectified and discounted. In South Africa, the Afrikaners have to perceive blacks as less intelligent, less civil, and less governable to substantiate apartheid. Likewise, an abusive man will no doubt refer to his partner as "the wife," "my old lady," or simply "her." In this process, he denies her true identity by making her some sort of appendage or possession. Similarly, pornography is employed as a kind of propaganda of misogynist ideology. As Andrea Dworkin states, "Male power is the raison d'être of pornography: the degradation of the female is the means of achieving this power."

15　　Not surprisingly, male power has its roots in the socialization of boys in our culture. For males to develop their gender identity, they must undergo a radical transformation from total vulnerability and dependence as infants to an adult display of complete mastery over both themselves and their environment. Like girls, boys must dissociate themselves from their mothers, who represent the entire world from which they came. This is essential for children to create their own sense of self. Yet boys must also separate themselves from this primary bond as they become aware of their maleness. Subsequently, boys learn to bury their "feminine" qualities as characteristics that are associated with mother. What boy hasn't been told not to show his pain because "only girls cry"?

As boys remove themselves from their mothers, they begin to identify with 16
the more distant male figures in their lives. Fathers, brothers, or the male roles portrayed in society give boys a clear role model of masculinity. Their emotionality must be renounced, as well as any interest they may have in "girls' stuff." Boys are discouraged from any traditional feminine roles of nurturing as they enter the competitive and aggressive world of men. The modern-day archetypes of He-Man, G.I. Joe, and Captain Power permeate a boy's perception of the impenetrable world of men.

From an early age, boys learn that aggression is a legitimate means of 17
resolving conflict. Be it in sports, the schoolyard, policing, or war — or, as Andrea Dworkin states, "[in] the mythology of heroism" — violence is acceptable. What boy doesn't want a toy gun or soldier? Now we have water pistols that look like Uzis. The toy industry markets war toys exclusively for boys. As a child playing road hockey, I vividly recall my friends and me throwing down our sticks and staging fights because this is what we saw on television. Similarly, the schoolyard bully may be emulating his abusive parents, and the batterer may be repeating his father's behaviour toward his mother.

This continuum of dominance, aggression, and violence isn't just a replay 18
of witnessed events or a resolution of conflict. It also gets results. The potential of this power transforms the individual man from a position of relative powerlessness to one of complete control. Nobody messes with John Wayne or the Equalizer.

Male domination allows men economic advantage, as women make only 19
$0.64 for every dollar men earn, and can give them sexual liberties as expressed by sexual harassment and assault. Historically, men's physical and emotional needs have been met by women — mothers, girlfriends, housewives, maids. Men control women not only in monopolizing discussions but in politics and business as well. Perhaps the question should not be "Why do men batter?" but "Why do they feel they need to?"

When men batter, they discount their partner's selfhood on a daily basis. 20
Society can be accused of the same crime, in that it has historically failed to respond to, much less identify, the victims of this male terrorism. Yet, things are changing for the better, now that we are no longer silently ignoring the needs of abused women. As a result, batterers are slowly being confronted. If

we demand that abusers be held accountable for their behaviour, we must also demand the same from the police, the courts, and other powers-that-be. It becomes painfully apparent that to change abusive men we must change our abusive society.

21   Part of this process of change must involve redefining power as an either-or concept. It is not a choice for men to consider that the only other alternative to having power over women is to be powerless. One of the greatest fears for abusers is that they will be "walked all over" by their partner if they give up their control. This false choice permeates our culture. We must strive instead for a society that honours a position of "power-from-within," a situation of mutuality and egalitarianism that honours all involved. By reclaiming the original definition of power as "to be able," we can evoke a sense of empowerment in both men and women. Since abuse cannot occur between equals, we must first restructure both interpersonal and gender equity.

22   We've got a lot of work to do before we can herald a major change. We are on the right track in addressing male violence by establishing programs for batterers; however, male abuse of power is an issue for *all* men to consider, not only those involved in violence programs. All too often, even those who receive counselling only modify their use of controlling behaviours. Much fanfare can be made over men's reduction of physical violence while they are in treatment. Unfortunately, many of the men only develop more subtle and sophisticated forms of verbal and psychological abuse to maintain their control. Feminists and social workers alike need to give more thought to what the mandate for these groups should be, in addition to what constitutes success.

23   Men's programs will not stop patriarchy. At best, they can provide a blueprint for change, if men *choose* to change. Batterers' groups deliver a strong message to society that men are responsible for their violence, and that their behaviour is unacceptable. We must not, however, be seduced into believing that therapy can be the vanguard of an egalitarian society. Male dominance must be recognized and rooted out wherever it is found in society. As men, we must start challenging each other in our sexism, as well as providing ourselves with support in our struggle to break free from it.

24   If we want to achieve equality between the sexes, then we will have to give up our power and control over women. It's only fair. Men are now beginning to question the psychological costs they pay to maintain their male dominance. Perhaps this is a start. What we do know is that, as men, we must begin the difficult process of relinquishing our masculine prerogatives. If not, whether we batter or not, our collusion with male violence will continue.

Style and Structure

1. (a) In his title, Goodwin suggests he is writing about the relationship between men battering women and power and control. Where in the essay does he actually make a direct statement about this relationship?

   (b) What purpose is served in delaying this **thesis statement**?

   (c) Do you feel that his strategy of repeating the title in the **thesis statement** is an effective one? Would you alter either the **thesis statement** or the title?

2. (a) The opening sentence of this essay contains a personal statement: "I recently worked with a man who was convicted of assault causing bodily harm." What purpose do you think the writer has in mind when he makes such a statement?

   (b) Students are sometimes advised to avoid making "I"-statements. Explain whether you think this is a general rule, or whether it applies only to certain situations.

   (c) Can you suggest situations where an "I"-statement is especially effective?

3. Goodwin makes good use of **topic sentences** throughout the essay. Identify which ones are particularly effective in focussing the reader's attention. Explain the reasons for your choices.

4. (a) Writers in several fields, sociology among them, have occasionally been criticized for using too much jargon in their communications. With the help of a dictionary, explain what jargon is. Do you find evidence of this habit in Goodwin's writing?

   (b) Identify those words you believe to be jargon. Do you think their use could have been avoided? Use a dictionary or thesaurus to suggest alternatives.

   (c) Examine the effect of jargon. Survey classmates about how they felt when reading the passage(s) you have identified and together make a list of reactions. What advice might nonexperts give to professionals who write?

5. (a) From paragraph 12 on, the writer makes frequent use of quotation marks: "female" emotions, "dark side," "effeminate" men, "female" qualities, and so on. Discuss Goodwin's probable intention in using these quotation marks.

   (b) Do you find that the quotation marks help or simply get in the way? Give reasons for your opinion.

6. (a) Examine paragraph 19: "Male domination allows men economic advantage, as women make only $0.64 for every dollar men earn. " Would you judge this paragraph to have strong **unity**? **Coherence**? (See pp. 211 and 212.)

(b) Rewrite the paragraph, starting with the **concluding sentence**, adding appropriate **transitional words**, and devising a new **concluding sentence**. Compare your reworked paragraph with the original and decide which is better, and why.

Warm-up

Many writers begin the essay-writing process by telling a story or recalling a vivid scene from the past. Take a few moments to remember a scene of children acting with violence, which you have either seen in real life or read about in literature. Tell (don't read) the story to the class, taking time to represent the scene as vividly as possible. As you are telling your story, try to note its effect on your listeners. Often, when a story strikes a respondent chord, listeners will nod or otherwise indicate agreement.

After all the stories are told, examine, as a class, which ones are especially effective and why. Discuss how you might use the storytelling technique as preparation for your next essay.

Thinking and Writing

1. Goodwin points out that he remembers playing road hockey, when the players threw down their sticks and staged fights because they had seen such behaviour on television. He suggests, "From an early age, boys learn that aggression is a legitimate means of resolving conflict" (paragraph 17).

    Make a list of three occasions when, as a child, you might have acted out aggression as you had seen others do, or perhaps occasions when you saw others behaving aggressively in imitation of a parent or other role model. For each occasion, jot down as many of the details of the scene and the behaviour as you can remember. Now, taking Goodwin's statement (above) as your **thesis**, and your examples as evidence, develop an essay in which you argue that children pattern their behaviour after a given model. **Audience**: someone who would question the validity of this thesis.

2. Although most of us would think of abusive people as sick or abnormal, Goodwin makes the point that abusive men are not much different from others: they are not "sick, pathological, or psychotic" (paragraph 9). Perhaps what we need, then, is a better profile of an abuser.

    Write an essay in which you describe a hypothetical abuser, using information from Goodwin's essay and giving examples to illustrate your case. Suggest what sort of man he is, what his background might be, and how he views himself and the world. You may want to consult some standard sources, such as journals of psychology and/or sociology, to get other expert opinions to validate your case.

Audience: young women who believe spouse abusers are easily recognized.

The Dispossessed

by Harvey Schachter

1   Dennis Barlett is wearing an open-necked white shirt with stripes, but he's blue collar to the core. On the wall of the brawny ex-steelworker's office, alongside the clippings about the latest swings in the economy, is a newspaper photograph of him addressing his workmates at the impromptu rally that sad day in 1992 when Canadian Building Systems Inc. announced its plant would be shut down, eliminating 200 jobs.

2   Three years later Bartlett is still addressing the fears of those suddenly separated from a steady paycheque. He is waving a ribbon of seven computer sheets, on which are printed the names of some 350 steelworkers who lost their jobs and who are depending on Bartlett, the job placement coordinator, to find them decent work.

3   Some already have jobs — "survival jobs," Bartlett calls them, paying $8 an hour — but they hope to return to the $15-to $20-an-hour glory days of the past. Others are without work, struggling on unemployment insurance or welfare, hoping to hope again.

4   They're just part of the carnage in the blue-collar ranks as the Canadian economy restructures. While reams of newspaper columns have been devoted to white-collar job losses, blue-colour workers have been hit far harder, without as much attention. More than 300,000 jobs were lost in manufacturing alone during the first three years of the decade, and nobody believes those jobs will be regained. "In the recession of the early '80s, the plants may have downsized but people eventually went back," says Paul Cloutier, administrator of income support for Durham Region, just east of Toronto. "This time, a lot of plants are gone. We're not riding out a few bad years." Like other welfare officers, he is having to deal with an increasing number of formerly middle-class, male blue-collar workers who have been driven down into welfare.

5   The epicentre for this largely unheralded earthquake is Southern Ontario, the manufacturing heartland of the country, although shocks and aftershocks have been felt across the land. The hardest-hit people in this recession, according to an unpublished Statistics Canada study, were male manufacturing workers in Ontario, aged 25 to 44, with a primary-school-or-lower level of education. In the long run, though, the bleakest prospects may belong to the older blue-collar workers thrown out of their jobs. Carla Lipsig-Mummé, director of the Centre for Research on Work and Society at York University in Toronto, sees them as "cast on the scrap heap of history"

and reaches back to catchphrases from the '30s for a harsh assessment: "Fifty has become old for these male blue-collar workers — too old to work and too young to die."

It's all part of a several-decades-long transformation of Canadian work. Manual occupations accounted for one-third of Canadian jobs in 1961, according to figures compiled by Noah Meltz, principal of the University of Toronto's Woodsworth College. By the end of the century, that will drop to about one-fifth of jobs. The shift amounts to an upheaval in the nature of work. The 1:1 ratio between white-collar and blue-collar jobs that for decades defined Canada's work force has abruptly flipped into a 3:1 predominance of white-collar positions. "Rarely do you look at economic data and see that magnitude of shift. In relative terms, it's a startling transformation," says Gordon Betcherman, former labor market research director at the Economic Council of Canada and now executive director of the human resources group at Ekos Research Associates Inc., a social-economic research group in Ottawa.

The transformation of work poses challenges to every sector of society. It is forcing unions to rethink their traditional antagonism toward working with management and pushing them to tap new sources to refill their depleted membership rolls. It is also pressing management to come up with new ways to educate its work force in the demands of a knowledge-based economy. And it is forcing governments to address the tremendous social issue of what place — if any — is left for the person who brings nothing more to the job market than a willingness to work.

Many male blue-collar workers are trained on the job, often learning skills that are not portable to another workplace. Today, that blue-collar worker is fighting for his economic life, at best hoping to hang on to a job until early retirement. Barlett deals with some of those who aren't that lucky: "When they lose their jobs, it's devastating. Often they've never looked for a job before. They don't know what a résumé is."

It's a steel gray day in Steeltown, matching the moods of the job hunters drawn to the employment centre tucked into the side of the old union hall. There's coffee and doughnuts in the back room, to promote socializing for those who need companionship through these troubled times.

Although only 28, Rob Hanc has sampled the good days for blue-collar work — and the bad. With only a Grade 12 education and little more to offer an employer than his brute strength, the tall Hamilton native followed his father and many male relatives into the foundry. He was a heavy laborer, grinding and chipping away, lifting and carrying — hard, physical work that he could feel taking a toll on his body.

11   A few years out of high school, he made $47,000 for the year. "I had it all. Good money. Great benefits. It was all there," says Hanc. Then suddenly, it wasn't. His company announced a massive layoff of 750 people. "I had seven years [seniority], working full-time. You figure you're in — but you're not. Now I have to start from the ground up again."

12   His marriage dissolved about the time of the layoff. Combined, the couple's income had been about $75,000 a year. He kept the house, but without his wife's help with the $1,100-per-month mortgage payments, he still needed to bring in big bucks. "I looked around for work. But everything came up short — $10 or $11 an hour. I can't work for less than $15 an hour. It sounds stupid — absolutely ridiculous. But I have to sell everything if I take a job for less," he says.

13   "Those jobs are around. My biggest problem is lack of education," says Hanc. "When I was in Grade 12, I was first exposed to computers. It's not enough today. Me and my friends say, 'Oh boy, are we in trouble.' It's scary how far ahead things are. I don't know how to do things. We used to fix cars. Now I'm scared to open the hood. Everything has changed. And it's changing every day. We can't stop and catch up. And heavy labor is a dying breed."

14   Hanc's father is retired now; an uncle took a buyout. The previous day's newspaper reported a comfortable $221-million profit for Hanc's former employers last year, which rankles: "All their debt's paid off. And we're out of there. We got nothing."

15   Hanc wasn't interested in retraining after his layoff: "Me and school don't go together. I need to work with my hands." He survived comfortably on unemployment insurance and considered going into business for himself by buying a centra-vacuuming operation. But only a week before his UI was to run out, his company offered him 10 months' work. When that runs out in December, he will receive a severance payment from the steel manufacturer. He sees little prospect of further work at the steelmaker. "I'd like to work for myself," he says. "But I'm like everyone else. I'm scared."

16   There's ample evidence to justify Hanc's fear of the future. York University's Paul Grayson studied what happened to blue-collar workers after two plant closures and found they "tend to be downwardly mobile when displaced. They drift in and out of part-time work. It's a slippery slope, with life precarious occupationally. Once they get displaced, they can't assume they'll have a long-term job again."

17   Two-thirds of workers do manage to find work, either full- or part-time, within a year of being laid off, according to a study by Statistics Canada. But almost 25% of workers simply drop out of the work force. And for those who do manage to find jobs, layoffs and closures often strike again: 10% of laidoff workers in 1978–1979 were laid off an average of six times in the following seven years.

Such desperation in male blue-collar ranks could be the breeding ground 18
for political revenge. Workers may take aim at those in governments that view male workers as advantaged and that bend their efforts to assist more politically correct job applicants.

That disenchantment can also fuel racism as blue-collar males struggling 19
in the labor force — or outside the labor force — watch high-profile government programs being launched for others. In the US, affirmative action programs are under assault by Republicans, who have drawn their votes disproportionately from men. A similar reaction could soon be felt here. Consider the potential for upheaval implicit in the image of desperate people lining up in the winter of 1995, 26,000 strong, for the possibility of good blue-collar jobs at General Motors of Canada Ltd. The scene, in Pickering, Ont., reminded York's Lipsig-Mummé of the '30s. She recalls that in the Great Depression the unemployed made a fuss that forced the government to react — but that hasn't happened yet this time.

While the blue-collar devastation has yet to affect politicians drastically, it 20
has had its impact on labor unions. Some of Canada's most powerful unions draw their strength from our largest manufacturing industries. As the companies they negotiate with have downsized, the unions have had to scramble to find new members in other fields. Some groups have merged. Several have also explored new avenues for growth, attempting to enlist workers in such businesses as hotels, nursing homes, taxis and retail stores.

To survive, unions have had to adjust philosophically as well. After 21
fiercely fighting free trade and after years of combat with corporations over workplace initiatives such as total quality management, unions have made a tentative peace. They have recognized that workplace restructuring is a global phenomenon and that it will be introduced unilaterally if unions don't get involved. One sign of optimism: unions and management have co-operated in the creation of sectoral councils that provide a mechanism for attacking common problems such as workplace training and adjustment programs for downsizing. If there's a sunny side to the battering in the blue-collar world, it's these councils and the innovative programs they've spawned.

The renewed emphasis on education and training they've offered is gener- 22
ally viewed as critical to job opportunity. Economist Lloyd Atkinson, of MT Associates Investment Counsel Inc. in Toronto, notes that from 1990 to 1993 employment for those with a high-school degree rose by 308,000 or 17%, while for those who didn't complete high school, it fell by 651,000, or 28%. Garth Jackson, the former president of Canadore College in North Bay, Ont., who is now CEO of the training and adjustment board, says, "The male blue-collar worker has to move toward being a knowledge worker."

23   But there's some skepticism in union halls. It relates to the question of whether blue-collar work — indeed, all routine work in the economy — requires more skills or has become deskilled, with technology serving as the brains of the operation. "We need to distinguish the rhetoric and public proclamations from what is actually happening," says Jim Turk, director of education for the Ontario Federation of Labour. "Contrary to the hype, the majority of jobs require less skill and less training. What confuses it is that [workers are] working on sophisticated technology." He points to the fact that the second most productive auto plant in the world is in Mexico, and it succeeds without a highly educated work force. And he cited the example of McDonald's. The fast-food empire has set the standard for more traditional manufacturing operations with its consistency from outlet to outlet and its ability to take advantage of a low-skill work force.

24   Paul Nykanen, vice-president of the Ontario division of the Canadian Manufacturers' Association, concedes that there's no question a lot of technological improvements simplify but, he argues, "to operate these sophisticated machines, there must be a fundamental understanding. Workers need a lot of skills and upgrading to do that."

25   The electrical/electronics industry is demonstrating how a sector can work with its employees to upgrade its work force. Companies in the industry target the equivalent of 1% of payroll toward training of current employees in programs that run from half a day to two weeks in duration. In 1993, as the initiative got under way, 3,481 workers were trained; last year that figure zoomed to 17,409. The program involved about 45% of employees at member firms, at a cost of $5.5 million.

26   Brock Telecom Ltd., a subsidiary of Northern Telecom Ltd. in Brockville, Ont., which deals with mechanical and circuit pack assemblies and the Meridian business phone unit, began its training initiative last August and managed to accommodate 33% of its employees by the end of the year. A few workers received funding to take short-term courses at Queen's University. But, for most, it was courses in the afternoon — half on company time, half on employee time — ranging from keyboarding and programming to so-called softer skills, such as critical thinking, problem-solving, personal effectiveness and presentation ability. Wander in one day and you might find a group of employees — most, but not all, blue-collar — practising presentations before a video camera or trying to solve a brainteaser using nonlinear thinking in a critical-thinking class. Although the skills extend beyond the workplace, the instructors and workers keep them close to home, relating issues to the workplace in discussions.

27   But for all such "upside" training, there's still a widespread need for "downside" training, helping employees to switch to other fields as their jobs

disappear. The steel industry, for instance, produced the same amount of metal in 1993 with roughly half the workers it required for the same volume of production in 1981. Anil Verma, a professor in the University of Toronto's Faculty of Management and Centre for Industrial Relations, expects more downsizing, amounting to another 50% of the work force over the next 10 years.

The Canadian Steel and Employment Congress has responded by establish-   28
ing an adjustment committee after each major layoff to help workers. Since beginning such efforts in 1988, the congress has set up 67 committees to serve more than 13,000 laid-off employees. Almost 11,500 of them — 88% — have made use of some service. About 60% of participants have received some training, ranging from short-term basic skills and skills upgrading to long-term training for up to three years to help them move into a new career outside of the steel industry.

The program is driven by the notion of steelworkers helping steelworkers.   29
The staff have all experienced layoffs or plant closures. Counselling is done by peers, with workers receiving emotional support against the stress of layoffs but also being forced to face a constant reality check on the feasibility of future employment thoughts. "Some people may want to be nuclear scientists. But we look at what's reasonable," says Bill Mouck, the labour adjustment coordinator in Hamilton, who himself was a casualty of the bankruptcy of Interlake Steel Inc. in Thorold, Ont., and who established a committee to help other workers. Another discipline is that employees seeking retraining must research and develop a proposal themselves, thus demonstrating some commitment.

Nationwide, only 74% of laid-off steelworkers find jobs. And blue-collar   30
work remains in decline. Indeed, blue-collar workers have been taking a pounding since long before the recent recession. Statistics Canada's Picot and Pyper found that each year in the 1980s, from the bust year of 1982 to the boom year of 1988, companies permanently laid off more than one million workers. In the scramble to find work, the lucky ones often land in what the Economic Council of Canada once labeled the "bad jobs" sectors of the economy. They shift to unskilled service jobs or lower-paying manual work, able because of their work history to take jobs away from others — particulary the young, who have even less to offer. Bernie Mason watches the struggle of the blue-collar worker from the welfare office he runs in Kingston: "You see a helluva lot more of them showing up here. Some 'bump and displace' [other] people having less experience, and get the $7-an-hour jobs." With the struggle has come a loss of security and inevitably some erosion of sense of self for all blue-collar workers.

It's a loss that counsellors such as Mouck and Barlett feel keenly. Today,   31
they won't find time for lunch, having to be content with some Timbits from the back room. A few job seekers have been in to check the job board and chat.

Others have phoned, keeping in touch. Barlett is on the phone, following leads and networking with company contacts, while simultaneously scanning the job ads in the seven newspapers he scouts daily.

32   "There's nothing better than when somebody goes through training and we find another job for them or they find a job for themselves," says Mouck. "It's like tasting the first strawberry of spring. You want more. You hunger for it. It's rewarding — every time it happens." It has not been a fertile period for blue-collar workers. All he can do is hope to pick a few more strawberries every now and then.

Style and Structure

1.   This essay, which appeared in a magazine called *Canadian Business*, begins with a description of Dennis Barlett. How does this **introduction** set the tone for the essay as a whole? What might the choice of this introduction say about the perspective of the magazine's editors?

2.   Most readers have a good idea what this essay is about right from the beginning, but can you find a single **thesis statement**? What do you suppose is the writer's strategy in this case?

3.   Throughout the article the writer employs many statistics to make his case. Evaluate his use of these statistics: has he made them understandable for the average reader? What qualities do such statistics bring to an essay of this nature?

4.   The writer employs a number of images to describe the employment situation and the difficulties faced by workers. He refers to the changes in the job market as an earthquake, for instance, and the term "blue collar" itself is a figure of speech.

   (a) Reread the essay, identifying as many of these figures as possible.

   (b) Which of these figures seem particularly effective to you, and why?

   (c) What effect do such figures have on the reader's ability to understand what the writer is saying?

5.   Several times the Depression of the 1930s is mentioned. It is unlikely that anyone old enough to have lived through those days is currently involved in the workplace upheavals that Schachter deals with here. In your opinion, what effect does the reference have on readers?

6.   Reread Paragraphs 10 to 15, in which Schachter describes the situation of unemployed worker Rob Hanc. What emotions do you believe the writer wishes readers to feel as they hear Hanc's story?

7. This essay deals with complex issues such as the future of work and the need for retraining. Unlike many argument-based essays, it proposes no definitive solutions to the problems.

(a) Identify areas where the writer shows two sides to an issue.

(b) In each case, does the writer seem to favour the arguments of one side or the other? Explain your opinion.

(c) Is the lack of a solution or solutions in this essay likely to worry or annoy the reader? What conclusions might the reader draw?

Warm-up

"Me and school don't go together. I need to work with my hands," says Rob Hanc, one of "the dispossessed" Schachter introduces in his essay. (See Paragraph 10.)

Take no more than 15 minutes to write a single paragraph in which you explain whether a person like Hanc might feel out of place in your school. Try to convey Hanc's emotions to the reader as accurately and sensitively as possible.

Thinking and Writing

1. Wally Beevor, national coordinator of a program aimed at helping high school students prepare for jobs in the field of electrical and electronics manufacturing, reports that 65% of young people in Canada do not go into postsecondary education, a figure he says has remained essentially the same since the 1950s. Given the demands of the modern workplace, some people would suggest that such a trend represents suicidal tendencies in the young!

With the evidence presented in this essay, supplemented by information you take from other sources or personal interviews, present an argument to convince young people to pursue their education past the high school level. Be sure to follow an acceptable style guide to cite your sources.

Audience: high school students and their parents, who may be worried about the problem of finding jobs in Canada but may not know the extent of the problem as laid out in Schachter's essay.

2. Some experts suggest that a perception problem exists in the minds of the public, who may see real "career-type" jobs as those of lawyers or

doctors while completely ignoring the need for skilled tradespersons. Some sectors of industry actually say they cannot find enough well-prepared candidates for jobs requiring math, science, teamwork and problem-solving skills.

Do some research, perhaps through your local employment counselling offices or through the print or electronic media, to discover areas where skilled tradespersons are very much in demand. Write a classification essay to describe the different types of jobs you have discovered. *Variation:* Using the research you have above, and information you find from local high school teachers and administrators (or from your own friends), write a compare and contrast essay to show the discrepancy between what industry is looking for and what young students expect from the workplace.

Audience: students in the last years of elementary school or high school who are contemplating their plans for education and a career.

Send a copy to your local high school guidance department or principal's office.

Muscling In on Madness
by Clarence Reynolds

It's no secret that for many bodybuilders and athletes, popping steroids goes hand in hand with pumping iron. Anabolic steroids — synthetic versions of the male hormone testosterone — allow users to develop more impressive pecs and delts than they could by weight training alone. But the quest for brawn may play havoc with the brain. Psychiatrists Harrison Pope Jr., at McLean Hospital in Belmont, Massachusetts, and David Katz of Harvard Medical School report that steroid use can lead to major psychiatric disturbances. 1

In the past, attention has focussed on the physical toll exacted by steroids. In men, steroids can cause breast development, shrinking of the testes, and decreased sperm production; in women, they can lead to deepening of the voice, growth of facial and body hair, clitoral enlargement, and menstrual irregularity. Long-term risks in both sexes include liver damage, hypertension, and atherosclerosis. 2

Much less attention has been given to the mental effects of steroids. Anecdotal evidence, however, suggests that the drugs can lead to unusually aggressive and irritable behaviour. When two patients turned up at McLean Hospital with steroid-induced psychosis, Pope and Katz decided to investigate. 3

The psychiatrists interviewed 41 bodybuilders and football players who admitted having used the drugs. (Although steroids can't be legally obtained without a prescription, they are there for the asking on a thriving black market.) Thirteen of the athletes reported that they had experienced manic or near-manic behaviour during steroid use. The most common symptoms were hyperactivity and inflated self-esteem, which increased their drive to train harder and intensify their workouts. They also described episodes of grandiose and reckless behaviour. One 23-year-old man bought a $17 000 sports car while taking the oral steroid methandrostenolone. When he stopped the drug, he realized he could not afford the payments and sold the car. A year later, during another steroid cycle, he impulsively bought a $20 000 sports car. Another respondent, convinced of his own immortality, deliberately drove a car into a tree at 65 kilometres per hour while a friend videotaped him. 4

Five subjects also experienced severe psychotic episodes. One person had auditory hallucinations that lasted for five weeks; another became extremely paranoid and thought his friends were stealing from him; yet another developed the grandiose delusion that he could lift his car and tip it over. These episodes ceased when they stopped taking the drugs. "We're not exactly sure what causes the mood changes," says Katz, "but we do believe that somehow 5 these drugs disrupt the normal functioning of neurotransmitters in the central nervous system."

6   Although steroids are sometimes prescribed for medical purposes (to treat men with low testosterone levels, for example), the doses are generally lower than those used by athletes, and Pope and Katz think that psychiatric manifestations are much less likely to occur. Athletes often "stack" steroids, taking up to five or six different kinds, including oral and injectable drugs and even veterinary preparations.

7   Since many athletes are wary of discussing their steroid use, says Katz, it's difficult to assess how common such psychiatric disturbances are. "But we're convinced that there's a huge subculture out there using the drugs. We've only touched the tip of the iceberg."

Style and Structure

1. (a) Judging from the vocabulary used throughout this essay, who would you think is included in the intended audience?

   (b) Make a list of any words you do not immediately recognize and guess at the definitions from the context by reading the passages in which they occur. Check a dictionary to see how accurate your guesses are.

   (c) Reviewing your list in (b), do you think the writer does a good job of showing the meaning of the words chosen through the context in which they occur?

   (d) Do you believe the use of these unusual words is necessary for the overall effectiveness of the essay? Put a check mark beside each of the words in your list that you believe is essential to the essay.

2. In this short essay, how many different **organizational approaches** have been used? What would you say is the overall **organizational approach**? (See pp. 212–213)

3. In the **concluding paragraph**, the researchers state that it is difficult to assess the psychiatric side effects of steroids because athletes are wary of discussing their use. Has the writer managed to show that there is not a large body of evidence to back up the essay? How?

Warm-up

Many writers begin their essay-writing process by highlighting questions that people have about a certain issue. Draw up a list of at least five questions that people have concerning the use of steroids. Be sure that your list covers the entire breadth of the issue, not just a single interesting aspect.

When you have completed your list, discuss what is achieved by writing down the questions. How might the reader of an essay on the topic benefit if the writer brought out these questions? Discuss with classmates.

Thinking and Writing

1. It has been suggested that we live in a society that believes there is a chemical cure for every problem. You're feeling down? — Have a drink! Feel a cold coming on? — Take a megadose of Vitamin C! We pour chemicals into our bodies, onto our foods — even onto our lawns to keep them problem-free. To the outsider, it would seem that we have enormous faith in chemicals.

   Write an essay, developed by example, in which you inventory the ways a typical family responds to its problems with chemical solutions. You do not need to have all the answers or to be fully aware of all the implications of the family's use of chemicals. Do try, however, to raise thought-provoking questions for your readers about lifestyles and chemical dependencies of all sorts.

   Audience: the average Canadian who is unaware of the extent to which we use chemicals.

2. The essay outlines a number of unpleasant side effects that steroids produce, and yet we hear almost daily about athletes using these banned substances to increase their stamina and ability. We must assume that, although these athletes are aware of the dangers, their desire to win is greater than their fear of the drugs' side effects.

   What is this drive to win all about? Is it always the admirable impulse to overcome obstacles and achieve excellence in whatever field? Or is it something less healthy, something that a great number of us don't have and are just as glad?

   Write an extended-definition essay, in which you examine the competitive drive. Develop your essay with numerous examples, but be sure to use appropriate transitions and to state your thesis clearly.

   Audience: aggressive young people who have not considered all the implications of competitiveness.

Autophobia

by Steve Vanagas

1   Imagine an invention that could carry you from your front door to virtually any destination across town and beyond at speeds of over 100 kilometres per hour. Imagine that you could choose your own audio entertainment, control how hot or cold it would be inside, and even choose what time to leave and how fast to go. Imagine enjoying this in complete privacy or with passengers — your choice. And imagine that this invention is affordable for everyone from corporate executives to high school students.

2   This invention, of course, already exists. It is the car. The culture and economy of North America revolve around the automobile. It is both an expression and a tool of personal liberty. Virtually everyone in North America of driving age either has a car or has access to one on a regular basis either as a driver or passenger.

3   In some areas, however, the automobile is on the defensive. For instance, its supremacy on the road is being challenged by provincial politicians and regional planners in the Greater Vancouver Regional District (GVRD) who believe that the car is an addiction causing pollution, noise and health problems, while also wrecking neighbourhoods and wasting resources.

4   But the prescribed cure for this addiction — discouraging car use through a series of incentives and penalties, and enlarging the government public transit monopoly — may be worse than the disease. Critics call it a recipe for higher costs to taxpayers with no guarantee that it will improve air pollution or traffic congestion. The only guarantee is that people will have less freedom to drive their cars, fewer places to park, and will have to spend more money doing it. Meanwhile, car-friendly, market-based solutions, such as road-pricing, have been left unexplored.

5   Indeed, automobile owners may face a future as second-class citizens. For example, "Greater Vancouver has concluded that heavy reliance on the private automobile is unhealthy," declares a 1993 report by the GVRD and the provincial government. Proposed measures to get people out of their cars and into public transit over the next 25 years include,

- Promoting car pooling by creating a network of high-occupancy-vehicle (HOV) lanes where buses and car-pools carrying three or more persons can bypass congestion while single-occupant vehicles simmer in rush hour.
- Giving buses the priority through new laws and dedicated bus lanes and by buying new extra-capacity "Rapid Buses" for the busiest routes.
- Building new rapid-transit lines including commuter rail and light rail.

- Squeezing cars out of downtown areas with parking restrictions, fewer parking spaces, and higher parking rates.
- Charging tolls for entering the downtown area in peak hours.
- Raising gasoline prices by 50% in real terms by 2021.
- Introducing traffic calming measures that make urban car travel slower and more frustrating.

"They're waging a war against the car," comments Marion Keys, executive vice-president of the B.C. Motor Dealers' Association (MDA). "Planners believe the car is the scourge of the planet and what they want to do is force people to change their habits. It's social engineering at its worst."

The justification for these measures? Ostensibly, smog. But if dirty air is not enough to persuade residents of the need for radical action, then dire predictions of the health costs stemming from exhaust emissions are expected to do the trick. The B.C. environment ministry, for instance, says studies show that if action isn't taken to improve the air in the Lower Fraser Valley, there will be 2,800 premature deaths, 33,000 more hospital admissions and crop damage of $75 million over the next 25 years — at a net cost of about $1 billion.

But cars will continue to clog our roads and neighbourhoods, creating congestion headaches, parking problems, noise and a demand for more and more roads. So cities are finding their own solutions. Vancouver, for instance, is trying to scare off the casual driver by lowering the maximum number of parking spaces included in new developments in the downtown core. Some cities are considering punitive "calming" measures, such as narrowed roads, speed bumps, exclusive public transit lanes, chicanes to curve previously straight roads, and traffic islands in intersections to make streets more appealing for pedestrians and cyclists.

Meanwhile anti-car activists may be adopting the same incremental tactics as their environmentalist cousins. Already commuters have been subject to protests by militant cyclists who clog key bridges in rush hour to publicize their demands for bike lanes. And car-haters have their allies in government. Thus, in 1993, politicians released a transportation plan for the Lower Mainland of B.C. called "Transport 2021" that established as goals a drop in rush-hour vehicle trips by 10%, an increase in transit ridership by one-quarter, and $1 billion in user charges to service the debt created by spending on public transit, bike networks and HOV lanes. The freedom to drive in the privacy of your own car may yet become a rare luxury.

The bottom line is that they dream of transforming a culture of cars and long commutes into environmentally-friendly walking and bicycling communities where people live, work and shop in town centres and use public transit to travel longer distances. "They're trying to make driving socially unacceptable

— like smoking," says the MDA's Ms. Keys. But, she points out that people use cars not to be "socially irresponsible" but to get to work.

10   However, moderate environmentalists embrace one plan apparently not considered by anti-smog zealots: "road-pricing." Drivers would be charged for using the roads — a higher price in rush hours, a lower price in off-peak hours. Although it may be unpalatable for many commuters, it would at least have the virtue of relieving congestion without turning car owners into second-class citizens. Under such a system, cars might be outfitted with electronic strips capable of being read by sensors measuring the time and distance travelled. The owners are billed later. Singapore has had such a pricing scheme since 1975 and its $2.50-a-day toll cut rush-hour traffic by 69% in four years.

11   Lawrence Solomon, research director of Toronto-based Energy Probe, makes the case for privately-run mass transit, now making great strides in the United Kingdom. Writing in *The Next City* magazine, he observes that "London's public transit system as a whole is costing taxpayers less, generating internal profits more, and looking forward to the day its surplus can finance its expansions, too. Car use? Why, in London it has been falling since 1990, losing market share to public transit."

12   Unless we decide to explore this and other less-expensive avenues, commuters will continue lining up to enter our cities. And for most car drivers, the sacrifice of long waits in rush hour will continue to be worth it. "People view their vehicles in very practical terms for travel to and from work, school, and shopping," comments Ms. Keys. "For most people, cars mean freedom of movement."

Style and Structure

1. (a) What is Vanagas' objective in the first two paragraphs of the essay? What is the primary appeal to the reader of the ideal vehicle he presents? Why is it important to put this idea into the reader's mind at the very beginning of the essay?

   (b) Underline the **thesis statement** for this essay.

   (c) Why would Vanagas choose to include the contents of paragraph 4 at this point in the essay?

2. (a) In paragraphs 5 to 8, Vanagas divides his discussion of the measures taken against automobile use by looking at two groups. What advantages does this approach offer him?

   (b) What information does Vanagas present in paragraph 9? How does it relate to the information presented in paragraphs 5 to 8? What advantages does he achieve by saving this material until this point?

(c) What are the advantages of using a bulleted list in paragraph 5?

3. What information does Vanagas include in paragraphs 10 and 11? In what ways does their inclusion influence the reader's attitude toward controlling automobile use?

4. Evaluate the effectiveness of the final paragraph as a conclusion.

5. A writer chooses words to establish a tone and imply an attitude toward an essay's subject, in the hope of convincing the reader. What tone does Vanagas establish in this essay? To support your answer, cite five or six examples of his word choice that set the tone.

Warm-up

1. Select a new car ad you have seen or read. Write a paragraph that examines whether or not the ad appeals to prospective buyers by offering a car as "an expression and a tool of personal liberty." (If it does not, explain how the ad does appeal to prospective purchasers.)

   In a group of classmates, exchange your paragraphs to see how many different types of appeals have been identified.

2. Working with a group of four or five classmates, do a survey of people to find out why they need a car. Make sure your survey includes a review of both males and females from a range of age groups, living conditions (urban, suburban, and rural) educational backgrounds, and work experience. Ask each person surveyed what year, make, and model of car he/she owns now. (You can use answers to this question to judge whether people actually buy the type of vehicle they say they want.) Pool your findings with the others in your work group.

   Construct a table or chart that shows your survey results effectively.

   Finally, write a paragraph to give the reader an overview of the findings presented in your table.

   Exchange your work with several classmates. Are there any suggestions you can make for ways they could improve their creations? Do they have any suggestions that would improve yours?

Thinking and Writing

1. Examine ads for a number of different cars. Explore the kind of prospective buyer to whom each ad is meant to appeal. You might begin by asking who would respond to the image portrayed, for example. Then write

an essay that compares the ways each type of car buyer is encouraged to see its purchase as "both an expression and a tool of personal liberty."

Audience: someone who works with an environmental group that is trying to understand the reasons for people's devotion to their cars.

2. Write an essay that compares the probable effectiveness of various forms of alternative transportation in actually cutting down on the use of cars. As part of your discussion, consider how well each would satisfy the needs people express for owning a car. You may also want to consider whether the reasons people give for needing cars are the real reasons they own them.

   You may want to do a survey and create a table such as that suggested in "Warm-up" 2, above, before you begin writing.

   Audience: someone who is interested in developing alternative forms of transportation.

   Send a copy of your finished essay to the public relations department of your local public transit service and ask them to comment on your ideas.

Living and Dying with AIDS:
A Banker's Story

by Hank E. Koehn

Hank E. Koehn died of AIDS on September 29, 1987.

At approximately 2 p.m. on Friday, February 20, 1987, my world came to an end in the San Jose, California, air terminal. 1

I had been in the San Jose area on a two-day business trip. Like most of my out-of-town visits, it consisted of two speaking engagements. 2

A week earlier, my doctor had convinced me I should have a test for the human immune deficiency virus that causes AIDS. He felt the results would allow him to treat me with greater knowledge. I had rejected the test. I suppose, like many other men, I was avoiding the information that I already suspected. 3

On Friday the 20th, I was scheduled to call my doctor for test results. I made the call while waiting for my flight to Los Angeles. The doctor informed me the test was positive. 4

I had AIDS. 5

With almost clinical detachment, we made an appointment for early the following week. According to the doctor, I "would have to be watched." 6

At the end of that visit, I, almost casually, mentioned that I was having difficulty using my left hand. For several weeks I had assumed this was due to some muscle I had pulled in my shoulder. 7

At my mention of this problem, my doctor sat up and took notice. After several questions, he said that this could indicate a serious problem linked with AIDS. The difficulty with the hand might be due to brain damage as a result of the now-active AIDS virus. 8

An appointment was made for me to have a magnetic resonance scan of my brain the following afternoon. That test required placing my head and shoulders inside a tubelike device that seemed to belong on a *Star Trek* movie set. 9

Within a day, the scan would indicate that there was a lesion on the right side of my brain. It could be the result of a tumour, or, more probably, the AIDS virus attacking my brain directly. 10

The doctor explained this in a cool, efficient manner. But, at the same time, he unwittingly transmitted the subconscious emotional message that I had a terminal condition — my future consisted of certain death. 11

It was arranged for me to go to the hospital for a complete diagnosis as soon as possible. Much to my doctor's displeasure, I delayed while I turned 12

79

over my client commitments to an associate and visited my attorney to arrange matters — should I not leave the hospital alive.

13   On the day I left home to go to the hospital, I took a final look at my liquidambar tree; it was budding and I thought it was highly probable that I would never see the tree with all of its leaves.

14   The hospital stay was not unpleasant. However, the multitude of tests did little to change my outlook for a limited future. They indicated the brain lesion was due to toxoplasmosis infection.

15   This protozoan is usually present in all of us, but our immune systems keep it in check. In my case, the infection in my brain was slowly taking away my ability to use my left hand and arm. Dressing and daily living became a one-handed exercise.

16   On the day I was to leave the hospital, I had my first seizure. My arm and hand jumped around for about fifteen seconds as a result of "short circuit" signals from the infected area of the brain. Utterly terrified, I was then told that this could become a common event — which it did — and I received my first capsule of Dilantin.

17   I left hospital convinced my days among the living were indeed numbered. The doctors were surprised at my acceptance of my limited prospects. I said I had led a full, happy, productive, and successful life. I did not feel cheated and could therefore face my impending demise calmly.

18   I had prepared myself for death and resolved to get on with it. I decided two things: I would most likely not live beyond the end of the year; and, when I thought it was time to die, I would merely get into bed and stay there. These feelings and an all-encompassing resignation remained with me for several weeks. My calmness was the result of an accepted certainty.

19   During this same period, I decided that I would no longer work. I couldn't bear the thought of having a seizure in the middle of a lecture. Also, I felt I would be rejected when the word got out that I had AIDS. I was sure that most of my clients would be appalled at accidentally learning about my choice of lifestyle.

20   I then decided to be comfortable in my remaining days. This decision led to two discoveries. First, I had lost my sense of self-worth, which I had not considered linked to my career. Indeed, I found I had little personal identity outside my work life.

21   Second, without my work, I had lost interest in the outside world. As a futurist and a social observer, I had previously spent most of my time watching and reading about change.

22   With no work to do, I was no longer reading and watching video. Instead, my days became empty. To fill the time, I began to sleep all day, as well as all

night. Weeks before, while in the hospital, I had found that I could stare at "nothing" on the ceiling for many hours.

In retrospect, the frightening fact was that I was very content doing nothing. Everything, including reading, became too much of an effort. Nothing seemed worthwhile, since I had only a limited number of days. Because of my relatively strong personality, there was almost no one to challenge my approach to my remaining time among the living.   23

I was well cared for in a comfortable home. I still felt deep inside that resignation seemed the civilized approach to my remaining life.   24

Then one day, while talking with a friend, I asked again if he didn't think I had become too resigned, too easily. As we explored this thought, I became convinced I had given up too quickly — even if giving up was the obvious course of action. From that point on I began to explore the alternatives. I had already been receiving some counselling to stabilize my emotional state — which I felt was stable without help.   25

To my surprise I found that, upon reflection, my inner needs were spiritual or metaphysical. When I mentioned this thought to more friends during the next few days, I found that during illness they had reached the same conclusions in their own lives. It was suggested that I read several books, including one written by Louise L. Hay.   26

Ms. Hay, a metaphysical healer, had been working successfully with both cancer and AIDS patients. Her Wednesday-night meetings held in Plummer Park had become legends in the gay community. I acquired several of her tapes and began to play them several times a day.   27

Slowly I began to understand that my future was in my own hands — perhaps mind is actually a better word. This is strange considering that, as a futurist, I had told my clients, "If you can dream it, you can do it." Louise Hay reminded me that each of us has the capacity to invest tomorrow with the thoughts we have today.   28

After a period of time spent listening to the meditation tapes, my attitude began to shift from resignation to a belief that I could play a major role in healing myself.   29

About this time, I developed an overwhelming urge to visit the ocean. I wasn't sure why I needed to see the ocean, but the need was very real.   30

We stayed in a Laguna Beach hotel that directly overlooks the surf. When I sat in a lounge chair, looking down at the waves, I realized why I had wanted to come to the sea. The pattern of the waves began placing me in a relaxed state.   31

My mind began to float and I recalled a long-forgotten feeling from early life, when I was an only child without parents. I had felt abandoned, and this feeling would be repeated both in my teen years and in two adult relationships.   32

33   My overpowering fear, now as a grown man with AIDS, was that I would once again be abandoned. This sudden, ocean-induced awareness shocked me. I had not realized I feared abandonment, at least not consciously. I realized how productive my visit to the ocean had been, and I returned home resolved to learn more about myself and healing myself.

34   The attempt to reach my inner mind and understand its abilities and effects on my life became a challenge, the biggest I had ever encountered.

35   I began to reach out to others who had attempted mentally to influence their health and well-being. To my amazement, many of my friends had accepted this line of thinking. They suggested several books that discussed the self-healing process.

36   There were many moments when I felt that I was succeeding as I reached deep inside myself for understanding and direction. There were many more moments of failure, but I continued on by reminding myself that I had shaped my career through personal determination for many decades — and had been successful.

37   I resolved that, at some time, I would place myself on a religious retreat in my own home as I began my spiritual search for a meaningful identity. It became clear that, whoever I became at the end of my odyssey, I would be far different from the person I was when I was diagnosed with AIDS. Obviously, it was time for me to make a transition in my life. I felt that having AIDS could be turned into a positive experience.

38   During the months since I had been diagnosed, I found that for the first time in my life I cried easily. I had never cried before — it isn't considered appropriate for a man to do so in our society.

39   My crying was not the result of fear as much as an emotional expression or outlet for pent-up anger and frustration. When my friends were very kind to me, I would cry then also. I had never thought that so many people would come forward openly expressing love for me. This saddened me because I had never understood how they felt about me.

40   I was frequently overpowered by a feeling of being all alone in a strange, dark place. Along with the crying and the loneliness, I developed an almost desperate need to be hugged and held closely — almost as if I were a small child.

41   I was being transformed from an independent person into someone who could no longer walk alone, who needed help to shower and to get to bed at night. My feelings and attitudes became so different that they seemed to belong to someone I didn't know.

42   The massive change in so short a time left me confused and surprised. I was not prepared either to understand or to control this new individual. For this reason alone the future would be very different, with a new set of values and objectives.

Even the closet full of executive suits now seemed to belong to someone 43
else. Frequently I would wake up still believing I could hop out of bed and
jump into the shower. Obviously, I had not adjusted to my new body and won-
dered how long it would take for the present reality to dissolve the memories
and actions of over 50 years.

The last few months have brought the steady loss of my ability to use my 44
left hand, arm, and leg. Over a period of 120 days I watched my disability grow
until I could no longer move freely under normal circumstances. I progressively became more crippled and more useless.

Standing up became a high risk, as I fell into objects around my home. 45
Once I lost the use of the arm and leg on the same side of my body, canes were
useless, and the manipulation of a wheelchair became a one-armed event.

AIDS is perceived to alter the life of one person, the patient. This is not 46
true, since the patient slowly becomes dependent upon someone else — finally
needing help all day, all week.

Thus the disease destroys the quality of life for two people, because the 47
care giver of the AIDS victim is also relentlessly held hostage by the disease,
trapped in a round of simple but indispensable tasks.

If there is anything worse than having AIDS, it is caring for the person who has 48
AIDS. The "significant other" can do little but wonder, "How long will this go on?"

The patient watches while the care giver's life and freedom become more 49
restricted, in the name of love; the relationship becomes one of self-imposed
duty. It is difficult to say who is the victim and who hurts the most. Joy slowly
seems to vanish in the eyes of both the patient and the care giver. The disease
dominates every discussion and action.

Over five months, I have learned how to help myself and take responsibil- 50
ity for my healing. Conversations with others have provided information concerning possible therapies and drugs to fight the disease. How others cope with
the challenge of AIDS gives clues and direction to my own efforts to maintain
a civilized quality of life. The overriding challenge is, "How can I be less of a
burden on my care giver?"

Accepting care and understanding limitations are skills one must learn. 51
Expectations must be adjusted to a new reality.

It was a great challenge for me to learn to reach out to others and to accept 52
their concern and love.

Fortunately my many friends, including business associates and clients, have 53
come forward to express their love and willingness to help. Indeed, I have been
surprised by their deep concern for my present and future well-being. I have
received dozens of calls conveying love, hope, and encouragement. To date, no
one has been appalled by the knowledge of my preferred lifestyle during the past

twenty years. I have deeply felt the love of others who I never thought would call and say "We love you."

54   My preferred life of 54 years is gone. Even if I were to go into remission or be given a cure, that life is over. My concern with my spiritual needs and metaphysical well-being is now central to my existence.

55   I can now empathize with terminally ill cancer victims and the helpless feelings of the elderly as they are forced to depend on others for their daily existence. I'm not sure what I'll be like when I complete this passage, except that I will be very different, able to accept my needs and the love of others.

Style and Structure

1. (a) Write a one-paragraph profile of the intended reader of this essay. Use evidence from the essay to support your conclusions.

    (b) Write a one-sentence summary of the essay's central topic.

    (c) How do the first five paragraphs of the essay relate to the central topic you have identified?

    (d) Would a single-sentence **thesis statement** such as your summary be a more effective way of introducing the topic to Koehn's intended reader? Justify your answer.

    (e) Which strategy would have been more appropriate if the essay had been written for an academic journal? Why?

2.   Many magazines and newspapers, like the one in which "Living and Dying with Aids" first appeared, use techniques to make their contents look easy to read. One is to break paragraphs into one- or two-sentence blocks. These blocks are then printed as if they were separate paragraphs.

    Examine paragraphs 46 to 48 in this essay, for example. They could be combined to form a single unified and coherent paragraph. All the elements are there: a **topic sentence** (in paragraph 46), relevant details in the body, and a **concluding sentence** (in paragraph 48).

    Identify two other passages in the essay where the same technique has been used. For each, identify the **topic** and **concluding sentences**. Then explain briefly how joining the shorter blocks together would create a unified and coherent paragraph.

3.   This essay uses the process-analysis format; i.e., it analyzes and explains the process of change that Koehn went through after his diagnosis. (See p. 212 for a further explanation of the process-analysis format.)

The most difficult tasks in writing a process analysis are (1) identifying the unique stages in the process and (2) creating appropriate paragraphs for them. Even when the paragraphs present natural stages, some writers forget to use **topic** and **concluding sentences** to guide the reader through them.

(a) Examine the body of Koehn's essay for any paragraphs that do not fit into the natural order of the process he went through. If you find any, suggest ways in which they could be changed to make them fit better (e.g., placing them elsewhere in the essay, adding a sentence, or providing a **transition**).

(b) Choose any two **topic sentences** from paragraphs in the body of the essay. Explain how each helps the reader understand that paragraph's stage in the process.

(c) Choose any two **concluding sentences** from paragraphs in the body. Explain how each helps the reader understand that paragraph's stage in the process.

4. Koehn faces a problem in dealing with some readers who might not be sympathetic to the gay lifestyle. Why could this problem be particularly acute in paragraphs 46 to 50? What techniques does he use in these paragraphs to avoid alienating these readers?

5. (a) How effectively do the last two paragraphs of the essay act as a **conclusion**? Justify your answer.

(b) What is the relationship between the statement made in the last sentence of the **concluding paragraph** and that made in the opening sentence of the essay? Is this an effective technique to use in a conclusion? Why?

Warm-up

Working with a group of four or five others, choose one of the following topics and, if necessary, do some background research on it in the library:

(i) the way AIDS develops in victims after they have contracted the virus;

(ii) the people who are in "high-risk groups" for contracting AIDS;

(iii) a history of the spread of AIDS;

(iv) the risk for the average Canadian of contracting AIDS.

On your own, write a one-paragraph explanation of the topic that can serve as a handout for all of your classmates. Then, as a group again, select the paragraph that best explains the topic and distribute copies of it to everyone else in the class.

Thinking and Writing

1. Write a process-analysis essay in which you explain the changes a person undergoes during one of life's major transitions (e.g., going from childhood to adolescence, moving away from home for the first time, or moving to a new town or a new school). Be sure to use specific details at each stage in the process.

    Audience: someone who has never gone through the experience and who may not be sympathetic to the problems encountered.

2. Koehn writes, "[Early in my illness] I was sure that most of my clients would be appalled at accidentally learning about my choice of lifestyle" (paragraph 19). Later, however, he is able to write, "Fortunately my many friends, including business associates and clients, have come forward to express their love and willingness to help. . . . To date, no one has been appalled by the knowledge of my preferred lifestyle. . ." (paragraph 53).

    Write an essay in which you explain whether or not most people in our society would have this type of sympathetic reaction if they discovered that a friend or business associate had AIDS. Give reasons for the reactions you identify.

    Audience: someone who deals with AIDS patients and is sympathetic to their problems.

    Send a copy of your final draft to a group that provides support for AIDS victims in your community.

Math's Multiple Choices

by Judith Finlayson

The world has been transformed in the past twenty years. Geared to microchips, floppy disks, and video display terminals, today's society demands a higher degree of mathematical skill than ever before. But, sadly and even dangerously misinformed about the realities of the working world, many teenaged girls across the country are repeating their mothers' mistake, a mistake that has propelled the majority of Canadian working women into low-paying, dead-end jobs. In high school, they are dropping out of science and math. 1

Today, a background in math is required for most high-paying technical jobs in fields such as computer technology and microelectronics, as well as for many apparently unrelated professions such as law, interior design, and urban planning. Some companies require Grade 12 math for all entry-level positions, even for caretaking jobs. 2

The need for mathematical competence has been heightened not only by the extraordinary technological change of the past two decades, but by social change as well. Women have entered the work force in unprecedented numbers. They can also expect to stay there — from 25 to 45 years, even if they choose to marry and have children as well as a job outside the home. And they should anticipate changing careers at least twice during that time. 3

As Donna Stewart, educational co-ordinator for WomenSkills, a Vancouver organization devoted to education and research on women's work, warns: "Whole fields of work are shrinking or disappearing entirely. We export enormous amounts of work to countries where labour is cheap, or we give it to machines. One result is that greater levels of competence are required, even for low-level jobs." 4

It's not surprising that a research report published in 1987 by the Economic Council of Canada stressed the value of flexibility in today's workplace. Not only are better-educated and highly skilled women more likely to benefit from technical change, but the report also concluded that their adjustment may be dependent upon how successfully they enter nontraditional occupations. It is important to note, however, that both higher education and nontraditional work are increasingly linked with competence in math. 5

Consider, for instance, that a minimum of high-school math is often required for entrance to university courses such as nursing, teaching, and law. It is also mandatory for many social-science courses such as psychology and sociology, as well as for admission to a substantial number of community college courses. The problem is, female students tend to drop math and sciences 6 as they progress through high school. This fact has led educators to conclude that math is an "invisible filter" denying females entry into the growth-related industries of the future.

7   Math and science avoidance in females is generally acknowledged as a serious issue, but unfortunately there are no national statistics that document the full extent of the problem. Research by the Toronto Board of Education, however, shows that even at the introductory level, the ratio of students in computer science courses is two-thirds male to one-third female. By Grade 13, approximately two-thirds of girls in Toronto schools have dropped out of maths and sciences.

8   "I'm still seeing the Cinderella myth at work," says Arlene Day, a resource teacher for equality in education with the Manitoba Teacher's Society. "Even though they see their mothers working outside the home because the family needs the money, girls are refusing to believe that the same thing will happen to them. They're still aiming for clerical jobs. Most are not even acquiring the computer skills that are necessary to be successful at office work." And her view is echoed in *What Will Tomorrow Bring?*, a 1985 Canadian Advisory Council on the Status of Women report that concluded, "adolescent girls still see their lives in very traditional and romanticized terms."

9   Statistics confirm that the majority of women (almost 60 percent) hold clerical and service-sector jobs, which are generally low paid, offer little potential for advancement, and may be in danger of becoming obsolete. Although women have made serious inroads into some male-dominated professions, such as business, medicine, and law, they are still segregated outside the more scientific fields, such as engineering and computer science. According to Statistics Canada, at the university level, the majority of women remain concentrated in the traditional fields of study, such as education, nursing, and the humanities. The pattern also holds true for community colleges, where most women continue to study secretarial science, community and social services, nursing, education, and the arts.

10   "To some extent, women have succumbed to the myths about women's work," comments Donna Stewart. "They want to be helpers and to work with people. They may be avoiding nontraditional jobs and careers that require a sound basis in math because they haven't seen the human context to these jobs. Social service agencies need to balance their books. And no one builds bridges alone. You're part of a team."

11   Women who avoid math may be ignoring more than the human context of working with numbers. Mathematical training has been linked with high salaries and job security in fields that have been targeted for future growth. Engineering technology, a profession that is 92 percent male, is one example of this trend. Two years after graduating from community college, an engineering student can

expect to earn $20 000 a year. Perhaps more importantly, engineering technologists who reach the senior level will likely make more than $30 000 and, if they rise in management, they can earn up to $50 000 annually.

Compare these salaries to those in a female-dominated field. Ninety-nine percent of secretaries are female. Not only is their average salary just $14 100 two years after graduation from community college, but according to a 1983 Labour Canada report, even those who reach senior levels earn on average under $20 000.

This kind of wage discrepancy alarms educators who see girls avoiding math. "Nowadays, a math and science background is necessary for most of the higher-paying jobs," says Linda McClelland, a science teacher at Crescent Heights High School in Calgary. "And girls are losing out on these credentials at the same time that more and more women are entering the work force. In addition, there is a rising number of women supporting families on their own who really need to earn a decent wage."

Tasoula Berggren, an instructor of calculus and linear algebra at Simon Fraser University in Burnaby, British Columbia, points to at least 82 careers for which math education is a prerequisite. Last November, she organized what she hopes will become an annual conference, Women Do Math, for girls in Grades 9 and 10 and their parents. Four students from each of 85 Vancouver schools were invited. "I thought we would get 100 people," Berggren recalls, "and 300 registered, with many more schools asking to bring more students."

Berggren designed the conference not only to introduce girls to women professionals but to provide an introduction to basic mathematical concepts. "Once they see the application of calculus — how a formula can give them the volume of a lake — they find it exciting. They say, 'This is great, I'm enjoying math!'"

She stresses the necessity of constant parental encouragement, something that Myra Novogrodsky, co-ordinator of women's labour studies at the Toronto Board of Education, observes does not come naturally. She is conducting a new program designed to make parents of Grade 7 and 8 girls aware of the importance of math and science education to their daughters' futures.

"I usually begin the workshops with a true-or-false quiz designed to test awareness," she says. "I've discovered that a lot of people haven't thought much about the implications of social change. They still think that most girls will live in a nuclear family and be secondary wage earners, if they work outside the home at all."

One result of this misconception is that many parents have lower career expectations for their daughters than for their sons. Their attitude is reinforced by negative role modelling, which can include apparently innocuous statements such as "Women don't have a head for figures" or "Her mother can't balance a chequebook." These stereotypes can seriously undermine the confidence of girls who may have an interest in technical subjects or nontraditional work.

19   "By Grade 10, I knew I was mechanically oriented, but people said that physics was too hard for me and I believed them," recalls Heather Bears, who is currently studying electronics technology at Red River Community College in Winnipeg. As a result, after graduating from high school, she spent two unsatisfactory years in the work force doing odd clerical or child-care jobs. Career counselling finally revealed her scientific aptitude and motivated her to return to high school as an adult student. Not only did she make up her physics courses, but she earned straight A's.

20   Today, as a second-year electronics student, she still feels the negative effects of gender roles. "When I entered the course there were only two other girls and approximately 100 guys. There was a real sense that we were bucking the system and it was scary. At its most basic, I'm only five-foot-two and most of the male students are in the six-foot range."

21   Although Bears admits that it is difficult being a pioneer — "some teachers pick on us and others favour us" — the satisfaction of doing what she finds fulfilling is worth the price. "If I had one piece of advice for girls in high school, it would be, 'Don't be afraid to enter a man's world.' I believed people who said I couldn't do it because I was a girl, and that's what held me back."

22   MaryElizabeth Morris, a math teacher at Castle Frank High School in Toronto, believes that the "my mother/my self syndrome" can also influence a girl's career expectations. "A woman who does low-level work could undermine her daughter's success because she might not convey the sense that work can be a rewarding experience," she says. "If her mother is a poor role model in terms of job satisfaction, a girl may cling to the Cinderella myth because she doesn't see work outside the home as desirable."

23   Studies such as *What Will Tomorrow Bring?* show that professional mothers tend to be positive role models for their daughters. But mothers who don't work outside the home can also encourage their daughters to develop an interest in traditionally male domains by organizing scientifically oriented excursions, such as a visit to a science museum, or by doing traditionally masculine tasks.

24   "We live on a farm, so my mother is a real handyman," says Robin Chant, a Grade 12 student at MacGregor Collegiate Institute in MacGregor, Manitoba, who excels at maths and sciences. "I think one of the reasons I do well in math is because, like her, I enjoy figuring things out."

25   Chant was the only girl in her physics class last year and there is only one other girl in this year's math class, compared to nine boys. "Most of my girlfriends have dropped math because they think it's too hard," she says. "They all want traditional jobs as secretaries and day-care workers. They plan to get married and have kids. I'm different because I really want to have a career."

26   Myra Novogrodsky believes that if mothers are to help their daughters overcome their negative outlook toward math, they must become aware of and

overcome their own negative feelings. If parents "suffered" through math class themselves, they may convey their anxiety and inadvertently undermine their children's performance. Equally important are the role models that girls receive outside the home.

"It's hard for girls to accept the message that they can have high career   27 aspirations and study maths and sciences if they don't see any other women doing it," says Linda McClelland. "We need more female math and science teachers as role models, as well as more women in nontraditional careers."

All the women math and science teachers interviewed for this article   28 strongly agreed. Moreover, those who kept statistics on the ratio of males to females in their classes reported that the fact that a woman was teaching the subjects had a positive effect on girls.

"In the past there was usually only one female student in senior-level   29 physics," recalls Shelagh Pryke, who teaches all the physics classes at Kwalikum Secondary School in Qualicum Beach, B.C. "Now as many as 42 percent of my students are girls, and I know the fact that I'm a woman who is married with a family has played a role in this change. The girls see that it's socially acceptable to be a woman who is interested in science."

Lydia Picucha, a math and science teacher at Mount Elizabeth Junior and   30 Senior Secondary School in Kitimat, B.C., shares this point of view. "I've been teaching here for seven years and I know my female students relate to the idea of a woman who enjoys her work and takes her career seriously. As a result, most of my female students — about 70 percent — have continued with science into Grade 11, when girls normally start dropping out."

The lack of female teachers as role models is complicated by the way   31 maths and sciences are taught in schools. Mathematics, for example, may alienate girls because it is typically taught in a masculine style. John Clark, coordinator of mathematics at the Toronto Board of Education, says, "Math is usually presented as a search for the right answer rather than as a process of enquiry. Some sociologists believe that females have a more collaborative style. They want to work by consensus and talk with other people."

Whether or not there is any inherent difference between the male and   32 female aptitude for mathematics remains a hotly debated issue. However, there is no doubt that the way girls are socialized undermines whatever natural ability they might have. For example, the kinds of throwing, jumping, and mechanically oriented play that boys engage in actually prepares them for an understanding of maths and sciences.

Consider the game of baseball. Most boys catch balls better than most girls   33 simply because by constantly playing ball sports they have learned how to estimate where the ball will land and, therefore, how to position their hands. What is less obvious is that this skill requires an understanding of the relationship between distance, force, and velocity that serves them well once they begin to study physics.

34   At the Institute of Child Study, a school that operates in conjunction with the University of Toronto's Faculty of Education, teacher Robin Ethier confirms that there is a division of play along gender lines by the time the children arrive at kindergarten. "The boys choose blocks and sand to build large spaces, whereas the girls prefer small paper projects," she says. "The few girls who prefer large motor-skill projects really stand out. They are identified as tomboys."

35   Even so, Anne Cassidy, the Grade 5 teacher at the school, says she is not aware of a gender difference in her students' approach to maths and sciences. To some extent, she believes the school's emphasis on intuitive and personalized learning has helped minimize the difference. Classes are small and teachers strongly encourage children to learn through their own activities. For example, to teach the law of averages, she might ask her class to count up the pennies all seven grades collected for UNICEF over Hallowe'en. When she asks her students to work out approximately how much each grade collected, they soon realize that to get an average they must divide the total number of pennies by the number of classes. In the end, they discover the mathematical formula all on their own.

36   This kind of hands-on learning validates the children's own observations about the world. It also reinforces their sense of themselves as autonomous problem solvers, a skill linked with success in math. Parents can play an important role in helping their children develop this problem-solving ability by transforming daily activities into informal lessons in maths and sciences. Children should be encouraged to play mathematically oriented games such as backgammon and chess. Cooking is an excellent activity for teaching fractions as well as the principles of chemistry. Similarly, carpentry teaches measurement and spatial concepts, and comparing sizes and prices at the supermarket can turn even shopping into a learning experience.

37   "People make the mistake of trying to introduce new math concepts with paper and pencil," according to Dr. Ada Schermann, principal of the Institute of Child Study. "Start with a game or a fun activity such as cooking, gardening, or playing a mathematically based card game like 21. Then children don't think they're being taught, and the learning comes naturally."

38   Girls' poor problem-solving abilities have been linked to the fact that they are not usually encouraged to assert themselves as individuals. So perhaps it's not surprising that they begin to retreat from maths and sciences during their teenage years. During this period their willingness to consider a nontraditional career also wanes.

39   It must be the responsibility of parents and teachers to erase the myth that an interest in math makes a girl "different" or "unfeminine." From preschool to high

school, maths and sciences should be as natural and nonthreatening subjects of study as English or history. Without a solid grounding in these subjects, the doors of opportunity will slam shut for yet another generation of young women — and, unfortunately, unemployment figures are the numbers *everyone* understands.

Style and Structure

1. (a) What is the overall **organizational approach** of this essay: narrative, descriptive, cause and effect, or compare/contrast? (See pp. 212–213.)

   (b) Having established the overall approach, identify other approaches Finlayson employs to support her opinions.

2. (a) In making her point, the writer cites a number of sources throughout the essay. Identify each of these sources and classify them as

   (i) professionals;

   (ii) institutions;

   (iii) nonprofessionals.

   (b) In a fully developed paragraph, explain how well you believe these sources serve the writer's purpose. Examine the appropriateness of the sources, the number of citations given, and the effect upon the reader.

3. (a) In paragraphs 11 and 12, the writer presents two career paths, one dominated by men and the other dominated by women. What do you believe the writer is hoping to accomplish?

   (b) Where has the writer obtained her statistics about salaries? How might these statistics affect the reader?

   (c) One of the primary rules about comparisons is that the writer must compare like things — not apples and oranges, as the old saying goes. Is the writer comparing apples and oranges in this case? (Suggestion: how might the comparison have changed if the writer had chosen nursing as a career dominated by women?)

4. Finlayson often employs a technique of making a statement and following it with examples to illustrate. Identify three instances of this technique. In each case, how does it aid the reader?

5. (a) What is the main point of this essay?

   (b) Does the writer manage to give both a positive and a negative picture of the situation? How?

   (c) Do you believe it is important to give the reader encouragement by pointing out the possibilities for success, even when dealing with what seems to be a very significant and widespread problem? Why?

Warm-up

Giving and following instructions are essentials in game playing, as well as in many of life's more important functions. Choose a board or card game, preferably one that would help teach mathematical concepts. Divide into small groups and teach the game using clear and concise instructions. Members of the group must listen closely to the instructions.

Test your success by playing the game. Count the number of times instructions have to be repeated to gauge how clearly you explained the rules and how well the participants listened. Compare with other groups and discuss.

Thinking and Writing

1. In her essay, Finlayson points to the advice of Dr. Ada Schermann: "People make the mistake of trying to introduce new math concepts with paper and pencil. Start with a game or a fun activity such as cooking, gardening, or playing a mathematically based card game like 21" (paragraph 37).

    Choose a mathematical concept that a primary school child would need to learn and devise a game that would allow the child to learn that concept. For instance, you might select working with volumes, and then work out a game in which the child would want to know how to halve a cookie recipe.

    Write an essay in which you explain the workings of the game you propose and the concept you wish to illustrate. Be as creative as possible, remembering that kids are severe judges of what is fun.
    Audience: Children and parents who are anxious to make mathematics an integral part of their family life.

2. In paragraph 18, Finlayson speaks of stereotypes that reinforce the myth that women cannot do math, or that they are not interested in the subject. Make a collection of cartoons, jokes, or household sayings that seem to substantiate the writer's opinion that these stereotypes are damaging to girls' confidence in handling mathematics.

    Outline and write an essay in which you argue that stereotypes are having a negative effect, using your collection as examples. Be sure to write a clearly defined thesis statement and, if possible, suggest how girls can overcome the image portrayed in these stereotypes.

Here is an example to get you started on your collection!

For Better or For Worse by Lynn Johnston

Audience: Grade 9 or 10 girls who are thinking of dropping out of maths and sciences.

Send a copy of your final draft to a high school guidance department for comment.

Let the Punishment Fit the Crime

by Philip Brickman

1   When a thief in Chicago stole a motorcycle, the press reported, the victim, who knew the thief, was not particularly interested in seeing the thief punished, just in getting his motorcycle back. By the time the police caught the thief, he had sold the motorcycle. He received a suspended sentence. The victim was told he would have to sue the thief if he wanted his money back.

2   What is wrong with this story? It does not satisfy our sense of justice because justice means that everyone gets what he or she deserves. Justice should mean helping victims as well as punishing offenders. This story and our criminal justice system ignore the problem of restoring fairness for victims as a principle of justice.

3   We set two primary goals for our criminal penalties. We want them to deter crime and we want them to rehabilitate criminals. In theory, these two goals should go together, since they amount to saying that we want to keep crime from happening in the first place, through deterrence, and to keep crime from happening again, through rehabilitation.

4   In practice, these two goals seem incompatible, since the harsh penalties that might work as deterrents offer little hope for rehabilitation, while the supportive treatments that might work as rehabilitation seem inadequate as deterrents.

5   Curiously, however, neither deterring crime nor rehabilitating offenders is a principle of justice. Our sense of justice requires that penalties be proportionate to their crimes.

6   Suppose we took restoring fairness as the first principle of our criminal justice system, instead of either deterrence or rehabilitation. What would such a system look like?

7   Simply put, offenders would be given sentences whose purpose, in the end, was to restore both the loss that the victims had suffered and the loss that society suffered through its investment in preventing, detecting, and punishing crimes. Where possible, this could involve labour directly related to recovering property, repairing damage, or making streets safer. More generally, it might involve contributing earnings from specified tasks to a general fund whose purpose was to compensate victims.

8   In informal systems, where victims and offenders are known to one another, restoring fairness is the common penalty that satisfies all concerned and preserves the social bond. It is typical of penalties that are meted out in healthy families.

Restitution as a principle of justice appeals to both liberals and conserva- 9
tives. Liberals like the idea that the penalty involves something more meaningful than just going to prison. Conservatives like the idea that the penalty
involves holding offenders responsible for their actions and making them pay
for their crimes. It appeals to people on moral and emotional grounds. It
appeals to people on practical grounds, in that it offers some hope of helping
both the victims and the offenders, as well as society.

Restitution can work in the service of both deterrence and rehabilitation. 10
The cost of making restitution should substantially outweigh the potential gain
of the crime, since both the victim's pain and suffering and society's costs of
enforcement may be included. At the same time, the act of making restitution
should serve to restore not only the offender's sense of himself or herself as a
worthwhile member of society, but, even more crucial, society's sense of the
offender as well, in a way that punishment alone could never do. The penalty
can and should involve real cost for the offender, but the novel and critical feature is that it should also involve creating something of value in both society's
eyes and the offender's own eyes.

The idea of compensating victims can be distinguished from the idea of 11
restitution by offenders. There are many crimes with victims needing help
where offenders are unknown. Even if an offender is caught and convicted,
restitution at best takes time, while the victim's needs are immediate. The solution is to use state funds to compensate victims, while offenders either replen-
ish these funds or provide other services.

To be successful, the principle of restitution must be implemented in a way 12
that is not seen as exploitation of offenders in the service of existing class interests. Most offenders are poor, and many victims are rich. It is doubtful that
making restitution to a corporation such as an insurance company will have
much meaning for people who do not see the corporation as a victim in the first
place. It is certain that chain gangs and corrective labour camps do not supply
work from which either victims or offenders derive any sense of meaningful
restitution. They are merely punishment and should be plainly so named. Restitution that is psychologically valuable will have visible and tangible effects
that can be seen by victims, offenders, and society.

Although not widely known, laws for victim compensation have been 13
enacted in a number of countries (including England and New Zealand) and a
growing number of states (including New York and California), while experi-
mental programs for offender restitution are under way in Georgia, Iowa, and
Minnesota. Preliminary results are encouraging, but they represent only a
beginning. Much remains to be learned about tailoring sentences to both society's needs and offenders' capacities, and we have yet to work out how to allow

prisoners to work without threatening jobs for anyone outside prison. These are reasonable tasks for social science and social policy. It is unreasonable to leave the field of criminal justice to the bankrupt debate between deterrence and rehabilitation.

Style and Structure

1. For what reasons does Brickman open his essay with the particular illustration that he chooses?
2. Underline the **thesis statement** and draft a plan of the essay's organization.
3. Trace the development of the writer's argument in paragraphs 3 to 6. Show how this development is logical.
4. What is the relationship of paragraph 7 to paragraph 6? How do paragraphs 8, 9, and 10 relate to paragraph 7? How do paragraphs 11 and 12 relate to paragraph 7?
5. In what ways does paragraph 12 function as a good **conclusion** for the essay as a whole? How does the author by his choice of words in the last two sentences attempt to win the reader over to his point of view?

Warm-up

1. Select a crime that is reported on tonight's newscast or in today's newspaper. Write a short essay that applies to this crime the principles of justice outlined by Brickman in paragraph 7.
    Audience: officers of the local police department.
    In a workshop setting with a group of three or four others, review the essay that each has written. Help the writer prepare for final revisions by identifying points at which the intended reader may have trouble understanding the ideas. In addition, look for improvements to the wording that will help overcome any preconceived ideas an intended reader might have about the content.
    Revise your essay and send a copy of the final draft to the public relations department of your local police force. Ask for comments.
2. Use the library to research the effectiveness of jail sentences in dealing with the type of crime you have identified in exercise 1. Write a paragraph reporting on your findings.
    Audience: officers of the local police department.

Review this paragraph in a workshop setting as you did your earlier essay, revise it, and send a copy of the final draft, along with your essay from exercise 1, to the police department's public relations officer.

Thinking and Writing

1. The benefits that Brickman outlines for the victim, the criminal, and society are needed nowhere more than in dealing with the crimes of murder and rape. However, no crimes offer greater difficulties to the judge who has to determine the sentence for a particular offence and to convince the general public that his or her sentence is "just" to all those concerned.

    Write an essay in which you assume the role of a judge who is sentencing a person for one of the following crimes; outline the sentence that you would give in accordance with Brickman's "restitution" and justify this sentence to the general public who may, at present, prefer punishment or revenge:

    (a) a woman with three children who has killed her husband in a fit of rage during a domestic quarrel;

    (b) a man who has no previous convictions and has before this offence been considered to be an ideal "family man," who has been convicted of raping a woman whom he had never met before.

    Audience: the "average" newspaper reader.

2. Write an essay in which you outline and present evidence to substantiate your personal point of view on the value and effectiveness of basing our system of criminal justice upon a theory of restitution such as Brickman proposes. Use concrete examples and logically developed arguments to support your thesis.

    Audience: someone who works in a field related to criminal justice (e.g., lawyer, judge, police officer, or social worker).

    Send a copy of your essay to a person employed in one of the positions listed under "audience," or to your MP or MPP.

Judy

by Esther Kershman Muhlstock

1   I knew a culture shock awaited us when we moved with our three little children from a walk-up four-room apartment to a four-fireplace, huge dream house. Spacious, on a quiet and charming street, with a Superior Court judge living beside us on one hand and a senator on the other, in a completely French Canadian neighbourhood with lovely green lawns and a beautiful park a few doors away.

2   I had perfect confidence in our Judy, age seven, already in the second-year program of the Jewish People's School and staunchly Jewish. I was sure she would skilfully handle this multi-language and multi-religion situation. So would Naomi, our four-year-old, who had declared to me, "Mother, you know that everybody in the world is Jewish, but some people talk French."

3   Judy had been playing with the judge's daughter. She confided in me, "I have been teaching Marie Hebrew. She's fine when she says 'David,' but she has a terrible time pronouncing 'Chaya.' Their family must be immigrants."

4   I had to laugh. Marie's great, great grandparents had come to Canada in the 1700s. In Marie's family's eyes, we were the invaders, the immigrants.

5   One morning, shortly after we had settled in, the doorbell rang furiously. There were about fifteen children in our doorway, with Judy in front. She was holding an old shoe box in her little hands. In the box, lined with grass, lay a tiny bird, moaning. It had fallen out of a tree and was hurt.

6   "Help it, Mummy," Judy implored. The children began to clamour.

7   With all those eyes focussed on me, what else could I do? I got an eye dropper, forced the baby bird's mouth open, and forced a few drops of milk into it.

8   "C'est tous ce que je peux faire, mes chéries," I told them. Marie took possession of the bird and they all left.

9   Shortly after, Judy came running in, tears streaming down her face. "What does 'noyer' mean? Does it mean 'to drown'? Marie's father said it would be kinder to drown the bird. He says the bird is crying for its mother. Please don't let them drown the bird, Mother, please!" she pleaded.

10   "Ask the children to come back and I'll talk to them," I suggested.

11   The news had spread, and a much larger group came to the garage door. "C'est contre la religion de le noyer. Il faut l'aider à vivre," I told them. Dramatizing the situation, I fed the little bird some of my children's vitamin drops, assuring them at the same time that I would get some bird seed at the pet shop for the little bird.

On returning from some errands later in the afternoon, as I approached the 12
house, the crowd came fairly flying at me. "Est mort, le pauvre petit," they
shouted in chorus.

"That's too bad," I replied. "Let's scatter this bird seed I have brought," I 13
suggested.

The children then pondered the question of interment. "Not in our garden, 14
Judy," I said. "Why not the empty lot down the street?" That suggestion
seemed satisfactory and the gang proceeded there.

At bath time that evening, I was informed of the progress of the grave- 15
digging. "We all dug the grave and it's lovely. Someone plucked a flower from
someone's garden and we put the flower on it."

In the morning, out sped Judy, and returned immediately. "All the kids are 16
there, Mother, and now there are thirty-five flowers all over the grave," she
shouted.

That evening, Judy appeared for her bath, nervous and irritated. "Do you 17
know what THEY did? They gathered up all the flowers and formed them into
a large cross on the grave. But when the kids all went home for their supper,
Naomi and I went to the grave and arranged the flowers into a Jewish star," she
whispered, secretly.

"Was that necessary?" I asked Judy. 18

"Yes," she replied. "It was also my bird." 19

The next day was Sunday. What with the *New York Times* with comics 20
and a "round" visit with Daddy to the hospital, it was late morning before the
children finally visited the grave site of the bird. They were back within five
minutes.

"Mother," Judy exploded, "what do you think? They changed it into a 21
cross again."

It was time for some talk. "Judy, is the air Catholic? Is the water French? 22
Is the flower Jewish? God didn't make crosses or stars. God made people and
birds and flowers. Only man made the other. Why not have a cross *and* a star?
Then the bird would be everybody's."

She agreed a little reluctantly. "Come with me," she urged. We pro- 23
ceeded to the grave, the other children following. Judith carefully arranged
the cross at the head of the grave and a Magen David, as best as she could,
at the foot. There seemed to be general approval and I sauntered back home,
a little disturbed.

At noon, the children came in beaming. "Mother," both children's words 24
tumbled forth. "We took off the cross and the star, and over the bird we made
a big heart. Now, it is really everybody's bird."

The little bird has made us friends. 25

Style and Structure

1. (a) A quick glance at this essay tells the reader that the paragraphs are very short. Give at least two reasons why, in your opinion, the writer has chosen to write this way.

   (b) How do you think the paragraphs in this essay compare with those of other essays in terms of effectiveness? Explain your reasons.

2. Is there a **thesis statement** evident in this essay? In a well-developed paragraph, explain the writer's strategy regarding **thesis** and the reasons why you believe this approach has been chosen. (The formal name for the approach is "implied thesis.")

3. (a) A great deal of the essay involves reported conversation of the characters involved. How useful is this technique in terms of reader interest? Why?

   (b) Much of the effect of reported conversation depends on how well the writer manages to portray a realistic sound. For example, most credibility is lost if small children are reported as speaking like learned scientists.

   How realistic is the conversation of the characters portrayed in this essay? Explain your answer by referring to specific portions of the text.

4. It is difficult to imagine a story in which nothing happens. In this story, what happens to the neighbourhood? to the family? In all, what progress is made? Why do you think so?

5. (a) There are three passages in the essay that are written in French. Why do you believe the writer has chosen to leave these lines untranslated?

   (b) If you do not understand French, what was your immediate reaction to the lines written in French? Assess the reactions of other classmates who do not understand the language. How are their feelings typical of people who encounter a language, culture, or religion they do not know? What bearing do their feelings have on the impact of the entire story?

6. (a) Volumes of philosophy and social science deal with theories about multicultural relationships. Why would this writer choose to write a short narrative about some small children from a mixed neighbourhood and their flower arrangements? In one paragraph, discuss the effectiveness of storytelling, comparing this narrative with non-narrative forms of expository prose.

Warm-up

Canadians understand the difficulties encountered when one cannot speak one's language of choice. Much has been written in the Canadian press about Anglophones not understanding Francophones, Francophones not understanding Anglophones, and governments restricting or promoting the free use of language, with or without agreement among voters.

Make a search of libraries and reading rooms for newspaper articles on language issues. Collect as many articles as possible, circulating them around the class to make sure you don't have duplicates.

Next, make a poster collage of headlines in order to give viewers a quick overview of the extent of the controversy and the range of emotions that are raised when language becomes a source of disagreement.

When you have completed your research, review the findings in a class discussion.

Thinking and Writing

1. It has been suggested by a skilled storyteller that the only good reason for telling a story is to relate something that the author has felt deeply, whether it is joy, anger, wonder, or some other emotion. We might add that sometimes a good story is worth a thousand volumes of explanation.

    Do you have a story about getting along in a bicultural or multicultural environment — a story perhaps about yourself, but especially one about which you feel deeply?

    Write your story in essay form and try your hand at using direct quotes. Pay careful attention, especially in your final draft, to the correct punctuation of quotes. (Note: in this case, it is all right to keep an implied thesis, as long as the purpose of your essay is clear to the reader from the story itself.) **Audience**: anyone concerned with keeping good relationships between different races and cultures.

    Send your best stories to a local newspaper and ask if the editor would like to publish them.

2. As the story "Judy" illustrates, the cross, the star, and the heart are all powerful symbols, even to children. What exactly do these symbols mean? Why do they have the potential both to unite and to break apart? What is a symbol?

    Taking this essay as an example, discuss the power of symbol in a well-developed cause-and-effect essay. Discuss why people adopt symbols and what effect their use has.

    Audience: adults who recognize such symbols but do not think much about either their meaning or their power.

Deliberate Strangers

by Charlie Angus

1   It's Saturday night and the kids want a movie. At the local video store, row after row of neatly packaged carnage assails the eyes. *The Toolbox Murders*, *Sorority House Massacre*, and *Three on a Meathook* compete with such old-time classics as *Texas Chainsaw Massacre*. There are video covers featuring victims being hunted with knives, chainsaws, hooks, and drills.

2   As you search in vain for an old Disney classic, the kids are crying out to see Jason. Jason? Who is Jason? They hand you a video called *Halloween*, a film that has spawned four sequels and countless imitations. The basic story line is rarely changed, movie to movie: a psychopath named Jason dons a mask and mutilates local teenagers.

3   "He's sort of a cult hero," the guy behind the counter explains.

4   Okay, so vampires, werewolves, and things that go bump in the night have always been part of our folklore. People love a good ghost story and always have. Bram Stoker's Dracula, the most famous figure in horror history, has been frightening people for generations.

5   It can be said that horror provides a way of synthesizing unexplainable evil. Tales like *Dracula* provide a safe way of confronting the darker side of human relationships. The reader is able to step over the line of the great unknown, comforted by the fact that the beast is always defeated in the end. The reign of darkness is broken by dawn, and Nosferatu is foiled in his evil plans.

6   Hollywood accepted this basic premise of horror for years. The heroine was always rescued from the fate of the undead, and Bela Lugosi always died before the credits rolled. But then, in 1960, Alfred Hitchcock released the film *Psycho*, and nothing has been the same since. For the first time, the monster in a horror film was another human being — a psychopath. Hitchcock tapped a growing fear that strangers could be monsters. Howling at the full moon was replaced with the brutal depiction of Janet Leigh being slashed in the shower. A generation of film-goers would never feel the same again about closing the shower curtain. In this one scene, Hitchcock changed forever the way viewers perceive fear.

7   A trip to the video store is enough to realize how far-reaching the effects of *Psycho* have been. Supernatural monsters have been replaced by Jason and the genre of psycho killers. The techniques of presenting horror have also continued to change. In the 1970s, Brian DePalma released *Dressed to Kill*, which used the camera as if it were the eyes of the killer. The audience was allowed to share in the excitement of the hunt, the gore of the kill. Our focus has been shifted from

the thrill of stopping the villain to the thrill of hunting down the victim. The modern horror movie has taught us to be wary of seemingly tranquil country roads. Who knows where someone might be waiting with a chainsaw or an axe?

Horror has made a clear shift from identifying with victims as subjects to regarding them merely as objects. Is this shift a harmless flight into fantasy, or have the borders of our culture, the substance of our collective soul, been altered? Welcome to the age of Jason, an age when the serial killer has become a cultural hero. 8

Meet Ted Bundy, all-American boy. He was popular and good-looking, and it was said that he had an almost Kennedy-like charisma. A former employer described Ted Bundy as a man who believed in the system. In particular, Ted believed in success. At one time he studied law. In 1972, he completed his degree in psychology and worked at a crisis clinic in Seattle. 9

Over the next four years, he raped and killed as many as 50 women. When finally apprehended after murdering two women and assaulting a third in a Florida sorority house, Ted Bundy became an instant celebrity. His trial was a classic event of the 1980s. Two hundred and fifty reporters, representing readers on five continents, applied for press credentials to the first televised murder trial in history. ABC News set up a special satellite hookup to bring the trial to 40 million American living rooms — a television horror drama. 10

The man of the hour did not let his public down. Bundy presented a persona that was charming and witty. When interest seemed to wane, he resorted to outrageous stunts for the cameras. The case moved further into the realm of absurdity when Bundy announced to the court that he had married a woman who fell in love with him during the trial. Those who missed such highlights the first time round could relive the experience when *The Deliberate Stranger*, a made-for-TV dramatization, was shown on prime time. Even radio claimed a piece of the pie with the songs *The Battle of Ted Bundy* and *Just Say It Ted*. Ted Bundy found the success he had craved. 11

The hype of the trial and Bundy's celebrity status served to underline America's fascination with serial killers. Bundy was a star in the quickly growing field of *lustmord*: killing for the thrill of it. Historically, there have been occasional instances of serial killers, but such cases were rare. According to Elliot Leyton in *Hunting Humans*, in the period between 1920 and 1950, the United States did not average more than two serial killers a decade. In the 1960s, this number rose to five (for an average of one new serial killer every twenty months). In the 1970s, the number of known serial killers rose to seventeen (for an average of one every seven months). Between 1980 and 1984, the figure jumped to 25 known serial killers, signifying a new serial killer every 1.8 months. 12

The rise of serial killers is disproportionate to population growth and to the increase in the murder rate in general. Newspapers are full of information on 13 the latest killers, their particular "styles," their kill ratios in relation to existing "records." The Son of Sam, the Hillside Stranglers, John Wayne Gacy, Henry Lee Lucas, Charles Ng, the Green River Killer, Clifford Olson — countless books, movies, and articles chronicle the exploits of these killers with a fascination that borders on adulation.

14   Ted Bundy became something of a spokesperson for this new breed of killer. He showed the world that psychopaths are not deranged. Most serial killers have passed previous psychological testing. They are well liked and never socially suspect. Psychopaths, however, relate to other human beings as objects. They lack the ability to empathize. Psychopathy is the extreme form of self-centredness.

15   The testimony at the trial underlined how easily such a disordered personality could fit in with social convention. At the time of Bundy's arrest, his friends were unable to reconcile the man they thought they knew with the brutal murderer described in the press. "He was one of us," one friend explained. Although it was overshadowed by the revelations of murder and mayhem, this detail is a key to unlocking the world of Ted Bundy. As a young Republican, as a yuppie, and as a brutal killer, he was one of us. His killings, like everything in his life, were a mirror image of the world around him.

16   After his conviction, Ted Bundy spent many hours being interviewed by his biographers, Hugh Aynsworth and Stephen Michaud. Calmly and dispassionately, he articulated the roots of his murderous inclinations: "If we took this individual from birth and raised him, say, in the Soviet Union or Afghanistan, or in eighteenth-century America, in all likelihood he would lead a normal life. We're talking about the peculiar circumstances of society and of the twentieth century in America." Ted Bundy knew he was a psychopath. Perhaps we all have some of the psychopath in us.

17   This is an age of impersonal violence. Television has brought saturation bombing in Vietnam, genocide in Cambodia, sniping in Beirut, and street wars in Los Angeles into our homes. Every night around suppertime, the living room is filled with footage of strangers killing strangers. Our response to tragedy has become shallow. Horrified for a minute, interested for an hour, we soon turn our attention from the dead and dying on our screen. The victims have become merely objects eliciting prurient interest instead of subjects eliciting heartfelt empathy. We no longer relate to them as human beings. Neither did Ted Bundy. "What's one less person on the face of the earth anyway?" he asked his interrogators.

18   Ironically, while becoming numb in the face of death, we are still aroused by violence. We have witnessed the deaths of thousands, both real and imagined. We have been spectators in an endless parade of shootings, stabbings, bombings, burnings, and stranglings. In the realm of fiction, Jason is just the latest in a long line of cultural figures who testify to the power of violence in

solving problems, settling scores, and putting zest into one's day. What makes fictionalized killing palatable is that the audience doesn't have to relate to those killed. Bad guys are dispatched with style and the audience is spared the messy details about grieving families and friends.

Ted Bundy did not kill to solve problems or expiate childhood trauma. He killed to possess status goods. His victims were all socially desirable women. "What really fascinated him," Bundy said, "was the thrill of the hunt, the adventure of searching out his victims. And to a degree, possessing them as one would a potted plant, a painting, or a Porsche. Owning, as it were, this individual." 19

In his world view, sex and violence were simply two faces of the same coin. "This condition," he told his interrogators, ". . . manifests itself in an interest concerning sexual behaviour, sexual images. . . . But this interest, for some unknown reason, becomes geared toward matters of a sexual nature that include violence." The stimulation we receive from media violence and sex rests on our ability to see others as objects. They become commodities to be consumed. "Once the individual had her [the victim]," Bundy explained, "where he had, you know, security over her, there would be a minimum of conversation . . . to avoid developing some kind of relationship." 20

This is indeed an era of peculiar circumstances. The days when one's neighbours were like family are long gone. We do not know our neighbours; perhaps we are not even interested in knowing them. This rift has been the price paid in the pursuit of commodity culture. In advanced capitalist societies, everything has a price, and every obligation is judged by its ability to advance individual interests. The ties of community, family, and even marriage have been weighed in the balance and found wanting. The modern ethic chooses pleasure over obligation, career over community, the self over the other. We have become a culture of deliberate strangers. 21

Serial killers are nurtured in this breakdown of community. In the absence of strong social interrelationships, the alienated mind begins to perceive others as objects for personal gratification, whether financial, sexual, or violent. On a spiritual level, *lustmord* is the logical extreme of our cultural sickness. Murder has become the ultimate act of self-worship. Gone are the crimes of passion, the relationships gone wrong, the fated love affairs. The killings reflect a cold brutality, the sterile control of subject over object. 22

Ted Bundy went to his death on January 24, 1989. His execution served as a gruesome conduit of hate and media sorcery. Two hundred reporters, camped out near the grounds of the prison, detailed every aspect of Bundy's date with the electric chair as if it were a major sports event. Cheering crowds gathered outside the prison gates. Street vendors reported a brisk trade in "I like my Ted well-done" T-shirts. 23

24   In the eyes of the public, it was not a fellow human being who was dying, but an object, a thing fit for ridicule and murder. His public revelled in the gruesome details, spurred on by reports of his fear and remorse. In the end, it was as mechanical and empty as his own crimes, again the sterile control of subject over helpless object. Ted Bundy died reaffirming America's belief in murder. No wounds were healed, no victims' families made whole once again. The beast is not dead but remains lurking in the gulf between neighbours. The electric chair and the cheering crowds serve only as reminders that Ted Bundy was one of us.

25   Ted Bundy was not a monster. He was a human being, and his path toward the ultimate in evil is a path that is well trodden in our culture. He made the choices that commodity consciousness dictates: pleasure, self-worship, and alienation from true relationships. His obsessions with violence and death were extreme, but the path that led there is a path we have all walked in our viewing and in our minds. If Ted Bundy's life and death are to have any meaning, we have to realize that the pursuit of self-interest is not a harmless choice. It fundamentally affects the fabric of human relationships. It is time to repair the bonds of community and stop being deliberate strangers.

Style and Structure

1. (a) In paragraphs 1 to 4, the writer establishes a chatty tone. Point to those words or expressions that seem to invite the reader into an informal discussion.

   (b) Why do you think the writer has chosen this strategy for his introduction? Given the overall purpose of the essay, why might such an introduction be particularly fitting?

2. (a) A change occurs in the fifth paragraph, where the writer begins a different approach. Which one of the **organizational approaches** does he use here? Why? (For **organizational approaches**, see pp. 212–213.)

   (b) In paragraph 9, Angus again changes the tone and direction of his essay by focussing on Ted Bundy, an American serial killer. As a reader, do you find these changes to be disturbing from the point of view of **unity** and **coherence**? Explain your answer.

3. (a) List the films that Angus mentions or alludes to in his essay.

   (b) The impact of the examples the writer uses will diminish greatly if few readers recognize them. How well known are Angus's examples? Have you or your friends seen or heard of any of these movies? What can you say about the success of Angus's examples in terms of recognizability?

4. (a) In paragraphs 23 and 24, the writer compares Ted Bundy's death to the death of his victims, but also suggests that the crowds thirsting for details were much like Bundy himself as he committed his crimes. As a reader, how did you react to this **conclusion**? Did you feel shocked or insulted, or did you see the **conclusion** as reasonable given the argument that preceded it?

   (b) Examine the text of the essay one more time. How has the writer set the reader up for the conclusions he draws?

5. (a) Is there a **thesis statement** in this essay? If so, where did you find it?

   (b) What do you think is the writer's strategy in dealing with a **thesis**? Explain your answer with reference to the essay itself.

Warm-up

Violence, like beauty and pornography, may be in the eye of the beholder. What seems violent to one person does not always seem violent to the next.

What is violence? Write a paragraph in which you define what violence is for people of your age category. Compare your definition with those of your classmates, and see if you can agree upon a single definition of violence.

Thinking and Writing

1. Angus has a theory that we have become a culture of deliberate strangers. He suggests that "the days when one's neighbours were like family are long gone. We do not know our neighbours; perhaps we are not even interested in knowing them" (paragraph 21).

   Is this true? Do people not know their neighbours, except perhaps in the most superficial way? List the number of your neighbours you know at least well enough to speak to on the street. Look back over your list, and put a check mark beside the names of those you feel you know very well (that is, you know all the members of the family and have visited several times over a year). Next, compare your list with those of your classmates to discover if there is a trend away from close neighbourhood bonds. What can you conclude about Angus's theory?

   Using the results of your investigation and discussion, write an essay in which you prove or disprove the following thesis: "We have become a culture of deliberate strangers."

Audience: the local police or members of Neighbourhood Watch or Block Parents (if there is such an organization in your area).

2.   When we discuss the most unattractive features of our society, our tendency to accuse television of playing a major role is almost automatic. Angus, for instance, points to television as being largely responsible for an age of impersonal violence.

Does television deserve the bad press it gets? Examine TV programming to determine whether there is a large proportion of violence offered to viewers. Write an essay showing which programs fit your definition of violence. Be sure to design your essay around a clear-cut thesis statement. **Audience**: members of your peer group who may be unaware of the real level of violence in television viewing.

Education for One World

by Jack Costello

From Plato to John Dewey, philosophers of education have insisted that a sys- 1
tem of education can be effective only if it takes account of social conditions.
Young people, they all agreed, must be trained for the society in which they are
to live. So most educators have conscientiously transmitted their cultural heritage while trying, with greater or lesser success, to relate it to their own times.

But something has happened on the way to the future that neither Plato nor 2
Dewey nor anyone in the centuries between them could have foreseen. Two
historical factors are distinctive about our situation: first, the massive acceler-
ation of all forms of change, and second, what can be called a "loss of faith"
in our civilization on the part of its own members. It has become increasingly
difficult to educate for a changing world.

After Alvin Toffler's *Future Shock* detailed the speed of change in our 3
high-tech society, many were relieved to see that their anxieties had some basis
in fact. Change that used to take a century began happening in a generation by
the eighteenth century and is now occurring at two or three times that speed.
Take, for instance, our consciousness of AIDS and *glasnost*, neither of which
was a major factor in our world a few years ago.

In 1949, when he was almost 60 years old, the Scottish philosopher John Mac- 4
murray gave a talk on education reflecting on the devastating impact the First
World War had on European civilization's experience of itself as a stable and rational social order. He confessed to his audience, "I have been trying to catch up with
a process of change that is too fast for me, and falling steadily behind — faint but
pursuing. Ever since 1919, I have felt that I was educated for a world in which I
have never lived; and have had to live in a world for which I was never educated."

Most of those who are middle-aged or older recognize themselves in this 5
confession. They were given an education in cultural ideals, career goals, scientific theories, social values, even notions of the right order of the world that
were meant to last a lifetime and beyond. But they now find themselves shaken
by what has happened to these notions in "real life." The world that produced
these ideas is no longer the world they live in. Along with Macmurray, they
have had to scramble to re-educate themselves, feeling all the while that the
world will always be moving faster than they can follow.

This leads quite naturally to the loss of faith that characterizes our society. 6
By faith, I do not mean primarily belief in a set of doctrines, but the shared
meanings and purposes that direct our choices as a society and give us the

111

capacity to act according to them. At root it must be religious. This faith is gone. Its disappearance is due partly to the breakup of the stable, nineteenth-century world and its world view that Macmurray described, and partly to our failure in the twentieth century to find new terms for a faith that can direct us. Because of that vacuum in our collective soul, we feel fragmented, drifting, caught up by events and technology rather than being directed by any unified purpose that engages our whole heart and soul. We have lost a capacity to choose and to act together, because without faith there is no common principle of valuation, and therefore no unity of purpose. This makes us a fearful and a grasping people. We define our problems in economic terms, constantly serving the economy as if it were some cruel ancient god demanding sacrifice. The truth is that we will never resolve our economic troubles until we have solved the dilemma in our spiritual life that produces them. And the same can be said for our quandary about how to educate ourselves and our children at this time.

7 Thus, education today carries a special burden: we want to educate our children to live well while having little collective wisdom to share with them about what the good life is or how to achieve it. At the same time, we are trying to educate them for a society that will be culturally very different from our own. No wonder educators are confused.

8 I am convinced we will get a fix on sound educational objectives only if we can come both to some shared faith in what the "way to genuine life" is for our world at this time and to some capacity to live graciously and creatively with constant change.

9 The search for a new faith for society could also be expressed in this religious form: In what direction is the Spirit of God leading the world at this time? If we can discern this direction and ally ourselves with the Spirit to bring this about, then we will have a sure (though moving) relationship to our own centre into which much change can flow without destroying our personal unity or making us constantly feel nostalgic.

10 The basic issues facing education in our society are contained in these questions: What is the way to fuller life for our world at this point in history, and can we choose to co-operate in that direction? If this is a fair appraisal of our dilemma, then we must reject any view that suggests the basic purpose of education today can be expressed by focussing simply on learning the heritage of the past, meeting the needs of the individual, preparing for careers, or simply acquiring "tools" or "skills" for survival.

11 The very fact that the world one generation ahead is so hard to foresee reveals that we ourselves live and educate in a time of permanent cultural revolution. If this is so, and I believe it to be, then we have no choice but to consider education as cultural action. It must be education that shapes not only the

way our children think about their own lives and goals but also the way they see the society they live in and the way they choose to judge it and act in it. And it must teach them not only to accommodate themselves to life as they find it but to be shapers of society itself, giving direction to its goals and structures that will lead to greater life.

Many people judge our era to be a time of revolution because the peoples   12
of the world are in the process of becoming a "world society" beyond the framework of national sovereign states and their partial alliances that have held sway for so many years. For the past several decades, the nations of the world have moved into deep interdependence with one another in their economic affairs, in spite of their presumed independence. This economic interdependence is a fact of life that will not go away but can only increase. The reality of our world relationships calls desperately now for a corresponding political interdependence that will place all nations under some commonly accepted system of planetary law in relation to areas of shared concern. The time for such an international order is here — and overdue — if we are to avoid further wars and even greater destruction of our planet. Finally, our times call out for a celebration of our human interdependence as an end in itself.

Teaching our children and ourselves to articulate, own, and promote this   13
human interdependence already beginning to shape our world should be, in my judgment, the most urgent educational objective in the dominant countries in the world today. Our times require nothing less than this: that the Western countries (the First World) and the Eastern Bloc (the Second World), along with Japan, learn to relinquish all claims to supremacy and begin to act in a genuinely co-operative and equal relationship with the rest of the world.

Our education systems must help us try to achieve this basic conversion. They   14
must help us move from seeing ourselves simply as citizens of one country to embracing our participation in a world order in which membership is determined not by skin colour or a country's economic system but by our common humanity.

Implicit in this revolution in our self-image would be a commitment to   15
change the way we live and our educational goals and strategies from kindergarten to Ph.D. As John Macmurray observed, "We are committed not merely to seek for knowledge but to live by it; and not merely as individuals but as communities with the goal of becoming the single community of humankind."

When this basic objective for education is embraced, a new light falls on   16
the more specific aspects of our educational efforts. First of all, it becomes clear that education must be a program for integration: a blending of learning and living. It becomes a challenge to apply our learning as a light for judging our way of living and as a help for finding ways of improving life. It fosters learning for cultural action that is at once critical and constructive.

17   This "critical" and "constructive" role of education can best be understood in relation to the current premises underlying our culture and our North American way of life. A conviction about the unitary nature of life on our planet and about the communal nature of human life leads to a belief in the unitary nature of all knowledge. We come to see that it's all meant to fit together and means something together. Once this belief takes hold, many questions and further convictions about our own society follow.

18   For example, it leads to a rejection of the opposition made in some religious — and business — circles between material and spiritual values, and works at showing the unity between them. It questions our liberal tradition in its separation of "private" and "public" morality and proposes the model of morality as a "seamless garment" in which the threads between individual and global issues are seen to be woven together. It challenges the split between thinking and feeling that leads to false categorizations of what is "objective" and what is "subjective" and wrongheaded views of what is masculine and what is feminine. It rejects the individual's — and the corporation's — separation of financial and career ambitions from concern for personal relations of intimacy and justice at home and in the larger community. It does all it can to formulate and propagate a genuine notion of the common good. Finally, even as it fosters a concern that each individual be free to hold and express his or her own views, it leads to the conviction that an educational process engaged in apart from belief and commitment is at best dangerous and at worst destructive.

19   If this conscious choice for world community is made in a school, then the administrators and teachers will constantly be educating their students not only toward an intellectual synthesis of all their studies but toward becoming an actual community in their life together. Utopian as it may sound, I believe that every school should aim at being a society of friends. After some years teaching in secondary schools and university, I am convinced this is best achieved — and inevitably will be achieved — if and only if the members of the staff have such a relationship with one another. All good primary and secondary school teachers know that they are teaching people, not subjects, and that young people learn best by imitation and only secondarily by information. If staff members have a vision of community for the school as well as for the world, and celebrate it with one another in shared purpose and friendship, the students will pick that up by osmosis. The student becomes a junior member in a fellowship that already exists.

20   These are some of the standards of this new age that it is the task of education to provide. There are, of course, vast limitations on our capacity to achieve them under the best of circumstances. First, this goal of educating for freedom in community is a value that has to be embodied in a new culture that

still awaits creation. Second, it remains true that the major part of education is done, well or badly, in the home. If the home training is bad or if it is shirked, the school will be helpless. And this does not even address the issues of over-crowding, overworked teachers, and lack of money and resources.

I have merely hinted at the role of religion as an agent in shaping this faith 21 and as an element in education, but the transformation envisaged here is essentially a religious one. The desire to form one community is not a political desire but a deeply human one that goes beyond the political structures that need to be part of it. I have already noted that this human response can be related to nothing less than the impetus of God's Spirit in the world.

As for the teaching of religion, we should acknowledge that the concern of 22 educators today has to be not simply how to teach religion in the schools but how to teach religion in the schools of a civilization that has thrown religion over. This same civilization has simultaneously made choices that have resulted in the near-disappearance of the family. These losses are two sides of the same coin. If a society refuses to try collectively to heal this rupture in family life by reordering its values, it could be said that it is a society with its heart set against community. There is no room for religion in such a society — except as a rebellion and a refusal to accept that kind of life. This creative rebellion was already suggested in my earlier examples of how the critical spirit shaped by the desire for community might look on the operating "truths" of our society.

Finally, I return to John Macmurray to have the last word on how our chil- 23 dren might learn to live in a world of constant change. In the same talk mentioned earlier, Macmurray concluded, "If we are to provide an education which will fit the children of today for the world they will have to live in, it must be one which embodies and expresses continuous transformation as the norm of life. It will not be enough to train them to adaptability so that they can make shift to live without stability while retaining the idea of stability as desirable. That is altogether too negative. What they need, in both the cultural and the technical field, is an education in which continuous transformation is both the law and the delight of life; a training which will make them happy and active agents in the transformation of their own society."

I believe that such an eduction is possible if we and our children can come to 24 believe in the community we are being invited to build with our learning and our lives.

Style and Structure

1. (a) In his introduction, Costello gives a historical overview of the philosophy of education. This, of course, is not the only way he might have chosen to

begin. Referring to pages 214–217, write two alternative introductions for this essay. Choose which you prefer, and give your reasons.

(b) Review one of your own recent essays and write an alternative introduction. Notice how the tone of the essay varies as the opening strategy changes. Comparing the two introductions you have now written for the essay, suggest what sort of readership might find each appealing.

2. (a) This essay is a challenging one, estimated at Grade 13 level on a standard index. How do you know that this is more difficult reading than you might have previously experienced in this text? Give at least four reasons for your answer.

(b) For what sort of readership do you believe this essay was written? Why do you think so?

(c) Do you believe that, given the readership you determined, the essay is written in a suitable style? Do you believe that the style and tone are suited to the nature of the subject matter?

3. (a) Paragraph 8 marks a change in the direction of the essay. What is the difference between the content of paragraphs 1 to 7 and that which follows?

(b) Do you believe that this shift in direction is natural and necessary, or is this a flaw in the essay? Give reasons for your choice.

4. (a) In paragraph 18, the writer uses the word "it" repeatedly. Jot down in your notebook the number of times the word is used and the accompanying verb in each case.

(b) What does "it" stand for? How do you know?

(c) Do you find the use of the pronoun "it" in this instance helpful or misleading? If you are not happy with the effect, rewrite the paragraph to clear up the problem.

5. (a) The writer makes a significant effort to assist the reader by providing a number of **transitions** throughout. (See p. 218 for a definition of **transitions**.) Make a list of all the **transitions** you find in the essay.

(b) Identify the **transitions** you believe are particularly effective and suggest why the writer found it necessary to include them.

Warm-up

In his introduction, Costello outlines a part of the historical background of the philosophy of education, "from Plato to John Dewey." Practise this technique by writing a paragraph showing a brief historical view of one of the following:

(i) the automobile;

(ii) the postal service;

(iii) tobacco;

(iv) public libraries.

Thinking and Writing

1. In paragraph 19, the writer lays out his vision of what a school should be. He suggests that young people learn best by imitation and that, "if staff members have a vision of community for the school as well as for the world, and celebrate it with one another in shared purpose and friendship, the students will pick that up by osmosis. The student becomes a junior member in a fellowship that already exists."

    Explore the idea of school as community. Looking at such aspects as relationships among faculty, administration, and students, list five characteristics such a "fellowship" might have. Using these five characteristics to form topics for the paragraphs in the body of your essay and adding an appropriate introduction and conclusion, write an essay in which you describe the sort of ideal school Costello has in mind.

    Audience: a parent–teacher group or the Board of Governors of your school.

    Send a copy of the final draft to the chairperson.

2. The writer of this essay suggests, "Change that used to take a century began happening in a generation by the eighteenth century and is now occurring at two or three times that speed" (paragraph 3). Discuss with an older person the one most significant change that has affected his or her life. Investigate the process in which the change occurred and the effects it has had, keeping in mind that those effects may be positive, negative, or mixed.

    Using the evidence of your conversation, write an essay in which you prove or disprove Costello's theory that the fast pace of change has led to the loss of faith that characterizes our society (paragraph 6).

    Audience: a religious leader in your community.

    Send a copy to this person and ask for comment on your ideas.

Is Plea-Bargaining So Bad?
by Leo Adler

[In a number of famous cases the public has had to face arguments about the justice of a plea bargain.

One case was that of Clifford Olson. Another was the Karla Homolka case.

In 1993, police needed Homolka's testimony to convict her husband, Paul Bernardo, of the abduction, sexual assault, torture and murder of two teenagers. She reached an agreement with the Crown Attorney: she would plead guilty to manslaughter and receive a 12-year sentence. In return she would testify against her husband. Later the Crown also agreed not to prosecute her for the sexual assault of a third woman or the death of her own sister. The trial judge accepted the agreement.

Soon afterwards, videotapes — made by Homolka and her husband — emerged to show she had been a party to the assaults. A public outcry arose that called for the deal to be quashed: over 300,000 people signed a petition demanding the Ontario government go back on the deal. Nevertheless, for all the same reasons Adler cites in this essay, the agreement was honoured. But the provincial government directed Justice Galligan to conduct an inquiry into the agreement. In early 1996 he reported that it had been necessary, it had served the purposes of justice, and it should be honoured. Homolka would be eligible to apply for day parole after serving four years. After eight years she could apply for release on mandatory supervision.]

1   When the British Columbia Supreme Court ordered that the $100 000 trust fund set up for the family of mass murderer Clifford Olson be declared null and void, it threw a wrench into the whole legal system of plea-bargaining. The fund had been set up by the Crown in return for Mr. Olson telling the authorities where he had hidden the bodies of the children he murdered, and for giving the Crown full details of these crimes to ensure his conviction. This is not the first time that the Crown has made "deals." In Ontario, a Mafia enforcer named Cecil Kirby has been granted full immunity, protection, a new identity, a financial allowance, and other benefits for helping the Crown prosecute the people who hired him to commit numerous crimes. Mr. Olson and Mr. Kirby are simply the two most graphic illustrations of plea-bargaining and the tactics used to gain convictions.

The courts have long recognized that if every accused pleads not guilty and the   2
Crown has to prove his guilt, our already overburdened courts would cease to function beneath the sheer weight of trials. For this reason, discussions are always being
held among the Crown attorney, the police, the defence counsel, and even the
judges. Through the negotiations, trial lists and costs are considerably reduced,
issues clarified, and sentences are usually set within acceptable legal principles.

For the most part, these discussions invoke the possibility of a plea to a   3
lesser offence, an agreed sentence range, or the withdrawal of other outstand-
ing charges. For the Crown and the police, a possible acquittal is averted and
an accused who is truly guilty is found guilty and made to pay the penalty. The
accused avoids the risk of a possible conviction for a more serious charge, or
is made aware of exactly what range of sentence he is facing. For the witnesses, there is the benefit of not having to come to court and be subjected to
occasionally embarrassing cross-examination. It is true that the ultimate decision is made by a judge — who can set aside, or ignore, a patently uncon-
scionable plea or suggested sentence.

However, when that situation occurs (which is quite rare), the judge either   4
sends the case to another court, or gives his reasons for not complying with the
request, thereby allowing a higher court to decide whether he was wrong. Significantly, in the Olson case, the trial judge was made aware of the "cash-for-
bodies deal," without which there could not have been a guilty plea or possibly even a conviction. The trial judge did not strike out the plea, thereby implying that he was prepared to abide by the arrangements.

Within the criminal justice system, the intricacies involved in plea-bar-   5
gaining are founded on the reputations of the defence counsel, police officers,
Crown attorneys, and often the judges. When an agreement is broken, it is
more than simply bad form; it means a loss of reputation that forever marks the
man who broke his word. He can never again negotiate or be trusted, and his
usefulness to his clients is virtually at an end. The British Columbia Supreme
Court, by overturning an agreement made in good faith, has thrown the entire
system into a quandary. If agreements cannot be made and maintained, what is
the point of making them?

The morality of plea-bargaining may be troublesome, but it is nothing   6
compared to the immorality of not having a plea-bargaining system and of having to subject the parties, and the public, to proceedings they could otherwise
be spared. We do not live in a perfect world where innocent people are never
convicted, nor do we live in a perfect world where all criminals are caught and
brought to justice. Our justice system may not be ideal for resolving disputes,
but it is the best of all other options. What makes it the best is the continuing
negotiation that usually leads to a correct resolution of a case.

7   With regard to Mr. Olson, the hard fact is that for $100 000 the parents finally know what happened to their children. Would the parents have preferred that the money not be paid, leaving them in the dark as to what happened? Without the $100 000, Mr. Olson might still be roaming the streets, murdering children. With the $100 000, society has assured itself that he will be behind bars for the rest of his life.

8   Is the moral and financial price really that high or that outrageous to ensure that this man never again sets foot outside jail? If the answer is no, then the deal was a good one and ought to have been upheld. If the answer is yes, then we must stop all plea-bargaining and admit that the Crown should have taken its chances without Mr. Olson's admissions, and that he may have been acquitted. This plea-bargain achieved its purpose. In that respect, it is no different from the hundreds of other plea-bargains made daily and that are not overturned by the courts.

9   There is nothing immoral or unethical about parties negotiating a resolution. It is called compromise and it happens in the real world as much as it happens within the criminal justice system. But it will not continue if individuals and lawyers do not have confidence that their agreements will be upheld. And if this lack of confidence actually permeates the criminal justice system, it is justice that will suffer the most.

Style and Structure

1.   What is the relationship of the first sentence in paragraph 1 to the rest of the essay?

2.   Why does the author follow the first sentence in paragraph 1 with the information contained in the rest of the paragraph? What does the inclusion of this information tell you about the intended reader of the essay?

3.   Make a list of the three arguments presented by the writer to justify plea-bargaining in paragraphs 1, 2, and 3. Note beside each entry in your list whether the argument is based on practical or moral considerations.

4.   What information is contained in the first sentence of paragraph 4? What information is contained in the second and third sentences of paragraph 4? By presenting the information contained in paragraph 4 in this order, what conclusion does the writer lead the reader to accept?

5.   What information is contained in the first three sentences of paragraph 5? What information is contained in the last two sentences of paragraph 5? By presenting the information contained in paragraph 5 in this order, what conclusion does the writer lead the reader to accept?

6. Make a list of the three arguments presented by the writer in paragraphs 6, 7, and 8 to justify plea-bargaining in general and in the Olson case in particular. Note beside each entry in your list whether the argument is based on practical or moral considerations.

7. (a) In the first sentence in his **conclusion**, the writer claims, "There is nothing immoral or unethical about parties negotiating a resolution" (i.e., plea-bargaining). Review your lists of the arguments made in paragraphs 1 to 3 and 6 to 8. Do these arguments prove the claim made in the sentence quoted above?

   (b) Why do the last three sentences of paragraph 9 form a more appropriate **conclusion** for this essay? Why, then, does the writer choose to include the first sentence of the **conclusion**?

Warm-up

1. Working in groups of three or four, research one of the following topics in the reference section of the library. Two groups may end up doing the same topic, but be certain that each topic is covered.

Clifford Olson	Cecil Kirby
Crown attorney	provincial supreme court
Supreme Court of Canada	unconscionable plea

   Working on your own, write a one-paragraph report on your topic for the rest of your class. Compare your report with those written by the others in your group and make any changes that might add to your readers' understanding of the topic. Then make enough copies of your report that, between those distributed by you and those distributed by the other members of your group, everyone in the class will have a report on your topic (but not one from each writer).

2. Read paragraph 7 of the essay "Let the Punishment Fit the Crime" (p. 96) and paragraph 6 of "An Alternative to Incarceration" (p. 41). Then write a short explanation of the possibility of applying the ideas contained in those essays to the Olson case or the Homolka case.
   Audience: someone who knows of both cases but is not aware of the principles outlined in the other essays.

   Working with the class as a whole, create a list of arguments both for and against applying these principles. Revise your explanation so that it takes into account as many of the objections listed by the class as possible.

Thinking and Writing

1. Review the background on *either* the Olson case or the Homolka case. Then, for the case you chose, write an essay to explain whether or not the agreement achieved by plea bargaining served the purposes of justice. Discussions of these cases can be highly emotional so try to remain objective as you write. In your argument, you might want to take into consideration the purpose of the police and the courts: is it to stop crime from recurring, to exact revenge, or to see that everyone affected by crime is treated fairly and equally?

    Audience: someone who knows little if anything about the case chosen.

2. Write an essay in which you argue that plea-bargaining either should or should not be used as a tool of the justice system. Whichever way you argue, consider the effectiveness of plea-bargaining for the justice system in dealing with crimes against property (e.g., theft, burglary, and fraud), crimes against society (e.g., smuggling, drug offences, and drunken driving), crimes causing bodily injury (e.g., assault and rape), and crimes causing death (e.g., murder and manslaughter).

    Audience: someone who knows how plea-bargaining works but would argue against your position.

    Send a copy of your final draft to the local Crown attorney's offices and ask for a response.

There's a Trickster Behind Every Nanabush

by Drew Hayden Taylor

Once upon a time, many years past, there was a man who told a story from his wayward youth. As he so bravely put it, it was a long time ago in a reserve far far away, when he was but a young and innocent aboriginal living with his family in the serene outdoors known today as Northern Ontario. Then one day, as often happens in tales such as this, a wandering group of archaeologists/anthropologists/sociologists (so grouped for they all looked and acted alike) appeared in his peaceful community. 1

Seems these intrepid academics were there in search of knowledge. They were fearless story hunters, wanting to document the legends and myths of these proud but oral people. Legends they wanted, and legends they were determined to get, for the annals of history and their publishers. First in their quest they went to the elders of the village, saying, "tell us your stories so that we may document them." 2

The elders, believing stories are meant to be shared with good friends and caring people, refused, saying to the puzzled academics "strangers do not demand a story, they ask politely." Thus they were chastised. With no stories to bring back, and no victory to print, the academics pondered and prodded until they found willing confidantes for their earnest though ill-conceived purpose. 3

The children of that community boldly approached these white warriors of writing. "We know the legends and stories of our people and we will gladly share them with you if you will honor us with gifts — financial ones," spoke their young leader. Eager and anxious, the academics gladly brought forth their small change in trade for the fables and myths of these proud people. Every morning for many days, the children would entice these eager men with a legend, often about the Trickster, Nanabush, and his mischievous adventures, or about the animals that abounded in this forest primeval, or occasionally about the people themselves. 4

Later, after the tale was told, the children of the community would retire to the woods and spend the afternoon enjoying the spoils of their barter. Down went the potato chips and pop while they pondered and created afresh each new tale they would tell these pale strangers. For they kept close to their hearts the real stories of their people, and instead, offered only the imagination and creativity of a child's mind. What they traded were new legends, barely a day old. 5

Many decades later, one of these children, now an adult, happened upon a bookstore. There, in a book of native legends published may years before by a 6

123

non-native researcher but still used frequently as source material, he came upon a story that was . . . oddly familiar. Then it dawned upon him. In the pages he held in his hand were those same spirited stories commissioned in that bygone era of free junk food and gullible academics. A smile played on his impish face as he replaced the book. The Trickster of legend was alive and well and living in the glorious halls of academia.

7   Some are tall, some aren't. Some are fat while others have a lean and hungry look about them. Most wear glasses or contacts but not all. And believe it or not, some could be your next-door neighbor. I am referring to academics.

8   There's an old joke in the native community. What's the definition of a native family? Two parents, a grandparent, five kids and an anthropologist (or academic). Get the picture?

9   Not a week goes by in the offices of Native Earth Performing Arts, Toronto's only professional native theatre company, that we don't get a call from some university or college student/professor doing research on native theatre in Canada. And each time I put the phone down I struggle to suppress a shudder. I can't help but wonder what wonderful images they are going to get from our work.

10   When is a door not a door? When it's ajar. When is a symbolic metaphor describing the native individual's relationship with the Earth, or Turtle Island as they call it, and the spiritual and physical sustenance that it provides, as well as the water being an allusion to the blood of said Turtle Island, or perhaps in this reference the term Mother Earth would be more accurate, not a symbolic metaphor? Sometimes you just wanna yell: "He's just fishing, for Christ's sake!"

11   This is a strange race of people who spend their entire life in the constant study and analysis of other people's writings and work (in this case native works) but seldom attempt the same work themselves. It's sort of like people who watch pornographic movies but never have sex.

12   British playwright Willy Russell, author of such plays as *Educating Rita* and *Shirley Valentine*, once related a story of a lecture he secretly attended, a lecture about his work. At one point the academic brought up for discussion the final scene of *Educating Rita*, where as a going-away gift, the former hairstylist Rita cuts the professor's hair. "This," said the man with letters behind his name, "was a direct metaphor to the Samson and Delilah legend where she is taking his strength by cutting his hair. The author obviously . . ." At that moment Russell stood up and said, "Uh, sorry, you're wrong. I just wanted to end the play on a funny and touching note. It has nothing to do with Samson." They proceeded to get into a rather intense argument over the interpretation of the scene.

13   As a writer I recognize the fact that all stories, in whatever form they are written, are the equivalent of literary Rorschach tests, all open to interpretation

and understanding. Oftentimes that's the fun of taking a literature class, dissecting the piece for the underlying imagery. And, I might add, adding subtextural elements into the stories I write adds a certain amount of fun to the writing process. However, as Freud used to say, sometimes a cigar is just a good smoke.

Case in point — a non-native friend of mine wrote his master's thesis on   14
native theatre in Canada. In one of the chapters he examined some of my work. One night in a drunken celebration after successfully defending his thesis, he let me read his dissertation. As he celebrated his newfound academic status, I sat there reading some new and interesting theories about the symbolism in my plays.

To put it bluntly, they were wrong. Completely, way off, not correct, inaccu-   15
rate, barking up the proverbial wrong tree. Especially the section where he thought a crow in the text was a manifestation of Nanabush, the Ojibway Trickster figure. I sat there for a while on that bar stool, quietly debating if I should tell him of the error. But looking at the sheer joy in his face — all those years of university finally completed — I held my tongue. I'd rather have him drinking happily than in a fit of depression. If he thinks a crow is Nanabush, let him. There's a whole flock of Nanabushes living around my mother's house. He'd have a field day.

That seems to be the latest fad with academics. Subscribing all actions and at   16
least one character in a written piece to the Trickster figure. As playwright/poet Daniel David Moses describes it — "they all like to play 'Spot The Trickster'."

But then again, these selfsame people, the academics of this world, are   17
responsible for introducing my books and other writings to the curriculums of various high schools, colleges and universities. The very computer I'm writing on I owe to their influences. I guess I mustn't bite the hand that feeds me.

So perhaps, just for clarity's sake, I should take the time to make sure these   18
no doubt intelligent people understand that it's just the inherent Trickster tendencies that exist on a subconscious level in all literary works penned by aboriginal writers. In other words, I'm not responsible for these views or criticisms, the Trickster is at fault here. The Trickster made me do it.

Yeah, they'll buy that.   19

Style and Structure

1.   There are several ways to prepare a reader for the central message of an essay. Most essay writers use an introduction that includes a grabber (attention getter), a **thesis statement**, and an **organizational statement**. Taylor takes a different approach in this essay.

(a) In what ways do paragraphs 1–6 prepare the reader for the essay's central idea?

(b) Each detail in the opening narrative prepares the reader to deal with the rest of the essay. How does each of the following passages help?

  (i) "Once upon a time . . . ." (paragraph 1)

  (ii) ". . . it was a long time ago in a reserve far far away . . . ." (paragraph 1)

  (iii) ". . . stories are meant to be shared with good friends and caring people . . . ." (paragraph 3)

  (iv) ". . . enjoying the spoils of their barter . . . ." (paragraph 5)

  (v) ". . . they kept close to their hearts the real stories of their people . . . ." (paragraph 5)

  (vi) "The trickster of legend was alive and well and living in the glorious halls of academia." (paragraph 6)

(c) What is the role of paragraphs 7 and 8 in introducing the reader to the essay's thesis? What reaction is Taylor trying to achieve by ending paragraph 8 with the question "Get the picture?" What picture?

2. (a) What device does Taylor use in paragraphs 9–10 to make his point? How does paragraph 11 relate to this device? How effective is this approach in convincing the reader?

  (b) How does using the same approach in paragraphs 12–16 develop his argument? What factors does he rely upon for the success of this approach?

  (c) How do the last sentences of paragraphs 10, 13 and 15 serve Taylor's purpose? How influential is this rhetorical device in leading the reader to accept Taylor's point of view?

3. What effect does the ironic approach in paragraphs 17 and 18 have on the reader? How does it influence the reader's attitude to the rest of the essay?

4. (a) What is the double meaning contained in the final paragraph? What earlier passage in the essay does it force the reader to recall? How does this reminder influence the reader's understanding of paragraphs 17 and 18?

  (b) In what ways does the final paragraph contribute to the impact of the entire essay?

5. (a) Who is the intended reader of this essay? Cite at least three specific passages to support your conclusion.

  (b) Examine three or four examples of humour employed in this essay. How does this use of humour help Taylor persuade the reader to accept his point of view?

  (c) What is the real thesis Taylor wants to convey to his reader? (Compare your answer to those of others in your class: see if any of you has fallen into the trap of being an academic!)

Warm-up

1. As you explore this subject you will be dealing with sensitive materials. Before you begin, agree that your group will use maturity and understanding of the feelings of others as it explores the topic.

    Working for 20 minutes with a group of classmates, identify jokes in common circulation that some people would find offensive and personally hurtful. (Do not restrict yourself to jokes about sex.) Discuss why the messages the jokes carry hurt some but not others. Then write a paragraph that summarizes your findings.

2. In paragraphs 10, 13 and 15, Taylor uses a single humorous sentence to make his point. Create a list of some of your pet peeves (e.g., tests in all your courses on the same day, transportation or parking problems at your school, men's attitudes toward women or women's attitudes toward men, and so on). Select one and write a paragraph, modelled on Taylor's, which uses a humorous concluding sentence to drive home your point.

    Working with a group of classmates, exchange paragraphs. How effectively have they achieved their objective? What suggestions can you make to help them improve their results?

Thinking and Writing

1. Someone once said, "Behind every joke there's a serious message. The brunt of the joke is always a target. A joke is always told at someone's expense." Write an essay in which you discuss the different types of serious (and sometimes frightening) messages jokes can convey. Use the example of a specific joke as the starting point for your explanation of each type of message discussed.
    Audience: someone who would usually respond, "Loosen up. It's just a joke."

2. Many people use humour to end a discussion or argument they might not win in any other way. Jot down a few examples of situations in which you have seen this technique used. Try to identify such factors as why it was so important for the person to "win," why the other(s) involved allowed the technique to work, and the effect its use had on the relationship of the people involved.

    Then write an essay that examines the effectiveness of using humour to win an argument. Use two or three specific examples to illustrate your points.
    Audience: someone who uses the technique frequently.

    Send a copy of your completed essay to someone who teaches psychology or sociology or who specializes in helping people with their relationships.

Stop the Music

by Bruce Headlam

1 The people in Section 45 of Exhibition Stadium in Toronto were particularly courteous as they waited for the concert to begin. They applauded politely when the stadium lights dimmed. And they applauded when The Cure, a British quintet that had ridden the crest of the nihilistic punk movement ten years earlier, was chauffeured to the grandstand stage in two white extended Cadillacs. Near the front of Section 45, a punk couple in their late twenties took their seats, and their appearance — all dark make-up and razor-sharp Mohawk haircuts — was admired by a sea of less severe imitators. Even in Toronto, there is just not enough black clothing to go around. Behind the punks, two young men in baseball caps boasted that they had attended four concerts and the monster truck mania show, but they agreed that concerts were better because afterwards more girls went to McDonald's. Three girls in identical Cure T-shirts sat behind them, eating caramel corn and telling each other that so many kids at the concert were "like, so obnoxious."

2 Not all of The Cure's memories of their August 1 concert in Toronto will be agreeable. Three weeks earlier, the Hamilton City Council had passed a resolution recommending to Queen's Park that the group's song "Killing an Arab" be banned throughout Ontario. On July 13, Mayor Art Eggleton informed Toronto City Council that The Cure had agreed not to perform "Killing an Arab" at the CNE. The council then adopted Hamilton's resolution without dissent. A motion to circulate the resolution to every Ontario municipality with a population of 50 000 or more was also unanimously accepted. It took the council less than two minutes to support the suppression of the song. Even the girls in matching Cure T-shirts, when asked about the ban, agreed that it was, like, so unreal. But Eggleton was pungent in explaining his determination to ban "Killing an Arab": if the song were in printed form, he argued, it would be called hate literature.

3 "Killing an Arab" was written in 1976 by Robert Smith, The Cure's lead singer, under the inspiration of Albert Camus' existential classic, *L'Étranger* — a book that, like most books, appears in printed form, but has not yet been classified as hate literature. Smith read Camus in his "A"-level French literature course in an English secondary school. The song's lyrics describe the critical event of the novel: the senseless shooting of an Arab on an Algerian beach. In the song, the chorus, "I'm alive. I'm dead./I am the stranger killing an Arab," is repeated three times over a quirky bass line and Hollywood-style harem guitar solos. The novel is meant "to illustrate the utter futility of the central action of

killing," Smith explains for the benefit of those of us without our "A" levels in French literature. Smith emphasizes that his intention, like Camus', was existentialist, not racist.

"Killing an Arab" attracted little attention when it was first released in 1977, but it happened to be re-released on a new collection of The Cure's singles after the American bombing of Libya in April 1986. When a student disc jockey at Princeton University broadcast the song with an anti-Arab crack, Arabs in the United States complained to Elektra Records, The Cure's recording label. In December 1986, Elektra and the American-Arab Anti-Discrimination Committee agreed that a sticker declaring that the song "has absolutely no racist overtones whatsoever" would be attached to the cover of all copies of the album. A week later, Smith — citing "brainless and irresponsible DJs" — requested that "Killing an Arab" be removed from all radio playlists.

In February 1987, The Cure's Canadian distributor, WEA Music of Canada, voluntarily started putting those same stickers on copies of the offending album sold in this country. In April, negotiations between WEA and Canadian Arab groups were undertaken under the auspices of the Race Relations Division of the Ontario Human Rights Commission. During those negotiations, WEA suspended distribution of the album. "WEA showed some sensitivity and positive corporate leadership," says Dennis Strong, then of the Human Rights Commission.

But the compromise reached in the United States came unstuck in Canada. The Canadian Arab groups were much less easily mollified than their American counterparts. Just a few months before, the Canadian Arab Federation had negotiated the removal of a boys' doll, "Nomad — enemy of Rambo," from Canadian and U.S. stores. They planned to be as tough with The Cure.

Rana Abdul Qadir, executive director of the Canadian Arab Federation, rejected the disclaiming sticker on the album cover: "The point is not [The Cure's] intention. The point is outcome. Ninety-five percent of people take this song in a negative way." Bernadette Twal of the Palestinian-Arab Association of Hamilton was even more adamant. "This song is a racist statement. . . . If the title were 'Killing a Jew' or 'Killing a Black,' it would not take so long to recognize this." Banning the song from further airing in Ontario would not be censorship, Twal claimed, because "it should not have been allowed in the first place."

As the group's Toronto concert neared, the Canadian Media Coalition, a lobby that claims to speak for minority ethnic communities, asked the Toronto City Council to ban any further sales of the song and to forbid The Cure to play the song at Exhibition Stadium. George Imai, vice-president of the coalition, has no patience with freedom-of-speech protections for The Cure. "If the so-called guardians of freedom were in the place of a minority child, what would their attitude be? Would they allow racist statements to be hurled at them? If that is what democracy is all about, God help us. Under the guise of freedom of speech, art, and culture, people get away with this kind of crap."

9   Meanwhile, Twal was writing to Ontario's attorney general, Ian Scott, urging that "Killing an Arab" be charged as hate literature. Scott's reply conveyed the opinion of his office's Hate Literature Committee that no such charge was possible. "He adopted the same argument as The Cure," Twal angrily remembers. "The attorney general is a very dangerous man."

10   There is no law empowering mayors or city councils to dictate what can be sold or performed in their cities. But Mayor Eggleton unhesitatingly telephoned Bill Stockwell, chief general manager at the CNE, and asked him to stop the song. Stockwell asked The Cure's management to assure him that the song would not be played. The Cure's management said only that the song was not in The Cure's current repertoire, but Robert Smith told the *Toronto Star* that he had made no promises. "It is untrue we've agreed to anything of the sort. If we want to play it, we will play it."

11   Nevertheless, the song wasn't played.

12   What did the Hamilton and Toronto city councils think they were doing when, beyond their legal powers and in possible defiance of the Charter of Rights, they tried to ban a song? By the way, Canadian Arab groups offer only one specific example of a racist incident directly caused by the song: a girl at a private pool in Hamilton claims to have been taunted when the song was played over a loudspeaker. But Toronto Alderman Joe Pantalone believes that municipal governments have "a moral responsibility for advocating positions that affect citizens." Petitioning the Ontario government to ban The Cure's song, and attempting to enlist support from other municipalities, is exactly that sort of moral leadership, not — to Pantalone — unlike posting multilingual street signs, arranging cultural exchanges with foreign cities, and cancelling council meetings that fall on Jewish holidays.

13   When The Cure failed to play the song, an interesting thing did not happen: indignation. A few irritated rock'n'roll columnists let off steam, but otherwise "Killing an Arab" was censored without protest.

14   The Cure was the victim of two double standards. If "Killing an Arab" had been opera, theatre, or literature, it's hard to imagine any city council, even Toronto's, attempting to ban it. The defenders of high art are so much more daunting than punkies.

15   And if anybody had suggested banning "Killing an Arab" because it was smutty, it's hard to believe The Cure would not have had some defenders. Censoring sex is at least controversial; but treading — or seeming to tread — upon the new taboos of race is uncontroversially forbidden.

And besides, the song was never very popular in Canada, where The Cure   16
is better known for whiny odes to adolescent angst such as "Boys Don't Cry"
and "In Between Days." The Cure have long abandoned their punk roots and
now their unimpeachable coolness appeals to the junior-high, funny-haircut
set, like the people in Section 45 who, after the band's third encore, were tired
from dancing and eager to leave the stadium. The two guys in baseball caps left
the concert early, no doubt to ensure themselves a good table at McDonald's.
One of the girls in Cure T-shirts was sick, not from drinking but from all that
caramel corn. Only the punk couple seemed disappointed that "Killing an
Arab" was not performed. As they climbed the concrete stairs toward the exit,
they sadly recalled braver days. "You know," said the man, "eight years ago,
they would have played that song for sure."

Style and Structure

Headlam's essay is very well written and extremely subtle in the way it
communicates its real **thesis** to its readers. Nevertheless, some of the
techniques he uses, such as the implied and delayed **thesis statement**,
require sophisticated writing skills and are not appropriate to more formal writing situations.

1. (a) Examine the *last* three sentences in this essay. Why would the author
       want readers to leave the essay with these ideas foremost in their minds?

   (b) Reread the last paragraph's description of the crowd (immediately pre-
       ceding the final three sentences of the essay). How do this description
       and the contrast it provides add to the significance of the ideas that con-
       clude the essay?

   (c) Examine the description of The Cure with which Headlam begins the
       essay's last paragraph. How does this description affect the reader's
       insight into the ideas in the rest of the paragraph, particularly the one in
       the last sentence?

   (d) What is the main point the author is trying to convey to the reader of this
       essay: the fact that the song was banned? the history of the song? the
       change in The Cure? or something else? Write a short summary of his
       main point.

2. (a) List three things that we learn about each of the following in the first
       paragraph of the essay:

       (i) the people in Section 45;

       (ii) The Cure;

(iii) the punk couple;

(iv) the two young men;

(v) the three girls.

(b) What ideas is the author trying to drive home by including these descriptions in his opening paragraph? What additional insights into them does the essay's final paragraph give you?

3. (a) What function does paragraph 2 serve for the reader?

(b) Of all the comments that would be available on the council's actions, what reasons might Headlam have for choosing to cite "the girls in matching Cure T-shirts"?

(c) Headlam chooses his words very carefully in the last half of this paragraph to influence his readers in the subtlest of ways. Give the meaning of each of the following words:

(i) suppression;

(ii) even;

(iii) pungent.

Try replacing them with synonyms (such as "ban" for "suppression"). How does this rewording change the emotional impact of this section of the paragraph? What reaction is Headlam trying to elicit in his reader?

4. (a) What purposes are served by including paragraph 3's background information so early in the essay? Why, specifically, is it important that it come before the reader learns the history presented in paragraphs 4 to 11?

(b) After examining each in its context, explain briefly why Headlam might include the following words and phrases in paragraph 3:

(i) inspiration;

(ii) existential classic;

(iii) appears in printed form, but has not yet been classified as hate literature;

(iv) senseless;

(v) those of us without our "A" levels.

5. (a) Choose any four words or phrases in paragraphs 4 to 11 that influence the reader's attitude toward the subject matter. Explain how each works. How effective is each in achieving its objective?

(b) Find three examples of words that Headlam uses to help the reader make **transitions** between the ideas in different paragraphs in this section of the essay. Explain how each does its job.

(c) Examine the quotations Headlam uses in paragraphs 4 to 11. Select one that *adds* validity to the speaker's stand. Select one that *undermines* the point the speaker is trying to make.

Explain how each achieves its effect. Would the same points have been made as effectively if Headlam had inserted some personal comment to guide the reader? Justify your answer.

(d) What effect does Headlam achieve by using a one-sentence paragraph (paragraph 11) contrary to the advice usually given to writers? In light of this effect, how would you advise budding writers about the use of one-sentence paragraphs?

6. (a) What purpose is served by beginning paragraph 12 with a question? Point out two ways in which the wording of the question attacks the council's stand.

(b) Writers will sometimes base an argument on a single example of a situation. How does Headlam point out the weakness of this strategy and use it to undercut his opponents? (What techniques might his opponents have used to prevent this attack?)

7. (a) In acting as a **conclusion** for this essay, paragraphs 13 to 16 function in several ways. What are they?

(b) Identify three techniques Headlam uses in paragraphs 13 to 15 to give added impact to his ideas. Explain the way each is used and the effect it has on the reader.

8. (a) How effective is Headlam's use of a delayed and implied **thesis statement** as a rhetorical device? Give reasons to justify your answer.

(b) What limitations does this device have? How would these limitations affect your own use of it?

Warm-up

1. Pay careful attention to the students entering your school tomorrow morning. Make notes on their appearance, behaviour, and general attitudes toward school. Write a one-paragraph description of the scene (similar to the one with which Headlam begins his essay) that drives home a point about students and schools.

Audience: a general reader who has been out of school for some time.

Before you do your final revision, exchange paragraphs with several others in the class. How do their observations differ from yours? Do they have trouble understanding any parts of your paragraph?

2.   Choose a song that you like. Write a one-paragraph description of the
       song that explains its significance and attractiveness to a reader who has
       never heard it. Headlam's approach in paragraph 3 may give you some
       ideas on how to describe your song.

       Find one or two people who know the song and test your first draft
       on them. After you have revised it, try it on someone who does not know
       the song.

Thinking and Writing

1.   Headlam implies that young people have lost interest in fighting against
       rules imposed upon them, even when the rules are blatantly unjustified.

       Identify a situation or incident in which young people have acted in
       a way that supports or contradicts this thesis. Write an essay in which
       you use this example to argue for or against Headlam's implication.

       Audience: people in the age range of the audience described in the article.

2.   Headlam's article seems to suggest that young people are kept from
       protesting by their interest in more material things such as Cure T-shirts
       or a good table at McDonald's.

       Write an essay that explains *your* ideas on the reasons for young peo-
       ple's reactions to rules that are imposed upon them by various authorities.
       Audience: someone in the same age group who is interested in activat-
       ing student involvement with issues.

       Send a copy of your final essay to the students' council in your
       school, your provincial students' organization, or the youth wing of one
       of the major political parties in your province.

How Jane* Is Fighting the Unkindest Cut of All

by Naomi Klein

My friend Jane* is suing her hairstylist. That's right, she's suing him and his 1
fancy salon because she asked for a trim and got a cut, and requested a color
retouch and got dyed. It's called a bad haircut and it has happened to everyone.
But instead of whining like the rest of us, Jane sent a lawyer's letter.

A portion reads as follows: "My client left in complete despair and very 2
concerned about her professional meetings and media attendances . . . . She
was forced to engage the services of a different salon to do 'damage repair' at
a total cost of $200." You get the picture.

What is truly revolutionary about this Hollywood Wives-style suit is the 3
way it turns the relationship most of us have with our hairstylists on its head.
Most of us act like Victorian women locked in unhappy marriages, thoroughly
unable to change our sad circumstances ("I, I told him what I wanted, but he
never listens to me," sniff, sniff). In this context, my friend Jane isn't petty and
vain — she's a cosmetic suffragette.

For starters, like Victorian women who were the property of their hus- 4
bands, most of us believe our hairstylists are the true owners of our hair. That's
why we act like we're breaking into our own chastity belts when we cut our
bangs with a Swiss Army knife ("Oh, no! My hairdresser is going to kill me").
If the women (and men) I have talked to are any indication, changing hairdressers is more emotionally traumatic than quitting psychotherapy, changing
thesis advisers mid PhD and blowing off a family member — combined.

I'm perpetually amazed that the same women who chant, "My body, my 5
choice," at an abortion rights rally will readily hand over ownership of their
heads to some guy in leather pants on Yonge St.

But we do. And since we don't own our hair, going to another hairdresser 6
is the stylistic equivalent of adultery with a scarlet A.

There are two scenarios for the adulterous style: leaving your stylist for 7
another and cheating on your stylist in a one-cut stand.

The first is pretty straight forward: You tell a friend to tell the stylist you've 8
joined some bizarre anti-hair-cutting cult and move on. After that, it's just the
occasional guilt flash, which may, depending on how neurotic you are, cause

---

* Names have been changed for fear of retribution.

you to avoid certain areas of the city — like the downtown core. (Personally, I still feel guilty about abandoning my childhood hairdresser in Montreal.)

9   The only snag comes when, by some unfortunate coincidence, your hairstylist sees you at the supermarket with your new do — and you feel like you just got caught at a sleazy motel with the Fed-Ex guy.

10   However, if your cheat was just a fling (maybe you sought adventure, maybe you felt under-appreciated, either way, you regret it) things get more complicated. First of all, you need a good story when you come slinking back, the most popular excuse for hair cheating being travel abroad. Ideally, your experience should have been so traumatic that it elicits pity rather than jealousy. For example, you were in Scandinavia when you suddenly discovered that your hair was waist-length, so you stumbled into some back alley dog grooming parlor where you were not only butchered but given fleas. One friend who had a torrid but ultimately unfulfilling hair affair claimed that her best friend had just graduated from beauty school and she had been forced, out of loyalty, to let the neophyte beautician practise on her head.

11   We concoct these alibis not because we believe we have acted immorally, but because we fear retribution. We will say anything to avoid the wrath of our hairdressers because the dynamic is perhaps the most power-charged of our times. They, after all, are holding the scissors. Of course, there is the surgeon-patient dynamic but those are only your insides. (I feel I must, at this time, mention that my hairstylist is flawless. In fact, I got a completely unnecessary cut immediately before this article came out just to tell him so. But back to those other women.)

12   In the classical patterns of abuse, the fear of retribution often can lead you to stay with a hairstylist who makes you miserable, endlessly giving him one last chance. "Maybe he'll change," you tell yourself. "He was having a bad day. He was rushed."

13   Why don't we protest? It's a tough question. Partly, we cling to the idea that the stylist is the trained professional, that he must have a plan for why he just carved satanic messages in our scalp, that it surely will look good once dry. Also, there is something about having a black plastic cape drawn tightly around your neck and wet hair plastered to your face that is infantilizing to the point of complete paralysis.

14   That's why my friend Jane, after looking in the mirror at her shorn head and freakishly streaked locks, thanked her stylist in drone-like fashion (wouldn't want to be impolite) and, fighting back the tears, told him she really liked the back when he held up the mirror (wouldn't want to hurt his feelings).

15   Then, she not only forked over the 80 bucks — she tipped 15 per cent.

16   But not any more. She's asking for $1,500 in damages. Some is the cost of the cut, some is time and money spent fixing it. The rest is hair alimony.

Style and Structure

1. The title of Klein's essay contains a reference to Shakespeare's *Julius Caesar*. How does the title help to set the tone for the entire piece?

2. Klein uses a number of quotations, often from no one in particular, to illustrate her point. How does she alert the reader that she is mimicking women in general? How effectively do you think she uses the technique?

3. Much of the force of Klein's essay depends on the way she likens the relationship between a woman and her hairdresser to a sexual relationship. Point to the instances where she uses simile and metaphor to make her point.

4. In paragraph 2 , Klein quotes a letter from a lawyer, which charges that Jane was in "complete despair" about her appearance when she left the salon. Near the end of the essay, Klein reveals Jane thanked her stylist, tipped him handsomely, and left without a word of complaint. What is the reader to make of this apparent contradiction? Does the reader see Jane as a "cosmetic suffragette" as Klein suggests?

Warm-up

Students and novice writers frequently overlook the value of a good title. Whether rushed to finish the job or at a loss for a creative response to the material at hand, they attach a title page that does nothing to announce the tone, the importance, or the scope of their work but merely labels its content, sometimes quite inaccurately. They settle for "Economics in Canada" rather than "An Evaluative Study of the Canadian Labour Movement in the 1990s" or "How I Broke My Leg" instead of "What Kind of Bunny Tested That Slope, Anyway?"

Test your skill at suggesting evocative titles for each of the following topics, first taking them very seriously, then as a possibility for some humour. Consider your peers as an audience.

(i) the price differential between men's and women's clothing;

(ii) tips for saving on your income tax;

(iii) methods of finding a summer job to pay your tuition fees;

(iv) composting.

Thinking and Writing

1. Male-female relations offer a veritable gold-mine for essay topics, or are they a mine field? Given the emotions that relationships involve, writers

often find they're stepping on trip-wires that trigger all sorts of reactions. For instance, one of the most enduringly popular essays in this book, "Power and Control:Why Men Dominate Women," by Rick Goodwin, never fails to stir up heated debate in the classroom.

Write an essay in which you look at the lighter side of gender relationships, assuming as Klein does the role of one looking on from the outside rather than someone involved directly. What insight can you offer readers about our behaviours and attitudes, especially when we are involved in situations that reveal unequal power structures?

Audience: someone of your own gender, who needs gentle prodding toward self-knowledge.

2. American writer Studs Terkel wrote masterful essays illuminating the life of the average working person in the 1960s and 70s. Ask your barber or hairstylist, or some other tradesperson, if you can observe his or her work for a day. Pay particular attention to the tradesperson's own expression of the ups and downs of the job, the nature of the work, and sights and sounds of the workplace. You may find a small tape-recorder helpful in capturing just the right impression of the day's activities.

With your notes from the interview, write an essay to give readers a new appreciation for the tradesperson and the work he or she performs. You may wish to design your essay as a process analysis showing how the day unfolds from opening to closing time, or you may wish to take a less structured approach for a descriptive essay. In any case, send a copy to the interviewee, with a note of thanks and a request for comments.

Audience: the average public; that is, those who use the services of such a tradesperson but may not appreciate all that the job entails.

Teen Runaways: Should We Force Them Home?

by Brian Weagant

Although the majority of runaways return voluntarily within two days, a small percentage find the harshness of street life an acceptable alternative to home or Children's Aid care. Some have run from abusive or dysfunctional families, others from institutions or foster homes where their needs were not being met. Still others find running the easiest way to resolve authority struggles with parents or child-welfare organizations. All of these children see running as the answer to their troubles. And until we recognize this fact, I see little hope of bringing them back home. 1

The press has made much of the risks facing runners, some of whom turn to panhandling, prostitution, and drug peddling in order to survive. According to conventional wisdom, these problems are exacerbated by toothless child-welfare legislation that hampers the police and the social services. But stricter and more intrusive laws are in my view both ill-conceived and unconstitutional. 2

Returning the teenager to the abusive family or inadequate institution or foster home fixes absolutely nothing. Moreover, legalizing the "arrest" of adolescents who are not at risk and then allowing them to be detained against their will may have the unfortunate effect of breeding more crafty runners, who are less likely to surface for help because of the response they expect from the authorities. 3

We make it legally and practically impossible for these adolescents to survive on their own, and then we hypocritically voice shock when they resort to crime or prostitution. If adults suddenly find themselves on the street without a penny, it does not take them long to find some welfare assistance, a meal, and a bed. Further, going for help does not result in being apprehended as "in need of protection" and sent to a group home with other adults in a similar situation. Teenage runners do not have the same options. 4

If we are truly committed to better lives for these young people, we must develop a legal procedure that allows them to emancipate themselves from parental or child-welfare care. Several jurisdictions in the United States have such legislation in place. Minors wishing to live apart from their parents or legal guardians can make an application to a court. If they show both a workable plan for living and a legal means of obtaining support or income, the court can grant a declaration of emancipation allowing a youth to find employment and housing, enter into contracts, sue, obtain welfare, 5 and get medical treatment without someone else's consent. Surely, a similar mechanism could give many young Canadian runners a safe and legal alternative to crime and prostitution.

6   Our legislators must face the constitutional implications of allowing competent adolescents to be effectively arrested simply because they have flown the nest. Such strong intervention should be reserved for the apprehension of alleged criminals or incompetents. By subjecting adolescents to this type of legal intervention, we would be denying them their constitutional right of autonomy not because of their lack of capacity or maturity but solely because of their numerical age. This is dangerous.

7   Arbitrary exclusions from the civil rights guaranteed by the Canadian Charter of Rights and Freedoms can only be justified if there is no other way to meet society's need. Yet there are plenty of other ways to protect teenage runners — and legally sanctioned emancipation is only a first step. We can develop social-service programming that offers runners a functional alternative to street life. We can provide shelters that are safe but noncoercive. Until we introduce these measures, we have no business considering a new law that makes running equivalent to a criminal offence, and we have no justification for curtailing the civil rights of runners.

8   The ability to make life decisions depends on the capacity to understand the alternatives. Accordingly, our common law recognizes no magic age at which one becomes competent to determine one's livelihood. Some argue that we can justify denying competent adolescents the right to make decisions about their own liberty because of their tendency to make bad or stupid choices. If this is the test for infringing basic civil rights, then most of us are in trouble.

Style and Structure

1.   Write a one-paragraph description of the intended reader of this essay. Base your conclusions on specific evidence in the text.

2. (a) Write a one-sentence summary of this essay's **thesis**.

   (b) Identify the sentence that contains the **thesis statement**. Examine this sentence carefully. How does it also serve as a statement of the essay's organization? How does such a statement of organization help the reader?

3. (a) Given the intended reader, why might Weagant have chosen to open his essay with the contents of paragraph 1?

   (b) What advantages does Weagant gain by presenting the other side's arguments in the first two sentences of paragraph 2?

   (c) Identify two passages in paragraph 2 that contain words that will subtly influence readers to question the opponents' arguments. Briefly explain how each achieves its effect.

4. (a) Compare the use of **topic** and **concluding sentences** in paragraphs 3 and 4. Which paragraph is more effective in conveying its main point to the reader? Why?

   (b) Write a **topic sentence** and a **concluding sentence** for paragraph 3.

5. (a) How effective in influencing the reader's thinking is Weagant's strategy of placing the contents of paragraph 5 after paragraphs 3 and 4? Why?

   (b) What reasons might he have for choosing not to open the body of the essay with the contents of paragraph 5?

6. (a) What aspect of the topic does Weagant discuss in paragraphs 6 and 7?

   (b) What is the advantage of saving the contents of paragraph 7 for the end of this section *and* the end of the body?

7. (a) Some conclusions simply summarize the contents of the body. What does Weagant do in this **conclusion**?

   (b) Write a short **concluding paragraph** that does simply summarize the essay. Which approach is more effective, this new conclusion or Weagant's original? Why?

   (c) Explain the effect of using the word "us" in the essay's last sentence.

8. Select any paragraph in the body of this essay (except paragraph 3). Write a short summary of each sentence in the paragraph, then comment briefly on the logical development (**coherence**) of the paragraph.

9. Identify three passages in which Weagant's word choice influences the reader almost subconsciously to agree with his position (e.g., "we *hypocritically* voice shock. . . ." in paragraph 4). Explain how each works.

10. Brian Weagant was staff counsel for a children's legal-aid clinic when he wrote this article. How does this position allow him to break the rule of never using the first person ("I") in an essay?

Warm-up

Weagant points out that "all of these children see running as the answer to their troubles" (paragraph 1). Discuss with a group of three or four others in the class the alternatives that runaways might have explored as options to running. Write a paragraph that presents alternate solutions. **Audience**: a potential runner.

Test your first draft of the paragraph by asking two or three people from the class to review its ideas (and presentation of them) with you.

Thinking and Writing

1. In an essay written to counter Weagant's, Howard Crosby (Conservative member of parliament for Halifax) wrote the following:

    > All the activities of our legal system have a price and the change I advocate [a law enabling police to apprehend runaways] is no exception. Besides the financial cost of searching for runaways and returning them to parents, there would be more work for overloaded police officers and hassles for youths hanging out in parks and shopping malls. There would certainly be restrictions on young people's freedom. But that is a small price to pay for saving countless children from exploitation.
    >
    > Responsible Canadians should realize that children are not small adults. They do have rights, but those rights are not licences to destroy future opportunities. And like everyone else's rights, theirs ultimately depend on a strong family unit, which will always be the heart of Canadian society.

    Obviously, Crosby and Weagant represent completely different views on the abilities and rights of adolescents.

    Make two lists, one representing the view of adolescents conveyed in Crosby's comments and the other, the view presented in Weagant's essay. Write an essay in which you compare and contrast these two views of adolescents. Even though you may support one view more than the other, be objective in your presentation of both. As you write, do not refer to the individuals (Crosby and Weagant) but simply use their ideas as representative of two different perspectives that are common in our society.
    Audience: someone who holds one or the other point of view on adolescents and has never considered another way of thinking about them.

    Submit all drafts of your essay to your instructor for evaluation.

2. Write an essay that explains (1) the view of adolescents that predominates in our society and (2) the ways adolescents are treated in the community (and particularly in schools) because of this view. If you believe the treatment adolescents receive could be improved, point out ways the basic view of them would have to change to achieve this improvement.
    Audience: someone who might be in a position to influence the treatment adolescents receive.

    Submit all drafts of your essay to your instructor.

    Send a copy of your final draft to the public relations officer of an organization in your community that helps teenagers.

Turning Down the Danger
by Ellen Roseman

"Turn down the volume and turn down the danger." That's the theme of a campaign by the Canadian Hearing Society, warning that walkaround stereos can be harmful to your health. The nonprofit group, which has distributed thousands of fact-sheets to high-school students, hopes to make them aware that permanent hearing loss can result from prolonged exposure to any intense noise — whether pleasant or unpleasant. "A lot of people think sound has to be annoying to damage your hearing — something like a jackhammer in the street," says Tani Nixon, an audiologist and researcher with the Canadian Hearing Society. "That's not true. It just has to be loud." 1

The power of a sound wave is measured in units called decibels. Normal conversations are about 60 decibels. Very busy traffic has been clocked at 80 decibels. A garbage truck operates at 100 decibels, a power saw at 110 decibels. The sound level at rock concerts and discotheques can go as loud as 120 decibels. 2

Research from industry indicates that prolonged exposure to sound over 85 decibels can cause permanent hearing loss. As noise level increases, exposure time should decrease. The Ontario Ministry of Labour recommends that at 110 decibels, no more than 15 minutes of unprotected exposure be allowed. 3

The Canadian Hearing Society measured the sound level of portable cassette players, most of which have volume control settings from one (softest) to ten (loudest). At two, the output is 85 decibels. At five, it's 104 decibels. At ten, it's 120 decibels. (Tapes are recorded at different levels, of course, and the sound output depends on the tapes used. If the input is 20 decibels lower, the output will also be about 20 decibels lower.) 4

Based on its research, the Canadian Hearing Society warns that prolonged exposure to any levels above volume two can permanently impair hearing. And short-term exposure can also be dangerous — damage can occur if the portable cassette player is worn at volume six for only 30 minutes daily. This is the same as listening to volume two for 40 hours a week. 5

How do you know you have a noise-induced hearing loss? The first sign is that you can't hear high-pitched sounds, such as "th" and "sh." Since 60 percent of speech intelligibility comes from the high-pitched consonants, you'll find that speech is no longer clear. People with a noise-induced hearing loss often say, "I can hear you okay, but you're mumbling." 6

When I asked manufacturers to comment, Doug Willock of Sony of Canada Ltd. said he didn't think it was fair to single out walkaround sound systems. The 7 stereo in your living room can deliver more power when hooked up to headsets than a portable stereo.

8   This point may be true, but portable stereos tend to be used in much nois-ier environments. If you're listening to your headset on the subway or in traf-fic, you have to turn up the sound to hear your music. This loudness tends to be greater than 85 decibels, the Canadian Hearing Society points out.

9   Music-induced hearing loss is starting to show up in young people. Dr. A.S. MacPherson, Toronto's medical officer of health, said there has been at least one case where an eighteen-year-old claims to have lost 95 percent of his hearing through the use of a walkaround stereo.

10   A Queen's University study of 60 students in Kingston, Ontario, ranging in age from 16 to 25, found a significant proportion with noise-induced hear-ing loss — 35 percent in the left ear, 28 percent in the right ear, and 12 percent in both ears. "You don't expect young people to have this kind of hearing impairment when they're not exposed to occupational noise," points out Janet Hatcher Roberts, the community health professor who did the study along with Dr. Ronald Lees and audiologist Zofia Wald.

11   When interviews with the students showed they liked to hunt, play in rock bands, listen to stereo music at high volumes, and go to noisy parties, the researchers concluded that leisure-time noise exposure was definitely associ-ated with the hearing loss.

Style and Structure

1. (a) Identify the sentence(s) in the introduction (paragraph 1) that best cap-ture(s) the central **thesis** of the essay.

   (b) Assume that the intended reader of this essay is someone who uses a walkaround sound system or who is close to someone who does. What would be the likely impact of the first two sentences of paragraph 1 on such a reader?

   (c) The author refers to the Canadian Hearing Society early in the first para-graph. What other authorities on hearing are cited in the essay? Given the intended reader, why does Roseman cite these authorities?

2. What information does the author present in paragraph 2? Given the intended reader and topic under discussion, why does she present this information at the beginning of the body of the essay?

3. (a) Using one sentence for each, summarize the information contained in paragraphs 3, 4, and 5.

   (b) How does the order in which Roseman presents the steps of her argument in paragraphs 2 to 4 lead the reader logically to the conclusion presented in paragraph 5?

4. What aspect of the thesis does the author develop in paragraph 6? Why is this a logical aspect of the thesis to discuss at this point?

5. Comment on how, in paragraphs 7 and 8, Roseman anticipates a likely objection from those who favour portable sound systems, and how she counters it in advance.

6. How does the evidence on hearing loss presented in paragraphs 9 to 11 differ from that presented earlier in the essay? Why would the author save this evidence for the closing of her essay?

7. For various reasons, Roseman has concluded her essay with a statement on the relationship of "leisure-time noise exposure" in general to hearing loss. Write a conclusion that specifically draws the reader's attention back to the danger of hearing loss due to walkaround stereos. Compare the two conclusions. Which do you think is more effective? Why?

Warm-up

1. Keep a journal of the types of noise and their levels that you encounter during the next 24 hours. Record all types, not just music. Based on the data you collect and the information provided by Roseman in her article, write a brief explanation of the danger you personally may be in.
   Audience: someone who can effect some change in your environment.

   Compare your report to those written by two or three others. Have they forgotten any that you included? Did they include some that you didn't even think of? Be sure to revise your work.

2. Who should be responsible for controlling the noise levels of radios, stereos, and so on? Should it be the government? What about the responsibility of the manufacturer who is producing a potentially dangerous product? Or should the responsibility be left to the individuals who use the products (it's their hearing, after all)?

   Decide which alternative you prefer. Then join up with the others in the class who think the same way. Working together, generate as many points as you can to support your stand.

   Working individually, use this list of points to write a paragraph that explains your personal point of view. Select what you consider to be the best arguments from the list.

   When you have finished the first draft, exchange papers with two or three others from the groups that proposed *different* solutions. Point out any weaknesses in their arguments and in their presentations, and have them do the same for yours.

Revise your paragraph into its final form, taking into account the others' comments.

Thinking and Writing

1. One implication of this essay is a criticism of the way in which people listen to rock music. Write an essay in which you explain why rock fans like their music to be loud. (Consider the psychological reasons as well as such things as quality of sound reproduction.)
    Audience: someone, such as a parent, who has read the article "Turning Down the Danger" and has difficulty understanding rock fans' listening habits.

2. Write an essay in which you explain why an educational campaign that distributes fact sheets and articles such as "Turning Down the Danger" either will or will not be successful in changing the listening habits of people exposed to high levels of "leisure-time noise" (like rock). If you do not think that such a campaign will be successful, suggest alternate approaches that might be taken.
    Audience: the person in charge of the educational campaign of the Canadian Hearing Society.

    Send a copy of your final draft to the nearest branch of the Canadian Hearing Society.

Peace at Any Price on Vancouver's Georgia Viaduct

by Ted Byfield

What is called the Georgia Viaduct in Vancouver is in fact a roadway access-   1
ing the downtown area. It is well illuminated, has a sidewalk, and is travelled
by several thousand automobiles most hours of the day. It was on this thor-
oughfare one early evening last month that a young woman was brutally
assaulted by two men, escaping with her life when she was able to leap over
the pedestrian rail into the path of the oncoming traffic and a motorist finally
stopped and picked her up. The police estimate that several hundred cars
passed her by as the attack took place. So did several pedestrians. The case has
been widely deplored in the Vancouver media. What's wrong with people, they
want to know. It's a good question. It should be asked, not just by police, but
by those in a position to shape our culture: television producers, novelists, journalists, literature professors, and, above all, the people who plan the social
studies curricula in the school system. Why is it, they should discover, that
these people did not stop — "these people" being you and I?

The sociologists no doubt will have an explanation. They will say that in   2
a small community, where everyone knows everyone else, and where antiso-
cial behaviour brings on social ostracism — meaning that if you beat up people on the street, no one will speak to you — law enforcement is largely handled by the citizenry. (A friend recalls a case of rape in a small Saskatchewan
town. The nearest police were miles away. "So the men," he said, "took that
guy out behind the barn and fixed him." There were no more rapes in that
town.) But as small communities become big cities, relationships become distant. You encounter many people you'll never see again. You don't need to
worry about being "shunned." Community self-policing becomes impossible
and we increasingly entrust it to uniformed officers. The crime you might see
on the street, therefore, is somebody else's problem.

Except that it isn't. The brute fact is that the police cannot function if   3
all of us, as it were, "drive past." They depend upon a high degree of public co-operation. When they don't get it, crime starts to pay, then becomes
rampant, and eventually renders large urban areas ungovernable. Already
certain sections of most western Canadian cities are unsafe after dark, particularly for women. In other words, this phenomenon of ungovernability
is already upon us.

4   Moreover, even as an explanation for our insensibility, this sociological account ignores a telling fact. Big impersonal cities existed and survived long before anything that resembled the modern police force had come about. Eighteenth-century London, for instance, was hardly a social paradise. Life was squalid, brutal, and dangerous, and the frequent hangings at Tyburn provided popular entertainment. You could buy good seats to see them. Policing was left almost entirely to the citizenry, and an assault or theft in the public market would set the whole crowd chasing the miscreant. Hence, I suppose, the phrase, "Stop thief!" If the poor wretch survived the beating and booting that followed, he lived only long enough to appear on the program at Tyburn. We today would dismiss such barbarity as all part of a brutish and uncivilized past. Yet in two ways those crude people demonstrated themselves more civilized than we are. That is, they understood two things that we do not seem to understand.

5   First, they knew that an attack on Joe Smith's fishmongering stand was an attack on the whole market, indeed on the whole city. If the assailant beats and robs Joe today, he will do it to one of the rest of us tomorrow. Stopping him and punishing him, therefore, is everybody's business. Joe isn't the only injured party. When a crime is committed, we are all injured. People knew that in London's Billingsgate market in the eighteenth century. They did not know it on Vancouver's Georgia Viaduct in the twentieth. This does not evidence social progress, but social decline.

6   Second, and more important, they knew that preserving the security of the city meant the distinct risk of violence and injury. The market thief was probably armed with a cudgel or a knife and, since his life was now in imminent danger, he would doubtless try to use it. Stopping him was therefore dangerous. But was that not always the way? To preserve peace you must be prepared to use violence. The eighteenth century knew this and taught it. The twentieth in theory knows it, but teaches something else.

7   Violence, we assure our children, is always wrong. We must cherish peace: we must eschew violence. Such is the message of our schools, and Remembrance Day exercises descend into an orgiastic deploring of the "waste and insanity of war." The fact is ignored that once the criminal is at large, whether on the international scene or on the Georgia Viaduct, then violence alone can stop him. We are not taught this, and therefore when we come face to face with the fact of it — as several hundred of us did last month on the Georgia Viaduct — we do not know what to do. Coming to the aid of that woman meant, purely and simply, involving ourselves in the immediate possibility of injury, even of death. So we drove on. We avoided violence, as our teachers had so fervently urged us. By doing so, we have lost one thing for a certainty. That is the Georgia Viaduct. It is no longer safe for the citizen to walk there, and heaven help him if his car should

break down on it, for he then stands the chance of joining company with that young woman. Thus, block by block and neighbourhood by neighbourhood, we cede our cities to the enemy. The eighteenth century didn't do this. We do. So has our sense of civic responsibility advanced from the eighteenth century? The answer isn't quite as self-evident as it once seemed.

Again, are we not ill-served in this matter by the luminaries of our media, the editorial writers, the columnists, the talk-show hosts, all those founts of civic wisdom who have been so busy deploring the timidity and apathy that left that young woman to her fate? Surely, if they are really going to confront this issue, instead of merely dabbling with it, then they must ask themselves whether the doctrines we espouse in the school system are correct. Curiously, those who most loudly deplore the viaduct incident are one and the same with those who endorse the "peace" program in the schools. They first urge pacifism upon us, and then deplore us when we behave pacifically. You get the impression they really haven't thought it through. Well it's time they did. The cure will not be quick, and the disease is far advanced.

Style and Structure

1. (a) The writer refers to "you and I" and "we" frequently throughout his essay. Suggest who "you and I" might include — that is, who his intended audience might be. Give reasons for your response.

   (b) What is the effect of using "you and I"? What other possibilities might the writer have chosen? Are these possibilities as effective for his purpose?

2. By the end of paragraph 1, do you have a clear idea of what this essay is about? Can you point to any one sentence that acts as a **thesis statement**? Explain.

3. (a) The **topic sentence** of paragraph 2 tells us, "The sociologists no doubt will have an explanation." What effect would have been lost if Byfield had used the word "reason" instead?

   (b) Point to other statements following the one above that indicate that Byfield intentionally used the word "explanation" rather than "reason."

4. In the middle of paragraph 2, the writer includes a portion in parentheses. Give two reasons why you believe he has chosen to use parentheses. Presented this way, what effect does this portion have upon the reader? Why?

5. In a well-developed paragraph, explain what the purpose of a **topic sentence** is and give examples from Ted Byfield's essay. Do you believe that the **topic sentences** in this essay do their job? Explain.

6. In paragraphs 6 and 7 of this essay, the writer addresses the question of fighting violence with violence. He makes the point that "once the criminal is at large, whether on the international scene or on the Georgia Viaduct, then violence alone can stop him." Was violence used to stop the crime committed on the Georgia Viaduct? What conclusions can you draw about (a) the suitability of the example of the incident cited and (b) the internal cohesiveness of the essay?

7. Is the writer of this essay offering any solutions to the problem of urban crime? How do you know?

8. Identify the question asked in paragraph 8. What might you say about the tone of this question? How does this question set the tone of the entire paragraph?

9. Are there any words in this essay that you did not immediately understand? What might these words tell you about the intended audience? Make a list of difficult words and, using a dictionary or thesaurus, suggest alternatives that the writer might have chosen.

10. Does the title of this essay accurately reflect the main ideas of the essay? Can you suggest alternative titles?

Warm-up

Invite a representative of your local police force to speak about crime prevention to your class. Prepare in advance a list of questions that will help you understand the situation in your own community, as well as help you prepare for an essay on the subject. Be sure that the invited speaker knows your intended questions so that he or she may prepare. Explain also that the class will be taking notes during the presentation.

After the presentation, have a class member review for the speaker one set of notes taken to make sure they accurately reflect the speaker's ideas and to give an opportunity for clarification. Another class member should prepare a short speech to thank the presenter.

After the speaker leaves, hold a class discussion about what you have learned.

Thinking and Writing

1. Byfield makes the point that "the police cannot function if all of us, as it were, 'drive past'" (paragraph 3). But is that, in effect, what people gen-

erally do? Many citizens have established such programs as Neighbour-hood Watch, Crime Stoppers, and Block Parents. In fact, the city of Van-couver itself instituted Crime Stoppers and reported that the number of solved cases doubled within a year, thanks to citizens' tips.* How is it that such programs are reporting overwhelming success at the same time that the media are reporting unprecedented violence and apathy in our cities?

In a well-developed essay, discuss the effectiveness of neighbour-hood programs for peace and protection. Examine a program that exists in your area, taking into account such factors as communication, co-operation, shared responsibility among neighbours, and their relation-ship with local police forces.

Variation: If no such programs exist in your area, write an essay in which you argue why one should be set up.

Audience: concerned citizens who live in your community.

Send a copy of your final draft to the local police department for comment.

2. Two essays in this book deal with social attitudes to violence: "Deliber-ate Strangers" (p. 104) and "Peace at Any Price on the Georgia Viaduct." However, the two writers differ in many ways in what they see as con-tributing factors and possible solutions to the problem.

In a compare/contrast essay, examine these two essays. (For the compare/contrast organizational approach, see p. 212.) Look at both the similarities and the differences in the writers' attitudes to violence. Be sure to include a clearly recognizable **thesis statement** in your introduc-tion, showing your reader not just that you are comparing these two essays but why you are doing so.

Audience: your classmates, who have also read the two essays.

---

* Tim Gallagher, "Has Vancouver No Good Samaritans?" *Alberta Report*, December 12, 1988.

Fashionable Ideas

by Barry Estabrook

1   An Inuit hunter insisted I write this column. I never learned his name, and little distinguished him from the other young men: he was in his early twenties, was sprouting a thin, black moustache, and wore a cap advertising a snowmobile company. But knowing his name, given the circumstances, didn't seem important.

2   A feast had just started in the village of Pangnirtung, tucked halfway up the eastern coast of Baffin Island. The excuse for the gathering was, officially, the opening of the Angmarlik Centre, a building that was to house a multiplicity of functions that, in the Inuit world view, belonged under the same roof: outfitters' office, community centre, drop-in centre, teen hangout, museum, library, art gallery, tourist information booth, and senior citizens club. To mark the occasion, five ringed seals had been killed, and a woman had just removed their meat from a cauldron bubbling over a bonfire when the Inuk accosted me.

3   "Never had seal before?" he asked, seeing my uncertain look as I gazed at the fatty, steaming gobs. "Here." With two fingers, he scooped up a piece that revealed too much of its original anatomical function for sensibilities shaped by buying cellophane-packaged meat at the local Loblaws.

4   I didn't want to lose face. So I swallowed quickly and was assaulted by a taste that combined the tang of mutton and the pungency of fish that has sat too long in the refrigerator.

5   "You a journalist?" the hunter went on, emboldened by my little act of complicity.

6   "Yes."

7   "Then tell your readers Inuit need to hunt seal."

8   Looking through Fred Bruemmer and Brian Davies' book *Seasons of the Seal*, I was reminded of my conversation with the young hunter. As an editor of a magazine that, in its pages, has tramped the length and breadth of Canada's Arctic, I admit with some embarrassment that last summer's government-sponsored junket was my first visit to that captivating land. But even under those less than favourable circumstances, the Arctic worked the magic so many visitors describe. The landscape, with surging rivers, tide-swept fiords and soaring snowcapped mountains, produced waves of awe I felt in my gut. It made me as proud to be Canadian as anything I have encountered.

9   It also gave me respect for the people who for the past 1000 years have made a living there. With respect came genuine liking. It's enough that a culture can survive in frozen desert, but Inuit do so with humour and generosity.

152

I am reminded of the two nine-year-olds who, in the twilight of 11:45 P.M.,   10
followed me down to the rock-strewn edge of the tidal flats. They had a few
laughs trying to trap me in a game of twenty questions, then, tagging along as
I made my way back to the town, insisted that they give me a lesson on how
to hand-capture the little minnows trapped in puddles.

And there was the last piece of luggage checked onto our outbound com-   11
mercial flight. Without my knowledge, the Inuk who had taken me fishing had
frozen the single char I had managed to catch, mummified it in green garbage
bags wrapped with duct tape, and then rushed it out onto the tarmac minutes
before the flight attendant closed the airplane door.

Against a dozen such memories, the young hunter's request stands out as   12
the one time an Inuk was brusque with me. But with the brusqueness came a
clear note of desperation. His demand, simple as it was, echoed the burden of
a century of mistreatment at the hands of Europeans. From about the time the
Normans crossed the English Channel until the mid-1800s, the young Inuk's
ancestors had survived by hunting in the waters of Cumberland Sound. That
changed in 1857, when British whaler William Penny established a permanent
station at Kekerten, near present-day Pangnirtung. Lured by an annual salary
of one gun, one harmonica, and a steady supply of tobacco, many Inuit
dropped their traditional way of life and moved to the settlement. For 50 years,
things went well, even as the whale populations were hunted to the brink of
extinction. Fashion — European fashion — demanded that women slim their
waists with whalebone corsets. The desire to look right pushed the price of
whalebone to $5.25 per pound ($11.50/kg) in the 1890s. By 1912, the fad had
passed. Whalebone fetched a meagre eight cents per pound (17¢/kg). The
Europeans went home, leaving behind decimated whale and seal populations,
disease, lots of mixed-blood children, and a population no longer able to survive by hunting.

The next seven decades are the story of a long struggle back for the peo-   13
ple of Pangnirtung. But by the early 1980s, the town was being described as a
"model" Arctic community. Its economy was anchored on government jobs,
printmaking, commercial fishing, and the beginnings of a tourist industry. A
referendum banned booze from town, so Pangnirtung faced fewer of those
problems than many Arctic communities. Most Inuit still went onto the land to
provide food for their families, keeping the social fabric together. And the sale
of sealskin enabled the people to fund hunting trips — no small consideration
in a land where hamburger is $8 per pound ($17.75/kg) and a wilted cabbage
is worth $6.

In 1983, leaders of the European Economic Community banned the import   14
of pelts from harp seal pups. No matter that the hunters of Pangnirtung shot

mature seals, the market for all sealskin collapsed. A hunter could get $40 for a good pelt in 1982. Today, he would be lucky to get $5, if he could find a buyer. The Pangnirtung Hudson's Bay Company outlet used to be one of the biggest sealskin dealers in the Arctic, employing one full-time fur grader and sending out planeloads of pelts. Today, the company is not buying. The grader is gone. The fur room is used to store excess stock. People can no longer afford to go out on the land, and the pelts of seals shot for food are thrown away, allowed to rot on the beach.

15   Northerners are convinced those are but the first ramifications of a campaign that will eventually destroy their way of life. Recent studies of native Greenlanders support this view. Examining suicide and accidental-death statistics that exceed those of virtually all the world's cultures, Greenland experts concluded that a genocide was under way, the inevitable result of a more powerful culture imposing its values on a weaker one. Canadian sociologists say the studies apply equally to our Arctic.

16   Conflicting cultural values are, of course, at the crux of the native-rights-versus-animal-rights debate. There is certainly no ecological explanation for why someone living in Liverpool or Lyons should object to a Pangnirtung hunter shooting a seal. At last count, more than five million ringed seals swam in the waters of the Canadian Arctic, making them the area's most abundant marine mammal. Some resource experts are even beginning to worry whether increasing seal populations will begin to cut into another important source of Inuit livelihood — char populations.

17   I recently put the question directly to a French friend of mine. Why does the average European support the seal ban? She shrugged and replied: "Fashion." It was an ironic use of the word. For it seems that once again, fashion is the villain, this time in the guise of fashionable ideas, but ideas no more applicable to life in the high Arctic than were whalebone corsets.

18   On the last full day of my visit to Pangnirtung, I was part of what has to be one of the strangest flotillas the eastern Arctic has seen. Two hundred people climbed into twenty-odd boats, ranging from open freighter canoes to Cape Islanders to heavy scallop draggers. We set sail in a blinding July snowstorm. The dozen Inuit aboard my boat included a two-year-old boy, who slept the entire voyage up under the foredeck on a pile of life jackets, and a 103-year-old woman, who joined us midvoyage, passed hand over hand from a bobbing adjacent boat so that she could talk with a friend. Our destination, some three hours away over the ice-studded waters of Cumberland Sound, was the ruins of Kekerten, Penny's whaling station. Our purpose was to consecrate them as a historic site.

19   It seemed like an odd thing to me: consecrating the site that in many ways marked the beginning of the end of a way of life for Pangnirtung Inuit. But

Inuit take some pride in their accomplishments as whalers. The elders remember Kekerten as their birthplace.

As I looked about, I realized I was ashamed. Aside from some ruins and rust- 20
ing machinery, the main historic artifacts at Kekerten are bones, the bones of the great whales and, strewn across the barren hillsides, the bones of Inuit employees of the whalers, shoved into broken barrels and rifle crates. (The remains of the white men rest in a nearby cemetery.) The symbolism was not lost. One of the world's great creatures, and one of its most resilient cultures, both nearly driven to oblivion because of a whim of Victorian European fashion.

On the way back from Kekerten, a pair of ringed seals made the mistake 21
of sticking their heads above the water near one of the boats. They were killed with two shots from a .222. I won't pretend there was anything romantic about the killings or what followed. The boat immediately pulled up to the edge of an ice floe to allow its passengers to disembark. In an instant, the seals were split up the bellies and Inuit began to eat, offal and all, sans benefit of the boiling pot. Ten minutes later, the snack was finished. The people continued home, leaving two bloodstains on the white ice and two discarded sealskins.

The skins are what stuck in my mind. It seemed like such a senseless 22
waste.

Style and Structure

1. (a) "An Inuit hunter insisted I write this column." What effect does this opener have on you, the reader?

   (b) Make a list of ten words that the writer might have chosen instead of the verb "insisted." Why do you suppose he chose as he did? What impact does the word "insisted" have that those on your list do not?

2. (a) In paragraph 3, the writer describes seal meat as it is offered to him by the Inuit hunter: "he scooped up a piece that revealed too much of its original anatomical function for sensibilities shaped by buying cellophane-packaged meat at the local Loblaws." What does the writer mean?

   (b) How would you describe the tone here? What does this tone reflect about the writer himself? Why do you think he chose such a tone?

3. (a) Estabrook gives his **thesis statement** in paragraph 7: "Then tell your readers Inuit need to hunt seal." What are the effects of having someone other than the writer give the **thesis**? Mention at least three effects. (Hint: Consider the answer you have given in 2(b).)

   (b) Do you believe that the delayed **thesis statement** in this case is a successful strategy? Why?

4.   In paragraphs 8 to 11, the writer speaks of the beauty of Canada's Arctic and the kindness of the people who live there. What relationship do these paragraphs have to the **thesis**? Why do you think the writer includes them?

5.   In paragraph 12, Estabrook begins to trace the history of Inuit fortunes. Why do you suppose he chose not to begin his essay with this piece of historical background?

6.   Count the number of words in each sentence in paragraph 14. What would you say about the writer's ability to vary sentence lengths? Looking over the paragraph once more, would you say that he has also used a variety of structures?

7. (a) Paragraph 17 is pivotal in this essay. Read it once again, and describe your immediate reactions to the French friend referred to there.

   (b) Compare your reaction to this woman with your reaction to the Inuit hunter introduced earlier in the essay. With whom do you more readily sympathize? How do you think the writer has prompted your reactions?

8.   This essay uses a number of **organizational approaches** in order to achieve its particular effect. Identify areas that are primarily

   (i) description;

   (ii) comparison;

   (iii) cause and effect;

   (iv) narrative.

      Which **organizational approach** do you believe best typifies the entire essay? Give reasons for your answer.

9. (a) The last part of the essay, paragraphs 18 to 22, tells of the writer's last day in Pangnirtung. Summarize what points the writer is trying to make in this section.

   (b) As a **conclusion**, this is a fairly lengthy one. Taking into account the points you made in (a), do you believe that the strategy is effective?

Warm-up

This essay makes excellent (although brief) use of direct quotations to bring home to the reader central ideas. Experiment with the use of direct quotations by imagining an old-timer who could report the information given in paragraph 13, the last seven decades of Pangnirtung's development. Rewrite the information, putting it into the words of the imagined character instead of the narrator.

Read your composition to the class or members of a study group. Compare the effect of reported conversation with that of the narration used in this essay.

Thinking and Writing

1. In paragraph 16 of his essay, Estabrook writes, "There is certainly no ecological explanation for why someone living in Liverpool or Lyons should object to a Pangnirtung hunter shooting a seal." And yet the Europeans do object, and the effects of their objections have drastically altered the way of life in Canada's Arctic.

    It is said that we live in a global village, that with communications networks and modern technology, no part of the world is remote from any other part. What happens in Alice Springs, Australia, may have an effect on Montrealers, for instance. We are, in short, "in this together."

    Take one issue of ecological importance, such as the burning of rain forests in South America, the hunting of elephants in Africa, the water shortage in the southern United States. Why should the issue you have chosen have any significance to the average Canadian citizen? For your essay, follow Estabrook's model, showing a concerned participant speaking out.

    In order to research your topic, you might wish to consult with a magazine that has an ecological or conservation-minded approach, such as the one from which this essay was taken (*Equinox*).

2. Make a list of the useful facts found in this essay. Once your list is completed, go back and rank the facts in order of least to greatest importance. From your list, develop the outline for an essay in which you argue for more understanding of the Inuit's hunting of seals and the effective promotion of the sealskin trade. Take as your **thesis statement** the words of the Inuit hunter who addressed Estabrook: "[The] Inuit need to hunt seal."

    After your first draft, check your paragraphs to see that you have provided colourful examples and variety in sentence length and structure. Be sure to use proper documentation, giving credit to the author of this essay.

    Audience: someone who is in a position to influence policy in native affairs.

    Send a copy of your essay to the Department of Native Affairs and ask for comment.

Policewomen on Patrol

by Cynthia Brouse

1   On a Saturday night in October 1985, two constables in a patrol car cruised through the quiet Montreal suburb of Dorval, on the lookout for a man who had been seen loitering in backyards. Suddenly the patrol car's driver saw a man rise up out of a clump of shrubbery and aim a rifle at them. Before the officers could take cover, a bullet shattered the rear window of the car, and the constable in the driver's seat died instantly, shot in the neck.

2   She was Jacinthe Fyfe, 25, and the first Canadian policewoman to die in the line of duty. Her death is dramatic evidence of women's new share in the fight against crime.

3   Traditionally, policewomen have worked behind the scenes, rarely being assigned to situations that might involve them in violence. Now, women are valuable additions to *all* phases of law enforcement, and especially to what many officials call "the hub of police activities" — patrol duty.

4   Until the early 1970s, only a few Canadian policewomen were entrusted with patrol duties. Today, all 2200 perform the same work as their male counterparts: they routinely patrol beats, operate in vice squads, handle undercover work, and serve in traffic control. In 1986, Const. Rose Budimir of the Downsview detachment of the Ontario Provincial Police became its first female motorcycle officer. Constable Cheryl Schneider pilots a Twin Otter airplane to cover her beat among the remote Indian reserves of the Hudson Bay and James Bay coasts. Constable Kathy McLaren patrols Vancouver's Stanley Park on horseback. In British Columbia, 377 out of 5780 police are women, the highest percentage in the nation.

5   True, the shift in policewomen's status has not come without controversy. Many male officers have stubbornly resisted the assignment of women to "field" duties on the grounds that they are "emotional" and physically unfit for the rigours of patrol. But the resistance is steadily ebbing in the face of day-to-day evidence.

6   Constables Kimberley Greenwood and Theresa Rynn, for instance, were staked out at a bank that had been robbed twice by a man wearing a ski mask. Greenwood, posing as a teller, and Rynn, who waited outside in an unmarked car, kept in constant radio contact. When Greenwood saw the robber enter the bank and vault over the tellers' counter, she alerted her partner. Rynn rushed into the bank with her gun drawn to find that Greenwood had already grabbed the robber. In seconds the two women had him handcuffed and were soon hauling him outside to a waiting police cruiser.

When Geramy Field was with the Vancouver Police Department's canine   7
unit, she followed her dog across a busy intersection in pursuit of a six-foot-
five-inch, 210-pound (195-cm, 95-kg) car thief. Turning into an alley, she saw
the suspect kicking the dog. Detective Field grabbed the man's arms, pinned
him against a wall and handcuffed him.

Policewomen were working in Canada as early as 1911, when Edmonton   8
became the first city in the country to hire "lady officers." Vancouver, Toronto,
and Winnipeg followed soon after; however, in these cities women were, for
the most part, limited to answering phones, searching, escorting, and guarding
female prisoners, and once in a while posing as prostitutes in undercover operations. Policewomen in Canada were not routinely given firearms until the
early 1970s. In 1974, the first troop of women began training at the RCMP
"Depot" Division in Regina.

Until about ten years ago, many female candidates for police forces were   9
eliminated by minimum-size requirements. Female recruits in Ottawa, for
example, had to be five feet ten inches (178 cm) tall. In 1977, the RCMP
adopted an evaluation system for recruits that placed less emphasis on stature
and more emphasis on education, experience, age, and physical fitness. Now
most police forces use similar systems, and many, such as Ottawa, Saskatoon,
and St. John's, Newfoundland, have abolished height restrictions altogether,
requiring instead that candidates meet height-to-weight ratios.

Little by little, male resistance toward female officers is moderating. The   10
men in the force realize that in many cases, particularly those involving young
children, getting information from victims of sexual attacks, and defusing family free-for-alls, policewomen can be a definite asset. "Policewomen often
have a greater ability to deal with areas of extreme sensitivity," says Phil
Crosby-Jones, director of the British Columbia Police Academy.

Officers in the field point to women's preference for verbal mediation over   11
physical aggression. Norman Wickdahl, president of the Winnipeg Police Association, says, "The women I've worked with were able to talk their way around situations that may have resulted in an altercation if my partner had been a man."

Female officers command as much respect from the public as their male   12
colleagues, but some experts feel citizens stay calmer with women. Deputy
Chief Keith Cole of the Dartmouth, Nova Scotia, police department explains:
"Most men will not hit a woman. In something like a barroom brawl, a woman
may be able to get things under control more quickly than a male officer can.
Sometimes a male officer walks in like he's the macho guy. But if a woman
officer walks in, the party seems to cool down."

Everywhere, law-enforcement officials are closely scrutinizing traditional   13
"tough" attitudes to policing. They are finding that skill in personal relations

may be just as important as physical strength in equipping an officer to cope with potentially dangerous situations. Inspector Walt Bennett of the Royal Newfoundland Constabulary — the only force in North America whose police officers don't carry guns — points out that all good officers, male and female, use force only as a last resort. "Police officers need good communication skills — they have to rely on their wits."

14　　　Most professional law officers applaud the work of policewomen. A study by University of Manitoba criminologist Rick Linden showed that female police officers did their jobs as well as male officers — and that their supervisors rated them highly. Says Keith Cole, "They perform excellently. We're no longer hiring policemen and policewomen — but police officers."

Style and Structure

1. (a) What is the relationship of the first two paragraphs to the central **thesis** of this essay?

   (b) What is the effect of concealing the driver's identity until the second paragraph?

   (c) For what type of reader would this opening be effective? Why?

   (d) Identify this essay's **thesis statement**. Does it summarize all of the points made by the **topic sentences** of the body's individual paragraphs?

2. (a) Identify the two paragraphs in this essay that do not have a **concluding sentence**.

   (b) Write an appropriate **concluding sentence** for each.

   (c) How would the sentences you have written help the reader?

3. Brouse makes extensive use of examples in the body of this essay.

   (a) Identify three different points that she supports by use of examples.

   (b) For each point identified, explain how she prepares the reader to understand the significance of the examples used to support it.

   (c) Comment on the appropriateness of the examples offered in each case. How does each help the reader to understand the point Brouse is trying to convey?

4. In the last half of the body of her essay, the writer depends heavily on the testimony of experts.

   (a) Identify three paragraphs in which such quotations are used.

   (b) Identify the **topic sentence** in each of these paragraphs.

   (c) Comment on the way each quotation contributes to the point being made in its paragraph. Is each appropriate?

(d) Was it a good idea for Brouse to include the credentials of each person quoted? What effect does this strategy achieve?

5. (a) How do the statements made in the final paragraph help the reader grasp the significance of the points made in the body? Do they form an effective **conclusion** for the essay? Why?

(b) How do the statements made here compare to the **thesis statement** in the introduction?

6. Identify three **topic sentences** in which Brouse uses words or phrases to make **transitions** from the ideas of the preceding paragraph. In each case, explain how the **transition** helps the reader.

7. Identify two places in the essay where Brouse uses dashes to set off groups of words. Explain the effect of each. If this is an effective technique, why would she not use even more dashes?

Warm-up

1. Write a list of the assets that officials say policewomen bring to the job (paragraphs 10 to 13). Make another list of the characteristics attributed to policemen in the same paragraphs. Compare these lists to those written by two or three others in the class: try to account for any differences in your respective lists.

Write a three- or four-paragraph essay in which you explain whether these characteristics are typical of the behaviours taught to all men and women in our culture.

Audience: someone who has never thought very seriously about these differences in behaviour.

2. Discuss with several of your classmates the positive behaviours and attitudes that each sex could learn from the other in our culture. Write a short essay on the topic.

Audience: an adult who has been exposed to our culture's typical sex-role training.

Thinking and Writing

1. Identify another occupation that has traditionally been associated with one sex (e.g., nurse, electronics technician, day-care worker, construction worker). Write an essay that explains

(i) the reasons one sex has dominated this occupation;

(ii) the benefits the other sex could bring to it;

(iii) suggestions for the process by which the other sex could be encouraged to enter this occupation.

Audience: someone who knows of the occupation but may never have questioned its being dominated by one sex.

2.   Make two lists of jobs, one under the heading "Predominantly Male" and the other under the heading "Predominantly Female." Examine each list to identify patterns or types of occupations that attract primarily one sex.

Write an essay that explains why the various types of occupations have traditionally been associated with one sex and not the other. Be sure to discuss the role of stereotyping, cultural training, and biological differences, in addition to any other factors you can identify.

Audience: someone who has never considered this situation.

Send a copy of your final draft to either your school newspaper (if there is one) or a newspaper in your community. Ask the editor whether the paper would be interested in publishing it.

So You Want to Move to the U.S. Eh?

by Camilla Cornell

Admit it. The thought of moving to the U.S. has crossed your mind. In fact, if   1
you're paying top dollar on your ever diminishing earnings, you're probably
thinking about it right now. And you're not alone. Thousands of Canadian professionals are packing up their degrees and diplomas and moving south. It's
called "brain drain" and it was once something that happened in Third World
countries. Having received an education, professionals would desert their
homeland for the monetary rewards of working in a G-7 nation.

But Canada *is* a G-7 country. One of the best places to live in the world   2
according to the people at the UN and they should know. But look at the statistics. From 1984 to 1989, the number of Canadian emigrants to the U.S. rose
from 10,791 to 12,151 — a mere trickle. But in 1990, the trickle showed signs
of becoming a flood when 16,812 left the true north strong and free for the stars
and stripes of the States. In 1993, the exodus reached a high of 17,156 hitting
us where it hurts, the private sector. It seems managers and executives were the
largest category to go. On the flip side, only 7,900 Americans moved here in
'93, even though their population is 10 times ours.

So what gives? What's driving our professionals south? Taxes, taxes and   3
more taxes. According to Satya Poddar, director of tax policy consulting at
Ernst & Young, taxes as a percentage of GDP constitute about 37% here compared to 30% in the U.S. What that means is, after adjusting for differences in
population and income, Canadians pay a staggering $50 billion a year more in
taxes than their American counterparts.

But what does that really mean for the average Canadian family? It doesn't   4
take into account our much-vaunted social services, our quality of life, our standard of living. It's difficult to make a mass comparison that tells you anything.
With the help of two families from north and south of the border, who shared
with us the details of their financial situations, we've put together a rough comparison of Canadian and American professionals. Donna Spector, 35, a former
partner with New York City accounting firm BDO Dunwoody who recently
hung out her own shingle as a consultant, and her 36-year-old husband, Donald,
a marketing consultant, share their three-bedroom apartment in upper-west-side
Manhattan with their two young children, Robyn, 6 and Gary, 2; they have a
combined household income of US$227,400. Clara Roca, 44, a widowed
teacher with a nine-year-old daughter, Alexis, lives in Stouffville, a small town

within commuting distance of Toronto, and has a total income of $68,000 a year. Apart from the taxes they paid, we looked at factors like cost of living, cost of housing, and even quality of life. We asked the people at Price Waterhouse, Canada and Runzheimer-Canada Inc. to estimate how much those same people would pay in taxes if they lived in two different cities — one in Canada, and one in the U.S. The results (in Figure 2) might surprise you.

Figure 1: THE SPECTORS IN NEW YORK (US$)
AND CLARE ROCA IN STOUFFVILLE (CDN$):
A COMPARISON

The Spectors: New York (US$)

Donna and Donald Spector admit that the cost of living in Manhattan is steep. When Donna visited her doctor and he asked what she was doing about birth control, she cracked "tuition." Kindergarten fees alone cost 14,000.

Clara Roca: Stouffville (CDN$)

Clara Roca, a widowed teacher with a nine-year-old daughter, Alexis, lives an hour's drive outside Toronto. Any money she'd save in tax by moving to the U.S. would largely be over-ridden by the increased cost of housing for a comparable home. What's more, she'd likely suffer a cut in salary.

The Spectors: New York (US$)	Clara Roca: Stouffville (CDN$)
Income	*Income*
Donna's salary: 100,000	Salary: 63,400
Donald's salary: 100,000	Miscellaneous earnings: 4,600
Rental income: 17,400	Total: 68,000
Investment income: 10,000	
Total 227,400	
Expenses	*Expenses*
Tax: 85,000	Mortgage: 7,378.56
Rent: 31,200	Property tax: 3,000
Maintenance: 9,912	Union dues: 366.41
Telephone/utilities: 3,000	Auto maintenance/gas: 3,600
Household expenses: 5,328	Pension contributions: 5,040
Car-lease: 4,260	Deductions (CPP/UIC): 1,951.19
Car-park: 3,900	Home/Auto insurance: 1,044.01
Transportation: 1,500	Life/Disability insurance: 800
Cabs: 1,000	Food: 4,800
Day care: 21,200	Entertainment: 2,400
Tuition/camp: 21,200	Income tax: 21,779
Pension: 1,000	Household expenses: 780
Auto insurance: 2,000	Utilities: 1,500
Home insurance: 1,000	Clothing: 2,500
Health/life insurance: 13,400	Savings/investments: 7,500
Medical deductible: 3,000	Vacation: 1,000

Food: 7,500	Gifts: 2,000
Clothing: 5,000	Miscellaneous: 960.84
Entertainment: 2,500	Total: 68,400.01
Vacations: 2,500	
Charitable contrib.: 2,000	
Total: 227,400	
Assets	*Assets*
Real estate: 80,000	Home: 210,000
Furniture/fixtures: 20,000	Furniture: 50,000
Investments: 250,000	Personal effects: 10,000
Pension-401K: 15,000	Investments/savings: 80,000
Total: 365,000	Car: 8,000
	Total 358,000
Liabilities	*Liabilities*
Credit line: 50,000	Mortgage: 70,000
	Credit Cards: 3,000
	Total: 73,000
Net Worth	*Net Worth*
315,000	285,000

Nobody can argue that American professionals pay less tax (the figures take into account federal and state/provincial taxes, as well as deductions for mortgage interest and real estate taxes which are available in the U.S.) Even in highly taxed New York City, the average tax level was 41% at the Spectors' income level, compared to a high of 46% in Vancouver and a low of 32% in Houston. By moving from New York to Houston, the Spectors could save themselves $27,639 on their tax bill. But if they move to Vancouver, they'd pay an extra $14,683. A Vancouver family at the Spectors' income level could save $42,322 a year in taxes, just by moving to Houston.

At Clara Roca's income level of $68,000, the differences are no less pronounced. An average tax rate of 34.3% in Toronto and 32.12% in Calgary,would drop to just 19.62% in Chicago. A move from Toronto to Chicago, then, would immediately cut almost $10,000 from Roca's tax bill and a move from Calgary to Chicago would eliminate $8,498.

But there's more to life than just taxes. When our experts factored in the cost of housing and cost of living, the results were somewhat different. For example, even with the tax savings, the Spectors would end up with more money in their pockets if they moved to Vancouver. Their housing costs of $45,537 (US$31,200) per year for a three-bedroom apartment in Manhattan would shrink to just $17,070 in Vancouver; saving them almost $30,000. And

Figure 2: CASH FLOW COMPARISON

Clara Roca	Toronto	Chicago	Calgary
Income	68,000	68,000	68,000
Housing costs	11,661	24,003	9,784
Goods & Services	18,369	18,964	16,894
Canadian taxes	23,321	N.A.	21,840
U.S. federal tax	N.A.	6,463	N.A.
State tax	N.A.	1,677	N.A.
Social security tax	N.A.	5,202	N.A.
Disposable income	$14,649	$11,691	$19,482

The Spectors	New York	Houston	Vancouver
Income	309,218	309,218	309,218
Housing costs	45,537	16,618	17,070
Goods & Services	88,081	65,992	69,376
Canadian taxes	N.A	N.A.	141,552
U.S. federal tax	77,016	84,967	N.A.
State tax	35,590	N.A.	N.A.
Social security tax	14,263	14,263	N.A.
Disposable income	$48,731	$127,376	$81,220

Source: Runzheimer Canada Inc.
All figures are in Canadian dollars; for continuity, income levels have been left unchanged.

they'd save $18,705 on a mixed basket of goods and services, including furniture and appliances, clothing, day care and other domestic services, medical care, entertainment and groceries. They're left with disposable income of $48,731 in New York, compared to $81,220 in Vancouver.

8   But keep in mind that New York is an anomaly — easily one of the most expensive cities in the U.S. in terms of taxes, cost of living and cost of housing. So if they lived in Houston, Texas, the Spectors would have a good $127,376 left over after the bills are paid. Runzheimer Canada estimates that the same downtown 1,300-square-foot apartment that costs them $45,537 in New York would ring in at a more manageable $16,618 in Houston. And chances are, they'd have invested in a house, giving them a heavy tax deduction,

since interest on mortgage payments is deductible in the States (but not in Canada). They'd also save about $22,000 on the basic basket of goods and services. Using the same figures, a Canadian family moving from Vancouver to Houston would end up with $46,156 more in disposable income.

For Clara Roca, on the other hand, any money she saved in taxes would be largely over-ridden by the increased cost of housing if she moved to a comparable three-bedroom home within a 20-minute commute of Chicago. According to Runzheimer, she'd also be paying about $600 more per year for the same mix of goods and services. Figure 2 shows she'd be better off moving from Toronto to Calgary, where slightly lower taxes, housing costs and goods and services might leave her with almost $5,000 extra in her pocket at the end of the year. What's more, a move to the U.S. would likely mean a cut in salary. The average teacher's salary in the States is $44,319 (in Canadian dollars), compared to $50,469 in Canada. 9

So before you take the jump and move to the U.S., look closely at the tax rates for the particular state you've chosen, as well as how much it will cost you to live in a comparable house in a comparable style, and what you'll be paid to do similar work. 10

However, the decision to live in one country or another, or even one city or another, does not stand or fall purely on the basis of finances. We asked Roca and the Spectors how they felt about their quality of life: Did they feel safe walking the streets? Did they feel well-served by the local school system? Basically, did they like living where they lived? They came up with some interesting answers. 11

Education eats up a hefty chunk of the Spectors' earnings. When Donna visited her doctor for a six-week checkup after Robyn was born and he asked what she was doing about birth control, she cracked, "Tuition." Indeed, their daughter Robyn stared kindergarten last fall at a cost of US$14,000. "You can find specialized programs in the public schools of Manhattan, but you have to look for them; you have to do your homework," says Donna. With both parents working full time, she says, "We just didn't." The Spectors also pay US$4,000 a year for their son's preschool program and US$400 a week for a babysitter. 12

What's more, the universal health care we take for granted in Canada just isn't available. As a partner at BDO Dunwoody, Donna pays US$700 a month for medical insurance for her family (this will continue for 18 months even though she resigned in November). Then there's a US$500 deductible for each person, and, she says. "It's a given that you're going to have a least US$500 in expenses each per year." So that's US$10,400 per year for basic medical coverage. 13

On top of that, the Spectors' insurer only pays a percentage of their overall hospital bills. Recently, says Donna, Robyn's continuing ear infections 14 resulted in an operation in which her adenoids were removed and tubes inserted in her ears. "The insurance company paid 80% of the US$2,250," she says. "So I'm still left with US$450-plus to pay on my own." Similarly, when her son was born, just the obstetrician's bill, "not the anesthesiologist or the hospital or anything else," was US$5,000. Of that, the Spectors paid about US$1,000. The maximum out-of-pocket expenses is US$2,500 per person or US$10,000 per family.

15   So what keeps them in The Big Apple? Says Donald: "It's a great city to live in. It's exciting in terms of the cultural, ethnic and racial makeup; and the opportunities in terms of museums and theatre, music and business."

16   Is it safe? Says Donna; "I wouldn't go to the park at night: it's New York city: let's not kid ourselves." When she gets on the subway, she turns her wedding ring around so potential muggers can't see the gems. "It's instinctive," she says, "It's safe, but I guess that's a relative term; I know what to do to be safe here."

17   And then there's the question of family. Grandparents and cousins are just a subway ride away: "Although some days we're ready to pack it all in and move to Vermont — get a barn, milk cows — we never really discuss it primarily because of our families," says Donna.

18   Clara Roca and her late husband Larry lived and taught high school in Ahoskie, North Carolina, for five years from 1986 to 1990, then moved back to Canada. Roca says about 23% of her overall salary went to taxes in the U.S. Here, she says, "after all of the deductions, I get about half my pay." What's more, she misses the warm climate, the beauty of the countryside and the small-town friendliness of Ahoskie. "Kids have a lot of respect for their peers and their elders. I felt very safe. Nobody locks their doors and they'll leave their keys in their cars."

19   While Roca and her husband paid only US$39,000 for a house in Ahoskie, a similar house here would cost about $150,000. Clara and Larry spent $217,000 for a home in Stouffville. As well, Roca admits she was shocked by the youth crime rate when she returned to Toronto. "In North Carolina, if you did something wrong, your face was splashed all over the paper," she said. "No one protected you. There's too much protection of criminals here."

20   Still, says Roca, "even after all the taxes are paid, I'm happier here." The things that convinced her to move back, she says, were "universal medical care, friends and family and our level of culture." With a population of 4,000, says Roca, Ahoskie was hardly a cultural dynamo. The centre of activity in town was church, and since Roca and her husband weren't religious, they never felt like they fit in. While she admits some American cities would rate highly in terms of cultural activities, she says "You'd get an even higher crime rate. For the numbers, Toronto is very safe."

In Stouffville, Roca feels she has the best of both worlds — a rural town, 21
an hour's drive from the big city. Her daughter Alexis gets to visit the zoo, the
art gallery and the Science Centre, for example, but she's not exposed to the
pace and crime of city life.

And universal medical care saves her a great deal of money. While she had 22
a health plan through work in the U.S., it covered only about 80% of her bills,
unless she used one of the health insurer's doctors. But when she gave birth to
her daughter, she refused to go to the hospital in town, "because they were
butchers." Instead, she went to a nearby city, where the bill came to US$6,000.
Roca paid US$2,400 of that herself.

What's more, had she stayed in the U.S., she'd be bankrupt. There was 23
never enough money to buy extra medical coverage for special expenses associated with diseases like cancer. "Cancer coverage alone was US$40 a month,"
says Roca.

But just three years ago, after the couple had returned to Canada, Larry 24
was diagnosed with cancer of the colon. After a year of chemotherapy and radi-
ation treatments, all of which would have been out-of-pocket expenses in the
U.S., he died in November, 1994. In the U.S., says Clara, "we would have lost
everything."

Style and Structure

1.   How do the approaches used and the information included in paragraphs
      1–3 affect the reader? Why is achieving these effects important for the
      writer?

2.   In what ways does paragraph 4 serve the writer's purpose?

3.   What features of the two countries does Cornell compare in paragraphs
      5–6? Why would she choose to look at these features first?

4.   Identify the features of the comparison Cornell examines in paragraphs
      7–10. What reasons would she have for placing this comparison at this
      point in her essay?

5. (a) What features does Cornell compare in paragraphs 11–24?

   (b) For a point-by point comparison, most textbooks suggest presenting the
       same details in the same order for each item being compared. Cornell has
       bent this "rule" in this section: she leaves out one detail (costs of educa-
       tion) altogether and reverses the order she used in discussing the Spec-
       tors (paragraphs 12–17) when she looks at Roca's situation (paragraphs
       18–24).

Why would she choose not to mention costs of education for the Canadian family? Why would she reverse the order in which she presents the details of her final comparison? How effectively does her approach drive her point home to her reader?

6. Most readers will finish this essay with a very definite conclusion in their minds. But can you find a formal conclusion in the essay? What strategy is the writer employing here? Evaluate its effectiveness.

7. (a) Throughout the essay, Cornell bases her comparisons on specific dollar figures. She could have used other approaches such as quoting expert opinions or restricting herself to anecdotes of people's experiences in both countries. How effective is her use of data and how does she try to maximize its impact?

   (b) What effect does her inclusion of figures summarizing the numbers have for the reader?

Warm-up

1. Write a short essay on the reasons that you personally have or have not been attracted to the U.S. Exchange your finished paper with two or three others in your class. How do the reasons for your choice differ from those of the others? How valid are the different reasons people gave?

   What suggestions can you make to help the others improve the presentation of their ideas?

2. Do a survey of people from as broad a range of backgrounds as possible to identify their reasons for staying in Canada or wanting to move elsewhere. Compare your results with those of others in the class. (You may want to pool your results if you find doing so adds validity to your results.)

   Write a paragraph that summarizes and interprets your findings. Exchange paragraphs with the classmates who shared their survey findings with you. Do their interpretations of the results differ from yours?

Thinking and Writing

1. Based on a survey like the one in exercise 2 of the "Warm-up" above, write an essay that compares and contrasts the reasons people give for wanting to stay in Canada or move elsewhere. Incorporate tables to summarize your findings.

Audience: a Canadian who may never have thought about leaving Canada.

2.   The reasons people give for wanting to leave or stay in a country tell us much about their values. They go elsewhere to look for the important things they cannot find where they are. They stay where they are, among other reasons, to avoid losing things that are not available elsewhere.

Based on a survey like the one in exercise 2 of the "Warm-up" above, write a classification essay in which you examine the characteristics of Canadian life that people value most (and least).

Audience: a general reader who has probably not thought through the topic.

Send a copy of your finished essay to a local newspaper. Ask if the editor is interested in using it as a feature for the Canada Day edition.

Respect: At the Heart
of Successful Marriage

by Annie Gottlieb

1   Respect is not mentioned in the marriage vows. No illustrated books show how to achieve it. Yet it is central to a lasting, satisfying marriage.

2   Yes, respect. It seems a quaint, almost formal word today. But it's one that couples who are successfully married mention with impressive consistency. For her book *Married People: Staying Together in the Age of Divorce*, author Francine Klagsbrun interviewed 87 couples who had been married fifteen years or more. She hoped to identify the factors that had enabled these marriages to survive and thrive in a time when some 40 percent end in divorce. Respect turned out to be a key element. "The vast majority of people I interviewed said, 'I respect him' or 'I respect her,'" says Klagsbrun.

3   What is this thing called respect? It's not the same as admiration. Says Dr. Alexandra Symonds, associate clinical professor of psychiatry at the New York University School of Medicine, "When you fall in love, you *admire* the other. You look *up* to someone, much the way a child idealizes a parent." Such romantic admiration thrives and even depends on the illusion that the other is "perfect for you." That's why it doesn't last. "You come to see that the person you married *isn't* exactly what you expected," says Francine Klagsbrun. "There are differences of personality, of approaches to life; different ways of doing things." It's now that real respect has a chance to develop.

4   You can try to change your mate back into your fantasy. But for the marriage to last, you must agree to disagree, learning to let the other be. For respect is between peers. It is for something really there, tested and proven.

5   The put-down is the chief symptom — and weapon — of lack of respect, or contempt. "Contempt is the worst kind of emotion," says Dr. Symonds. "You feel the other person has no worth. I have one patient whose husband loves sports. She would prefer to go to the theatre or to stay home and read. She could simply say, 'We have different tastes.' Instead she says, 'How can he waste his time and money that way?' She puts him down."

6   We've all seen marriages in which one or both partners attack the other quite savagely in the guise of "It's for your own good." Any "good" is undone by the hostile tone of what claims to be constructive criticism. A wife nags her husband to be more ambitious and makes him feel like a failure because he prefers craftsmanship or community projects to the competitive business

world. Or a husband accuses his wife of wasting time whenever she gets together with a friend: "Why isn't she doing something productive?" In good marriages, partners nurture each other's self-esteem. They never make the other person feel like an idiot.

Respect, then, is appreciation of the *separateness* of the other person, of the ways in which he or she is unique. These things take time to discover, accept, and finally appreciate. That's why respect is a quality of maturity in a marriage, not of the first heat of romance. But this doesn't mean that married couples who respect each other are simply saying, "You go your way, and I'll go mine." On the contrary, says Francine Klagsbrun. "Respect often helps you to learn from each other, because you've taken on some of each other's ways of thinking."   7

My husband and I are from different worlds and generations. He's a European, eighteen years my senior. Sometimes we clash. But we've learned to respect each other even for some of the differences that once annoyed us most. As a result, we've grown more alike. I've absorbed some of his authority and definite standards; he's absorbed some of my tolerance. I've gained a genuine appreciation for jazz, he for rock'n'roll. That's the paradox of a good marriage. Only by respecting each other as you are do you open the door to change.   8

The root meaning of the word *respect* is "to look at." Respect is a clear yet loving eye. It sees not only what is really there, but also what is *potentially* there, and helps bring the latter to fruition. Respect is the art of love by which married couples honour what is unique and best in each other.   9

Style and Structure

1. (a) Identify the sentence in the first paragraph that acts as this essay's **thesis statement**. Give reasons to support your choice.

  (b) Examine the other sentences in paragraph 1 and the first two sentences of paragraph 2. What point are they trying to convey to the reader? What do they reveal about the writer's attempt to deal with the attitudes her intended readers may have toward her **thesis** before they read her essay?

2. Given her intended reader, why might Gottlieb have chosen to begin the body of her essay by referring to Klagsbrun's book?

3. (a) In this essay, the writer defines respect in several ways. What method does she use in paragraphs 3 to 6?

  (b) Considering her intended reader, what reasons might she have for beginning this definition by talking of love and admiration?

(c) What reasons would she have for following up this definition with the contents of paragraphs 4, 5, and 6?

4. (a) In what ways does the definition of respect offered in paragraph 7 differ from those offered in earlier paragraphs?

(b) What method of definition does Gottlieb use in paragraph 8? Why is it effective?

(c) What benefits does Gottlieb gain by saving the definitions presented in paragraphs 7 and 8 for so late in the essay?

5. In what ways does paragraph 9 act as an effective **conclusion** for the essay? Why would the writer begin her **conclusion** with a definition derived from a dictionary?

6. Count the number of words in each of the sentences in the first two paragraphs. How does this variation in sentence length help drive home to the reader the points being made?

7. The tone of an essay may be friendly or angry, formal or informal. The tone chosen can subtly affect the reader's acceptance of the ideas being presented.

(a) Identify three passages in which Gottlieb uses contractions. What tone do these contractions help establish? Is it an effective way of dealing with her intended reader?

(b) Given this tone, in what kinds of writing would it *not* be appropriate to use contractions?

Warm-up

1. Working with a group of four or five others in your class, choose a word that represents a concept important in our society (e.g., "friendship," "hatred," "equality," "democracy").

(a) Write a paragraph that defines the word by describing what it does *not* mean (as Gottlieb does in her essay).
Audience: someone who may not have thought very seriously about the implications of the word.

(b) Write a paragraph that defines the word by describing what it does mean.
Audience: same as above.

(c) Write a paragraph that defines the word by using an example.
Audience: same as above.

(d) Compare your paragraphs to the ones written by the other members of your group.

Thinking and Writing

1. As Gottlieb points out, most people enter marriage without knowing the most important ingredient for success. Most of us who fall in love never realize *its* most important elements either. Write an essay in which you define "Romantic Love." Use a number of different methods of definition. (Suggestion: you might want to write a humorous essay.)

    Audience: a typical Canadian who is amazed at the array of emotions involved in loving.

2. Gottlieb draws a clear distinction between romantic admiration and a successful married relationship. Yet in our society most people marry because they are in love (i.e., share romantic admiration). Write an essay in which you briefly define romantic love and explain the role it plays in a successful marriage.

    Audience: someone who is in love and plans to be married.

    Send a copy of your final draft to someone who deals with people having difficulties in their marriages, such as a priest, minister, or marriage counsellor. Ask for comments on your ideas.

Second Opinion

by Ivor Shapiro

1   In a conference room on the top floor of an Ontario hospital, a group of staff members are discussing starvation. Their undernourished patient is not an Ethiopian refugee but a 77-year-old woman who has spent more than a year in hospital and now lies dying in a nearby ward. There is an intravenous tube in her arm, but it provides no nutrients, only dextrose and water. An ethicist quietly takes notes as nurses and therapists recount the case history. A month ago, after meeting with Mrs. X's family in the wake of her unexpected recovery from the complications of a stroke, the attending physician instructed staff to stop feeding her. Then, the day before yesterday, again with the family's consent, a new order appeared on her medical chart: when the last available intravenous site deteriorates in a few days' time, the water supply will end with it. No attempt will be made to lead a life-giving tube into her stomach.

2   Mrs. X herself has taken no part in the series of decisions that guarantee her imminent death. She suffers from dementia and floats in and out of mental clarity. Dementia does not kill, but Mrs. X's chronic frailty seems to amount to an agonizingly prolonged death. After the latest crisis passed, her family confessed to feeling worn out by deathbed scenes, and her son told the doctor that his mother would want to make an end of it. It is 31 days since the physician agreed that there was no point in continuing to feed her, and now, with the decision to stop providing water, the doctor may as well write out a postdated death certificate. Her nurses and therapists, distressed by that stark reality, decided to ask for a second opinion — not on a matter of medicine, but on the ethics of beckoning death.

3   Abbyann Lynch was at another hospital, leading the first of a series of staff discussions on "bioethics case studies," when the manager of Mrs. X's nursing team phoned the Westminster Institute for Ethics and Human Values, where she works. When the message reached Lynch, she rearranged her schedule and set up a meeting. This is not the first time Lynch has dropped everything to lead a discussion about whether or not a patient should be "allowed" to die. Over the past decade, it has become accepted practice for physicians to disconnect life-support systems in advance of patients' inevitable deaths — accepted, but never routine.

4   The legal and customary conditions for terminating treatment can be quite vague, so in these and other cases, an ethicist will often be called in to help doctors (or, as in the case of Mrs. X, the lower ranks in the health hierarchy) cut a moral Gordian knot.

Over the past decade or so, clinical ethics has become one of North Amer-   5
ica's growth industries. Most ethicists say the main stimulus for the increase in
their business is an abundance of new technologies that present ever-widening
choices — and dilemmas — to physicians and patients. But Benjamin Freedman, ethicist at Montreal's Jewish General Hospital, says the issues he and his
colleagues most often tackle were around long before the advent of high-tech
medicine. There is nothing new about patients' rights: receiving full information about risky medical procedures, having the power to refuse any or all
treatment, and being guaranteed confidentiality by medical professionals.
What is new is that patients and their families have become increasingly more
aware, and therefore more demanding, of their rights.

From the doctor's point of view, there is no harm in taking out an extra   6
piece of malpractice insurance by getting an ethical opinion on a tricky
judgment call. For whatever reasons, the nation's hospitals are following
the U.S. example of establishing ethics committees, and a dozen or so,
mainly in central Canada's biggest cities, have hired professional ethicists
to teach and counsel. An important part of the ethicist's job is to sort out
the conflicting feelings and needs of patients, their relatives and friends,
and the doctors and nurses. George Webster, ethicist at three Catholic hospitals in Toronto, says of the family's role in deciding about ending the
treatment of an unconscious patient: "We do not routinely ask what they
want, but rather ask them to reconstruct what the patient would want done."
And who is family? A dying AIDS patient's estranged wife, his hostile parents, or his current lover?

Freedman says the proliferation of applied-ethics positions is reducing "a   7
glut of philosophers." The new career options have been welcomed by a generation of philosophy Ph.D.s like himself, who, uninspired by the idea of a life
spent probing ageless metaphysical questions, were looking for new markets
for their wares. The jobs have also been a godsend for theologians who find
earthly debates more attractive than spiritual exercises in a secular society. At
the same time, says Abbyann Lynch, medical schools have been churning out
a new kind of graduate class: more women, more members of minorities, older
students with a background in the social sciences. Today's medical graduates,
she says, are more willing than many of their forebears to think about the
meaning of their vocation and to seek help in dealing with the agonizing questions about life and death with which their jobs confront them.

Some of these questions can be seen in the seven faces that watch Lynch   8
with a touch of disappointment as she tells the troubled nursing team that her
role is not to provide clear-cut answers but to ask more questions and try to
help them clarify issues. She is not here, she says, to make judgments.

9   Not all consulting ethicists would agree with so limiting a definition of their profession. It's a matter, perhaps, of personal style. Lynch has the manner of a teacher of philosophy, which is exactly what she has been since 1954. Her present assignments include sitting on hospital ethics committees, teaching groups of doctors and nurses, and conducting "ethics grand rounds," a monthly meeting at which hospital clinicians discuss complex cases — "The Case of the Extremely Low-Birth-Weight Infant" or "AIDS: Ethical Dilemmas." But with her gentle questions and tentative, self-effacing suggestions, she still plays convincingly the role of tame philosopher, criticizing logic and probing diagnostic assessments in the light of policies and laws.

10   By contrast, David Roy hunches over his pipe and delivers unambiguous epigrams with a punchy fluency oddly reminiscent of Joe Clark during Question Period. Roy runs the Centre for Bioethics at Montreal's Clinical Research Institute and provides consultancy services upon physicians' requests. His basic task, he says, is to build accurate descriptions of patients and their conditions. Is a particular brain-damaged child capable of experiencing happiness (and should she therefore be given the chance offered by an emergency operation), or is she a virtual vegetable who should be allowed a merciful death? Discovering the answer to such questions is not a job for a detached philosopher, he says, but a case for an "espionage agent."

11   The investigation requires detailed discussions with everyone involved: a shy nurse may hold the crucial piece of information about the patient. And then "a point comes in consultation when I put my opinion down on the patient's chart just like anybody else," Roy says. "To put it crudely, I've got to put my ass on the line."

12   When invited to put her opinions on charts, Lynch always refuses. "I'm not a clinician," she says. "I help people sort out and order their thinking and give them possible avenues to discuss." Similarly, because she is not a psychologist or social worker, she refuses to get involved in meetings with families.

13   But Roy says he would never consider doing a consultation without talking to the patient's family. He says ethicists cannot do their jobs properly without some of the skills of clinician, philosopher, and psychologist. The profession requires, he says, a broad humanities training "with a strong dose of, and interest in, science."

14   Lynch presses on with her questions to the nursing team about Mrs. X. What are the patient's chances now? Could she survive if feeding were to be resumed? Was she dying a month ago, before her food was withdrawn? Was she in pain?

15   She reads from a draft policy statement still under consideration by the hospital's ethics committee. Treatment must not be withdrawn, it says, unless the patient's death is imminent. She reads quickly through the rest of the document,

pausing before the last sentence, which says: the purpose of withdrawing treatment must not be to hasten death but to prevent needless suffering.

A competent patient has a legal right to refuse treatment, Lynch reminds her listeners, and if the patient is not competent, the family may be consulted about what to do. But unless the patient is dying anyway, and the decision will affect only the timing and the circumstances of her death, the family's wishes should not necessarily be the "first priority." 16

In the case of Mrs. X, Lynch suggests to the hospital group (in the first indication of her opinion in nearly an hour of discussion) that the family's wishes may have dominated the decision. Over a month ago, before her feeding was stopped, Mrs. X was not about to die, was not even in any great pain. She was recovering from a respiratory infection, and while her dementia affected the quality of her life, her illness was not a terminal one analogous to cancer or AIDS, where, in the final stages, all a medical team can do is provide comfort and perhaps adjust the timing of an imminent death. 17

"This patient may be dying," Lynch says quietly, undramatically, "but she may be dying because she is not being fed." The starkness of that statement is greeted by a slightly dazed silence. No one disagrees. Lynch seems to have put into words a possibility no one at the table was eager to face: that a patient has been condemned to die for no good reason other than relieving her family of their burden of responsibility. But now it has been said, and within five minutes there is consensus about the next step: Lynch should raise the matter with the hospital authorities. Later, having visited Mrs. X, the hospital administrator will ask the ethics committee to consider the case. 18

The array of ethical paraphernalia available to hospitals — committees, consultants, guidelines, teachers, patient-advocates — may not always be an advance over old-fashioned agonizing on the part of patients and their families and doctors. Whatever else they do, the new procedures can have the effect of shifting decision making further away from vulnerable people in beds and closer to the people who have power over them. And the process offers doctors a chance to shuck off a burden of guilt. 19

Michael Yeo, a researcher on Lynch's staff, says people have a disturbing tendency to relinquish moral authority to other people: priests and rabbis in the past, now ethics committees and ethicists. He thinks there is something "potentially dishonest or cowardly" about doctors deferring to a committee on a matter of morality. "I shudder when I see someone quoted as 'an expert in medical ethics,'" Yeo says. "I'm inclined to say the guy's just a schmuck like anyone else." 20

For good or ill, the age of the ethical consultant has dawned. The specialty is still so young that its practitioners' tasks, methods, and qualifications are far 21 from standardized, but ethicists are likely to contribute ever more frequently to medical decisions — at best influencing them, at worst simply lending them moral weight. Since the ethicists can only function effectively with the good-will of physicians, they potentially have a conflict of interest when their consciences call them to stand up for patients. While today's consultants seem to possess a compensating bias toward recognizing patients' interests, the unenviable tightrope they must walk could make them reluctant to recognize abuses that are not glaringly apparent.

22   The ethics committee's ruling on the case of Mrs. X may help resolve some future dilemmas. A shadowy area of policy has been illuminated, and if a revised draft statement is passed, the hospital will clearly forbid the arbitrary withdrawal of treatment from a patient who is neither about to die nor already rendered vegetative by an irreversible illness. But things have moved somewhat more quickly in the starving body of Mrs. X than in the hospital's body politic. Within 48 hours of the emergency ethics consultation, she has had "a cerebral accident," lost consciousness, and died. No one is suing the doctor or the hospital. No one is pressing for a public inquiry.

23   And no one enjoys dwelling on the question of what would have happened if the ethicist had been called in earlier. No one enjoys thinking about whether being without food for the last month of her life may have helped to kill Mrs. X.

Style and Structure

1.   What type of person does Shapiro expect his typical reader to be (e.g, medical professional, legal expert, philosophy major, etc.)? How can you tell?

2. (a) Identify the main topic of this essay:

   (i) the story of Mrs. X;

   (ii) the customary conditions for terminating treatment;

   (iii) the increase in the number of ethicists;

   (iv) the role of an ethicist.

    Write down the sentence in which Shapiro announces his **thesis**.

  (b) How does the presentation of Mrs. X's case in paragraphs 1 to 3 relate to this **thesis**?

  (c) Reread the **thesis statement** as if it were the opening sentence in the essay. Then reread paragraphs 1 to 3 as if they followed this **thesis statement**. Given the intended reader, which opening, Shapiro's or this new variation, is more effective? Why?

3. (a) What information does Shapiro include in paragraphs 5 to 7? How does knowing these facts near the beginning of the essay benefit readers as they continue through the later sections?

   (b) Paragraphs 9 to 13 use a compare/contrast format. What advantages does Shapiro achieve by presenting these contrasting opinions at this point?

   (c) Paragraph 8 takes the reader momentarily back to the case of Mrs. X. Why do you think Shapiro might choose to do so?

4. In what ways do the events presented in paragraphs 14 to 18 relate to the paragraphs preceding and following them? How important are these events to the reader's understanding of Shapiro's **thesis**?

5. (a) In what ways do the final three paragraphs of the essay act as a **conclusion**?

   (b) Shapiro returns to Mrs. X's case in the last two paragraphs. How effective is this technique in helping to convey his message to his reader?

   (c) How many times does Shapiro use the word "no one" in the last four sentences of the essay? What effect does this repetition have on the reader? How does the length of these sentences reinforce this effect?

6. Half of this essay is devoted to the case of Mrs. X. Reread the sections that do *not* deal with her specific situation (paragraphs 5 to 7, 9 to 13, 19 to 21). In what ways did including Mrs. X's case help the reader come to grips with this essay's **thesis**?

Warm-up

1. Make a point-form summary of an ethicist's work. Then write a one-paragraph job description for an ethicist aimed at someone who has never heard of the profession.

   When you have finished, look at two or three of the job descriptions written by others in the class. Compare them to yours for completeness and accuracy. Suggest details that might be added or changed in the others and make any changes to your own paragraph that would improve it.

2. Should an ethicist work in the way that Roy does (see paragraph 11) or as Lynch does (see paragraph 12)? Write a paragraph that explains your preference and the reasons behind it.
   Audience: a classmate who prefers the other way.

   Find someone in the class who disagrees with your preference. Read each other's paragraphs and then try to convince the other person that your choice is preferable. When you have finished, make any revisions to your paragraph that might make it more convincing.

3. Working with the class as a whole, create a list of the types of cases in which an ethicist might play a role. Then write a short report on the class's findings.
   Audience: someone who has never heard of an ethicist.

Thinking and Writing

1. Shapiro's essay raises serious questions about decision making in the field of health care, particularly when those decisions involve such life-and-death choices as the ones in his example. Who should decide whether or not to remove life-support systems — the doctor, relatives, nurses, a team of people? Should such decisions be made at all? Should they be reviewed both before and after being put into practice? By whom? How often? At what stages should family members, doctors, nurses, ethicists, and ethical committees be a part of the decision-making process? What role should each play? Who should have the final say?

   Write an essay in which you outline the process you would like followed if you or a member of your family were the patient in such a situation.
   Audience: a medical professional.

   Send a copy of your final draft to your family doctor and ask for a response.

2. The case of Mrs. X brings us face to face with the dilemma of euthanasia, or causing death to end suffering. Some people see euthanasia as an act of mercy. They believe a quick, painless death is preferable to facing extended periods of suffering from a terminal illness or from mental incompetence. However, another large segment of our society considers any act that speeds the process of dying to be a form of murder.

   The dilemma becomes even more complicated in such cases as that of Mrs. X, where patients cannot tell others what they would like done, and those who are left to make the decisions may have opposing ideas on what course to follow.

   Underlying this dilemma, of course, are the fundamental questions: "Who has the right to take life? Should euthanasia be practised at all?"

   Write an essay in which you argue either for or against the practice of euthanasia. (Do not try to present the arguments for both sides.) As part of your planning process, try to identify the objections that would be raised by someone who holds a view opposed to yours, and deal with them in your essay.
   Audience: someone who has not given much thought to euthanasia.

Integrated Sports:
A Question of Fair Play

by Fran Rider

Full integration for all ages and in all sports will mean drastically reduced opportunities for female athletes. With uncontrolled emigration of girls to boys' teams, girls' teams will fold, and many girls unwilling or unable to compete with boys will have no chance to play. This is equality? **1**

Sports-minded girls already have enough trouble honing their abilities. Too often, boys' teams monopolize both practice time and funding dollars. But the way to correct such problems is to promote and develop a female sports system leading to Olympic competition and professional events. This effort is now well under way. **2**

Time was when girls either played against boys or hung up their hockey skates. As recently as the mid-1970s, ten-year-old goalie Gail Cummings of Huntsville, Ontario, had no girls' team available to her and was rejected by a boys' team because of her sex. The OWHA helped Cummings take her cause to the Ontario Human Rights Commission. Although she lost, girls have since gained the right to play on boys' teams when no local girls' teams exist. They have also gained teams of their own that equal or even surpass the boys' in coaching and calibre of competition — and are much more sportsmanlike to boot. **3**

Take the teams open to Justine Blainey. The Toronto and surrounding area offers the world's best female hockey opportunities, ranging from provincial championship teams at the novice level (girls aged nine and up) through to the senior A Team Canada, which captured the McCallion World Cup last year. **4**

Blainey has been touted in the press as an exceptional player simply because she qualified for a male team. Few noticed that the team was playing at the lowest competitive level in boys' hockey, and this kind of shortsightedness has coloured the entire debate about sports integration. **5**

Many people now assume that the best female athletes should be moving up to male events. What an insult to world-class athletes like runner Angella Issajenko, skier Laurie Graham, and our Canadian Women's Field Hockey Team, who are every bit as skilled as their male counterparts! Should we dismiss these women as second-rate just because they can't outmuscle equally trained men? **6**

No one disputes the notion more forcefully than female athletes. In most sports, the vast majority of girls want to play in an all-female environment where they can enrol at an early age and progress to the upper levels. They want to match their competitors in size and strength as well as dedication and mental acuity. **7**

8   Integrated teams may meet girls' needs in a few sports, such as shooting, where a more muscular opponent cannot dominate competition. But in many others, integration would make females the losers. Each sport's promise for integration is best evaluated by its own governing body, not by ill-informed feminists.

9   Like it or not, male and female bodies do not perform identically. Medical evidence indicates that the differences are negligible until puberty, when girls gain a temporary edge in size and strength. But the situation reverses at about age fourteen. And if teenage girls are to have the teams they deserve, we must nurture and protect the entire female stream.

10   If we allow girls like Justine Blainey to play on inferior male teams, how can we deny boys the chance to play on often-superior female teams? Last season, the OWHA's male applicants included a fourteen-year-old boy who felt that the girls' program offered better opportunities than the boys'. But letting boys in creates a new problem: displacement of girls by more powerful players.

11   Integration will lead to exploitation of female athletes. Girls will be lured from top female teams by coaches of male teams who want sensationalized media coverage and increased funding (often allocated on a per-capita basis). These girls will be recruited at puberty to help bring the male team a championship, and will then be discarded when biology overtakes them.

12   Meanwhile, the loss of girls from the female system will leave their former teammates with fewer opportunities. The defection of one or two players has been known to kill a team, and those that survive such blows will then face a shortage of money. Cost-slashing governments will likely decide to fund only one team per sport. Universities, now fending off requests for increased funding of women's teams, could well go the same route.

13   In Quebec, which has allowed integration since 1978, female sporting opportunities have not expanded. Only 35 girls' hockey teams exist, compared with 286 in Ontario, and almost 300 girls play on boys' teams, compared with 55 in Ontario.

14   If we really want more opportunities for female athletes, then let's start giving girls more funding, facilities, media coverage, corporate sponsorships, and elite opportunities. And let's stop demeaning female teams with cheap talk about integration. We need not defeat men in head-to-head combat on the playing field to prove we're their equals.

Style and Structure

1.(a) The writer has chosen to begin her essay with her **thesis statement**: "Full integration for all ages and in all sports will mean dramatically reduced opportunities for female athletes." Do you believe this is an effective opener? Explain your answer.

(b) Regardless of whether you like the opener or not, you can experiment with alternatives. Review the suggestions on introductory techniques (pp. 209–214) and choose two different approaches that might work in this instance. Write two new beginning paragraphs on this subject, proposing the same **thesis**.

(c) Which of the three introductory paragraphs you now have do you prefer? Why?

2. (a) Count the number of sentences in each paragraph of this essay. What might you conclude about the variety of paragraph lengths?

(b) Taking the information provided and using appropriate **transitions**, combine paragraphs 4 and 5. Do you feel that the longer paragraph formed this way is more satisfactory? Give reasons to support your decision.

(c) Contrast the paragraph formed in (b) above with some of the writer's shorter paragraphs, such as paragraph 2. What tone do short paragraphs give to the essay?

(d) Review one of your recent essays, looking for short paragraphs. Do you believe that you could now improve the tone by developing the paragraphs further? Choose one and rewrite for fuller development; then compare with your earlier attempt. Which do you prefer?

3. In paragraph 13, the writer presents statistics regarding women's sports in the provinces of Ontario and Quebec. What impression do these statistics make upon the reader? Do they strengthen the writer's case? Why?

4. (a) Point out areas in this essay in which the writer uses different **organizational approaches** to help further her argument. (See pp. 212–213 if you need to review **organizational approaches**.)

(b) Which approaches do you think are most helpful in proving the writer's case? Would you suggest others that might also be effective? If so, which?

5. (a) In her **concluding paragraph**, Rider introduces the pronoun "we." To whom does "we" refer?

(b) How does the use of the pronoun "we" change the tone of the essay? What impressions will the reader likely take away from the essay, in light of this change? Do you believe that the strategy is effective? Explain your answer.

Warm-up

Investigate the difference between primary and secondary research techniques. Divide the class into two groups. The first group will conduct primary research by polling other students and staff outside the class about their attitudes toward government funding in the area of sports.

This will involve meeting together first to compile a list of questions to ask participants. The second group will conduct secondary research by going to the library to find as much current information as possible on what Canadians believe their government should be doing about funding organized sports.

Bring the two groups together for a class discussion of findings and experiences. Investigate such questions as which technique produced more helpful information and which technique was more enjoyable. Try to draw some conclusions about the use and the effectiveness of each of these two techniques.

Thinking and Writing

1.   A poll among readers of the magazine in which this essay was published showed that 60 percent favoured integration of males and females in sports teams, 29 percent opposed, and 11 percent were undecided. Evidently, those favouring numbered more than twice those who opposed.

Write an essay in which you explain why you believe there is such a large proportion of people favouring integration. Give specific examples of social attitudes that you feel might have promoted the response given. You might also cite cases such as that involving Justine Blainey, mentioned in this essay, to support your opinion.

Audience: anyone interested in community team sports.

2.   In her essay, Rider speaks of "cost-slashing governments" (paragraph 12), suggesting that they are looking for ways to reduce the amount of funding they give to sports.

Many people suggest that governments are frequently less than generous when dealing with the needs of sports. On the other hand, there are those who maintain that, particularly in times of economic slowdown, governments have far more important issues to address, and that sports should be the last of their considerations.

Write an essay in which you argue for or against increased government spending in the area of sports. You will probably find information to support your ideas if you look through the pages of the sports section of your local newspaper. Organize the research material you find, using a number of approaches.

Audience: a local member of parliament.

Choose two essays expressing opposing opinions and seek publication for them in the school newspaper.

Crowd Control

by John Colapinto

George "The Animal" Steele and Bam Bam Bigelow hit the spotlit ring, and   1
Marilyn is up out of her seat bellowing. "Tear his eyes out! Rip his ribs out of
his chest! Hey, ref! That wasn't fair! What're you, blind?"

A cashier at a restaurant, Marilyn usually attends wrestling matches with a   2
couple of friends. She's a small-boned woman in her forties with beige hair,
beige glasses, beige slacks, and a beige sweater. She's been a wrestlemaniac
since the age of fifteen, when she attended her first show. Except for karate
(she says her bedroom is wallpapered with Chuck Norris posters), Marilyn's
favourite sport in the whole world is wrestling.

It's a passion she shares with millions of others in 26 countries who have   3
caught wrestling fever. NBC-TV's monthly wrestling show is now a top-rated
program; *Piledriver* (an LP of wrestlers growling pop tunes) went platinum in
1988; sales are brisk for Ricky "The Dragon" Steamboat baseball caps, King
Kong Bundy posters ("Suitable for Framing!"), and even the plastic Hulk
Hogan light-switch cover ("HULKASIZE YOUR ROOM!"). Wrestling may
not be making the cover of *Sports Illustrated* and *Newsweek*, but the sport is
more popular than ever.

The question is, "Why?" Why does Marilyn spend her nonworking hours   4
combing The Sports Network for wrestling updates? Why drop fifteen dollars
on a ticket?

Seen live, without the flash and dazzle of TV editing and the distracting   5
commentary, wrestling seems an unusual sport indeed. A match between two
of wrestling's biggest stars, Greg "The Hammer" Valentine and Jake "The
Snake" Roberts, is little more than a listless, slow-motion tussle in which lum-
bering, sun-lamped men with shaven chests and Spandex bottoms execute
somersaults with the assistance of their "opponent." Jake throws a "punch" that
misses by a yard, yet sends Valentine flying against the ropes. When the now
"enraged" Valentine retaliates, tossing his tormentor out of the ring (onto the
conveniently placed foam mat), the "victim" is seen to give a little *hup* with his
legs to help himself over the ropes. Frequently, it's possible to see the supposed
adversaries communicating with each other to agree on the next move: a knee
drop, a body slam, or that ever-popular but mystifying moment when both
wrestlers, in tandem, trot back and forth across the ring, "bouncing" off the
ropes, narrowly missing one another in the centre until they pretend to collide
and one of them falls down.

6   Wrestling is often compared to the throwing of the Christians to the lions — a communal outlet of violent tendencies. But if it's blood-letting people want, they don't go to wrestling. There's always hockey or, better still, boxing, where the athletes are sometimes killed. Marilyn, for instance, grimaces at the mention of boxing. "Can't stand it," she says, mere minutes after hurling her invective at Jake and Valentine. "Too violent!"

7   It can't be the spectacle that draws the crowds. Occasionally a wrestler will perform an impressive acrobatic leap or fall, but such moments are rare. The wrestlers can't be blamed. They're simply too exhausted to do much except roll around a bit. Billy "Red" Lyons, now retired from the ring, recalls what it was like working the North American wrestling circuit in the 1950s, during the sport's earlier boom. Wrestlers fought five nights a week without benefits or health insurance, and they were paid only for their time in the ring. "It's a tough life," Lyons says. "In some ways it's even worse for the boys today, because they work all over the world. Jet lag. Monday they're in Toronto, Tuesday in Tokyo, Wednesday in Australia." If the travelling doesn't wear them down, injuries do. (Just because the fighting is faked doesn't mean they don't get hurt.) Wrestlers are often performing with torn ligaments, twisted joints, bruised muscles, sprains. Or worse. "I knew guys who'd broken a leg," Lyons says. "They'd get it put in a cast. Then, after a day, they'd cut the cast off, tape up the fracture, and go into the ring. You had to. You only get paid when you fight."

8   Signs of this frantic life are clearly visible in today's top stars. When the "titans" enter the ring, you can see the boredom, fatigue, and pain that makes the skin on their faces sag. They trudge into the spotlight, favouring swollen knees, limping on twisted ankles, growling like very tired and unconvincing bears.

9   And yet. . . . The audience is rapt. A half-hearted knee drop in a bout between two unknowns can raise a more ear-splitting shriek of joy from the crowd than an overtime goal by the home team in hockey. Ask Marilyn why she screams herself hoarse, and she shrugs and smiles. "That's just the way I am. I'm very excitable when it comes to this. You get caught up in it. I know it's fake," she adds cheerfully. "But that's okay. I still love it. I JUST *LOVE* IT!"

10   In 1952, the French philosopher Roland Barthes pondered wrestling and concluded that it is a "sum of spectacles, of which no single one is a function." Possibly — but this isn't much help in explaining wrestling's appeal to fans like Marilyn. Anthropologist Jim Freedman, in his book *Drawing Heat*, offers a class explanation for the sport's popularity. Wrestling often presents a simple drama. A rule-abiding good guy is pitted against an unscrupulous bad guy who has supposedly rigged the contest by bribing the referee, using concealed

weapons, or working in collusion with one or more colleagues outside the ring. The struggle is a metaphor for the real-life injustices and inequities suffered by simple, hard-working folk. Freedman says that wrestling's predominantly blue-collar fans "recognize [in the ring] an economy that's rigged against its basic [free-market] principles of opportunity for everyone, and rigged against them and their jobs in factories and small businesses." But Freedman doesn't explain why people angry about being duped by society will pay fifteen dollars for the privilege of being further duped by the powers that rig wrestling.

Philosophers, academics, and even fans can go only so far in solving the   11
riddle of wrestling. As with everything else about the sport, answers can be arrived at only through the promoters. At 53 years old, Jack Tunney is one of the most successful wrestling impresarios in the world. A bearlike man six feet three inches tall, Tunney likes to show people how far a kid from Toronto's tough east end can go on a high-school diploma. He wears a dark blue business suit with a gold World Wrestling Federation lapel pin, a chunky gold pinkie ring, and a gold bracelet. His salt-and-pepper hair is conservatively cut, except for the hint of Elvis in the curling wave that crests over his forehead.

Tunney has been in the wrestling game for more than 30 years, having appren-   12
ticed with his uncle, Frank Tunney, the legendary promoter who, in the 1930s, was one of the first to recognize the vast potential for profitability in the sport. Together, Frank and Jack built a wrestling empire unparalleled in Canada. In the early 1980s, after his uncle's death, Tunney threw in his lot with the New York–based World Wrestling Federation, and in 1984 was elected its president. Tunney is as vague about his role as WWF president as he is about all aspects of his business. "Well, I'm kind of like the head of the Kiwanis Club," he says, "or the Lions Club . . . I chair meetings . . . and so forth . . . make decisions on the rules. . . ."

Tunney has been a major player in creating the worldwide wrestling boom   13
of this decade. It was the WWF that came up with the highly successful marriage of rock'n'roll and wrestling. (Cyndi Lauper was hired to act as "manager" to a woman wrestler, generating immense publicity.) The WWF has crammed cable-TV airwaves with wrestling extravaganzas. And the WWF has, for better or worse, made Hulk Hogan a household name.

At heart, Jack Tunney is a promoter, and when he's feeling particularly   14
expansive (which, admittedly, isn't often), he can be slyly sardonic about the sharp young MBAs who have invaded wrestling's back rooms with their flow charts and demographics and marketing strategies. "Those are smart guys," Tunney says. "They come up with some real good ideas. But they don't know how to sell tickets."

Tunney does. He has spent 30 years filling arenas with hysterical fans.   15
He's done it, he explains, by giving people exactly what they want. Tunney

actually stands at the exit as the fans file out after a show. He eavesdrops on what they are saying to each other, trying to learn what moments they enjoyed, which wrestlers they liked. "The *fans* choose the favourites," Tunney says. "Give 'em what they want, and they keep coming back."

16 And what *do* they want? "Well," Tunney says, "put it this way. Hulk Hogan won all his matches for four years. Obviously, people weren't coming to see him lose."

17 It has been revealed by renegade wrestlers that promoters not only rig the outcome of each match, they can stage-manage every moment of the struggle. Tunney, of course, denies this, just as he denies any role in engineering the off-stage dramas that run like a soap opera through the wrestling season. "Natural tensions develop between the wrestlers," Tunney explains, patiently. "What we do, as promoters, is *play* on those tensions. By hanging around in a dressing room, you can tell who doesn't like who." For instance, "Ravishing" Rick Rude and Jake "The Snake" Roberts have a running dispute over the overtures "Ravishing" repeatedly makes toward Jake's wife. "Ravishing" often approaches her at ringside in full view of the fans and wriggles his pelvis suggestively. Invariably, Jake, wielding his trademark eight-foot boa constrictor, hurtles himself from backstage and chases "Ravishing" around the ring. Though this scenario is repeated in city after city, Tunney insists it is perfectly spontaneous. "There's very bad blood between those two," he says. "Naturally the fans are looking forward to a big match between them. So, at the appropriate time, we'll schedule one. You give the people what they want."

18 Tunney prides himself on being a keen observer of human nature. "I really make a study," he says. "I can sit in an airport, watch the people, and really enjoy myself. You look at them, size them up, try to guess where they came from, where they're going, what they have at home, what they do." Tunney calls this his hobby ("like stamp collecting"), but it's the same skill he uses as a promoter — probing the buried desires, dreams, and frustrations of total strangers. Not that Tunney and his promoter cronies are always successful in tapping those deep-seated feelings. Sometimes they guess wrong about the way the fans' sympathies will go. He gives the example of the Honky Tonk Man, an Elvis impersonator who was originally conceived as a "baby face" (promoter jargon for good guy). But audiences reacted differently. They turned on him, jeering, booing, and railing against what they took to be an overweening arrogance. "We made a mistake," as Tunney puts it. But he and his fellow WWF officials decided to play on the outrage of the crowd, converting Honky Tonk Man into an arch heel by pitting him against baby faces whom he threatens with his "killer guitar." In this modified incarnation, Honky Tonk Man has become one of the sport's top stars, the fighter a crowd loves to hate. "What you want," Tunney explains, "is some strong reaction — love *or* hate.

Doesn't matter which. The worst thing is *no* reaction. They hate Honky Tonk Man," Tunney adds, permitting himself a rare chuckle. "So they *love* him."

Listening to Jack Tunney, you come to realize that wresting isn't about wrestling at all, or about class anger, or the struggle between good and evil, or even about fakery. It's about the dialogue between promoter and fan. Why don't audiences mind that the outcomes of matches are prearranged and the dramas fabricated? Because they want them to be. Everything is tailored to their own desires, shaped according to the fluctuation of their every mood, all in the interest of bringing them back for more. This accounts for why the crowd doesn't mind the awful tedium of a live show. They yell, scream, jump up and down — because wrestling is about being *heard*. 19

It's the last match of the night, a tag-team duel between the Killer Bees and the team of Bobby "The Weasel" Heenan and Ted "Million Dollar Man" DiBiase. Marilyn is heaping special scorn on "The Weasel," an aptly nicknamed heel who continually interferes with the match from ringside. "Get outta there, &#!*!" Marilyn screams. Turning to her companion, she adds, "He calls us humanoids. But he should look at himself. He's the biggest humanoid of all." 20

To the uninitiated, Marilyn's harangue might seem futile. Busy pretending to fight, "The Weasel" is clearly paying no attention (even if he could hear her voice above the 14 000 others screaming at the same time). But this doesn't bother Marilyn, or shut her up. Like everyone else in the arena, she seems to have an implicit understanding that someone is listening to her, that she's making some kind of difference, that she's affecting events in some way. And, of course, within wrestling's specially constructed universe, she is. 21

Style and Structure

1. Describe, in detail, the intended reader of this essay. Use specific evidence taken from the text to support your description.

2. (a) Marilyn probably said many things at this wrestling match. Why might the author have chosen the specific quotation he uses in paragraph 1? What is the effect of saying she was "bellowing" (as opposed to, say, "yelling" or "shouting")?

 (b) Colapinto presents a detailed description of Marilyn in paragraph 2. Why would he describe her as "small-boned" and repeat the word beige? What is the effect of ending the paragraph with the phrase "Marilyn's favourite sport in the whole world"? What general impression of her does this paragraph convey? Why would the author want to create this impression?

(c) How does paragraph 3 relate to the paragraphs that precede it? How does Colapinto make the **transition**?

(d) The author makes extensive use of parentheses in the first three paragraphs. What effect do you think he is trying to achieve by using them?

(e) What purposes do the first three paragraphs of this essay serve? Are they effective, given their intended reader?

3. What is the function of paragraph 4? What are the benefits of using questions here?

4. Identify the **topic sentences** in paragraphs 5 to 11. How does their relationship to the **thesis statement** contribute to the **unity** and the impact of this essay?

5. What aspect of the thesis does Colapinto explore in paragraphs 11 to 17?

6. (a) In what ways does the opening sentence of paragraph 11 help the reader?

(b) The author devotes two paragraphs to a detailed description of Jack Tunney (paragraphs 11 and 12). How does he avoid having this description distract the reader from his central **thesis**?

7. In spite of the announced **thesis**, more than half the paragraphs in the body of this essay refer to Jack Tunney (paragraphs 11 to 18).

(a) How do these references add to or detract from the **unity** of the essay?

(b) List the ways in which Colapinto uses references to Tunney to develop this part of his **thesis**. For each, explain the benefit he gains from using Tunney.

(c) What methods does he employ to get readers, almost without their realizing it, to accept the fact that using Tunney in these ways is valid?

8. (a) As part of the **conclusion**, paragraph 19 fulfils several functions. What are they?

(b) How does paragraph 19 complement the introduction's presentation of the **thesis**?

(c) What is the effect on the reader of Colapinto's choosing to return to Marilyn in paragraphs 20 and 21? How does he capitalize on her behaviour?

9. Colapinto uses several interesting stylistic devices in his final paragraph to give impact to his ideas.

(a) How does the variation in the length of the sentences help him convey his message to his readers?

(b) What contribution is made by the repetition of "that she's . . ." in the second-to-last sentence?

(c) Normally, it is not a good idea to begin a sentence with "and." Why would Colapinto have chosen to break this rule in his final sentence?

Warm-up

1. Make a brief list of the things a professional wrestler must do (and put up with) according to Colapinto. Discuss with some of your classmates the kind of personality someone would have to have to become successful in this field.

    Write a short character sketch of what a person must be like to become a successful professional wrestler.

    Audience: someone who has not read Colapinto's article.

    Compare your character sketch to those written by the others. Can you see any ideas or techniques you could use as you revise your work?

2. Write a one-paragraph description of a person you know, which subtly makes a point about that person as Colapinto does about Marilyn in paragraph 2.

    Before you begin, jot down a number of your acquaintance's physical features. Then identify some character trait, interest, or behaviour that can be related to a number of these features.

    Audience: someone who has never met the person being described.

    Test the success of your first draft before revising it: give it to two or three people to read. Then ask them questions that will tell you how well they have understood your point.

Thinking and Writing

1. Choose a sport you enjoy watching and write an essay explaining its popularity (or lack of it). Try to outline the underlying reasons rather than falling back on such old excuses as "it's fun," or "it helps people relax." (If you are not a sports fan, choose a popular sport such as hockey, football, or baseball and explain why people would enjoy watching it.)

    Audience: someone who is not a fan of that sport.

2. Sports viewing is so popular in North America that it has spawned multi-billion-dollar businesses. Write an essay in which you explain why so many people in our society watch professional sports.

    Audience: someone who is familiar with sports.

    Send a copy of the final draft of your essay to a sportswriter for one of your local newspapers.

Saying Goodbye

by Stevie Cameron

1   Minutes before the prime minister and his wife left the official residence at Harrington Lake for the last time, their household staff gathered on the drive to say goodbye. It was Monday, June 28, 1993, a hot summer morning, and the maids, the chef, and the butler were hoping for a few days off.

2   Unfortunately their prospects were not good; the new leader would shortly move into the white farmhouse, which would serve as headquarters for the forthcoming election campaign, and the staff had promised to see the new-comer through the summer months. After that, who knew? If the party won again, they'd keep their jobs. If not, chances were they'd be fired, just like the political staff on Parliament Hill, to make way for a new government and its appointees.

3   But the plans for the out-going PM and his wife were set. They were off to the Riviera for the summer while their recently purchased Montreal home was gutted and renovated; after that, he would be rejoining his old Montreal law firm. This morning, the limousine was packed and stood idling in the driveway, ready to take the couple to the airport for the flight to France. When Madame came out of the house, she was in tears. Her husband followed and solicitously handed her into the back seat of the car. Straightening up, he turned to the cluster of grim-faced servants and tried to smile. "We're just a phone call away," he muttered, his eyes not meeting any of theirs, "just a phone call away."

4   No one knew what to say. Finally one young man, who had worked for them since 1989, mustered his courage. "What's the number, Boss?" he asked, a smile twitching at the corners of his mouth. There was no reply. "What's the number?" he asked again.

5   "Uh, just a phone call away . . ." the former PM repeated, his eyes on the ground as he bent and slipped into the back seat beside his wife.

6   The door slammed and the limousine pulled away, followed by the RCMP escort car and watched in silence by the servants. As the car slowly rounded the curve a few hundred feet down the driveway, it suddenly stopped. The staff froze. Maybe they were just having a last look at the house, maybe they'd forgotten something.

7   The tension was too much for one of the maids; she could not stifle a heartfelt shout: "Don't come back!"

8   The car started up again and soon it was just a speck in the distance.

Style and Structure

1. This piece represents a departure from others in this book, since it is the preface to a book rather than an essay published separately. Point out the differences between this piece and traditional essays you have studied.

2. In this narrative the writer captures what she believes to be a defining moment, an instant in which a whole series of events and the personalities involved can be seen in their full significance, if the observer has keen insight and a talent for making relevant details come to life for the reader.

    (a) From your reading of the narrative and your knowledge of recent Canadian history, what events have led to this scenario?

    (b) How does the writer manage to emphasize the tension in this climactic event? Point to words and phrases that convey this impression.

3. Jot down your reaction to the people portrayed in the piece, under the headings "husband," "wife," and "staff." With whom do you think the writer wants you to sympathize? What makes you think so?

4. Discuss the impact of the repeated words, "Just a phone call away."

5. The climax of this short narrative is the maid's heartfelt shout: "Don't come back!" What significance might the writer have seen in this utterance? Why does the writer call it a shout — not "a plea" or "a scream" or "a warning?"

Warm-up

Novelists call them "epiphanies." Educators, "teachable moments." Whatever they are called, we all know those rare but recognizable *ah - hah!* moments when we finally understand the significance of an event or a discovery.

For no one else's viewing but your own, write a list of such moments of discovery you have had in the last five years. You might consider, for instance, the very moment you knew when you were in love — or you knew when it was over — a problem you solved or a mission you resolved to take up. Try to record as much about the moment as you can, including where you were, what people said, what the mood was like.

Thinking and Writing

Essayists who write on historical or political themes often favour moments such as the one Stevie Cameron describes in the beginning of her book, partially because such events speak to our own experiences while at the same time highlighting an instant of high drama. All of us know of such moments in our own lives, and although we seldom stop to record them we never really forget them either.

Research a particular event that falls into one of the following categories. You may consult newspapers or the personalities themselves in private interviews. Find out as much as you can about the people involved and what they said or did that made the moment an event. Then, using Stevie Cameron's example, provide as many details as you can in a descriptive essay to make readers understand the significance of the chosen moment-in-time.

(i) a leave-taking

(ii) an experiment that led to changes in our lives

(iii) a decisive moment in a political or academic career

(iv) a moment when a group of individuals became unified

Audience: a member of the general reading public, who has a casual interest in historical, social, or political events (especially when they are written about in an appealing manner), but who is not a serious scholar.

The Making of a Wasteland

by Mayo Mohs

The fires are elaborate undertakings, choreographed destruction. A virgin
tropical rain forest is too wet under its canopy simply to put to the torch.
Men with axes and chain saws must first fell many of the trees, let them dry
in the sun, and only then set fires that clear thousands of acres at a time.
Afterward, if they are farmers, they plant their crops in the ashes, rich with
the fertilizing chemicals released from the burnt logs. If they are cattlemen,
they may sow a crop of hardy Australian grass to turn it into grazing land.

Yet this wholesale razing of the forest produces only short-live profits.
The ash disappears quickly. Denuded of its protective canopy and deprived
of its fertile carpet of decaying plant life, the thin topsoil typical of much of
the Amazon basin is soon washed away or leached out by tropical down-
pours. Within a few years it can support neither man nor beast. The farmer
and the rancher must cut still deeper into the forest, leaving behind only des-
olate scrub land, or even near-desert.

The Amazon basin is immense. The great river, second only to the Nile
in length, rises in the Peruvian Andes and meanders 6500 kilometres to the
sea, draining some 7 million square kilometres of land through its vast web
of tributaries. About 324 million hectares, 46 percent of the basin, is rain forest — a third of all that remains in the world. Just since the Second World
War, almost half of the rain forest in the tropical belt girdling the earth has
disappeared, lost to logging, farming, ranching, mining, and road building.

Estimates of exactly how much rain forest is being lost or irretrievably
changed range from 8 million to 20 million hectares each year — between
one and two percent of what is left. In the Caribbean, where Columbus first
wrote in awe about the rain forests of Hispaniola, they are all but gone. They
are dwindling fast in West Africa, Southeast Asia, and Central America.
Only in Zaïre and the Amazon is there a chance to save large, unspoiled
tracts.

What is lost is literally irreplaceable. Notwithstanding the cliché, the
jungle does not reclaim its own. Even where healthy second growth arises,
the species it breeds are not the same. A primal tropical rain forest reaches
back through epochs of evolution. Its flora and fauna reflect the drift of continents and the ebb and flow of ice ages. The sheer abundance of plant and
animal species in any rain forest is staggering. In the 1970s, Ghillean
Prance, a tropical botanist at the New York Botanical Garden, counted

235 species of trees in a one-hectare patch of rain forest in the Amazon; a comparable parcel of New England woodland might yield ten. Scientists fear that as the forest disappears, a million species could become extinct by the year 2000 — many of them before they are even found and named, let alone studied seriously. Potential foods, medicines, and valuable products for agriculture and industry may be lost without them, along with a lode of unique genetic material that researchers are just beginning to mine.

6   In the Amazon, one singular species is succumbing to disease and dispossession. The Indians, the aboriginal human inhabitants of the rain forest, numbered as many as nine million in the basin by 1500. By 1900, only one million were left, and now there are only 200 000. More than one hundred tribes have become extinct in this century; others are certain to follow.

7   Because the Amazon rain forest is so vast, its loss would pose other dangers. Scientists estimate that the respiration processes of forest trees and plants return at least half of the rainfall that drops on it to the air, to fall again and again within the same region. As the forest shrinks, the Amazon basin could dry out irreversibly, grow warmer, and shift weather patterns in the United States and Canada, pushing the grain belt northward. The widespread burning of rain forest could also compound the buildup of carbon dioxide in the atmosphere, intensifying the threat of a greenhouse effect that could warm the global climate, melting polar ice caps and raising sea levels dramatically.

8   The Brazilian government is finally beginning to worry about the rain forest's future. Brazilian scientists of the National Institute for Amazonian Studies have joined Americans of the World Wildlife Fund in a twenty-year effort to determine how much rain forest must remain intact in a single piece if its thriving life is to survive. Meanwhile, development continues. A far-flung network of huge hydro-electric projects, together with mammoth new mines, may carve up the forest even more quickly than did earlier schemes.

Style and Structure

1.(a) After reading the essay, write a one-sentence summary of its main **thesis**.

(b) Identify in paragraph 2 the sentence that best captures the theme you have identified.

(c) What is the relationship of the rest of paragraph 2 to this sentence?

2. Since the author states his theme in paragraph 2, why does he preface it with the information contained in paragraph 1?

3. (a) Why does the author choose to include the information contained in paragraphs 3 and 4 at this point in the essay?

   (b) What does the inclusion of the information contained in paragraphs 3 and 4 tell us about the intended reader of this essay?

4. (a) What three consequences of the "wholesale razing of the forest" does the author deal with in paragraphs 5, 6, and 7?

   (b) Why does the author choose to present these consequences in this order?

   (c) What further conclusions about the intended reader of this essay can be made from the information in these paragraphs? How does the author stress the relevance of the destruction of the tropical rain forest to this reader?

   (d) Why in paragraph 5 does the author refer to "a comparable parcel of New England woodland?

5. Identify a number of words and phrases employed by the author that reveal his attitude to the subject.

6. (a) What two approaches to the management of the Brazilian rain forest are contrasted in the concluding paragraph?

   (b) These two approaches could have been presented in a different way. For example, read the last two sentences of paragraph 8, and then read the first two sentences of the paragraph. How does this changed order affect the "message" of the paragraph?

   Given the main **thesis** of the essay, the writer's attitude toward it, and the reaction the author wants to create in the intended reader, which order of presentation makes for more effective conclusion?

Warm-Up

1. The people involved in projects such as those described by Mohs are not inhuman monsters out to destroy the world. Write a one-paragraph character sketch of your idea of a typical Brazilian farmer or rancher who clears these huge tracts of land.

   Audience: a conservationist trying to understand the thinking of Brazilian farmers in order to find ways of persuading them to change.

2. In paragraph 5, Mohs uses a comparison between the rain forest and something with which his intended reader is probably more familiar to help drive home his point. Write a one-paragraph comparison that will help the same reader grasp the significance of the statistics on the natives contained in paragraph 6.

Test the efficiency of your paragraph by having two or three people from outside the class read it. Try to judge from their reactions the extent to which your efforts have been successful. Try another version of the paragraph on one or two more people and compare the results.

Finally, exchange paragraphs with two or three classmates and compare the effects you have achieved.

Thinking and Writing

1. Identify a local project that is now having or will soon have a negative impact upon the environment (e.g., deforestation, conversion of farm land to other uses, the dumping of untreated sewage and/or wastes, or the use of chemical sprays). Write an essay that explains the project and its impact.

    Audience: someone who knows little, if anything, about the project.

2. Write an essay in which you explain the probable motives and attitudes of people who promote, or participate in, projects that have a negative impact upon the environment. Go on to suggest realistic measures that could be taken to convince such people to abandon or modify such projects.

    Audience: someone who may not have thought about the long-term effects of such projects.

    Send a copy of the final draft of your essay to a minister in the provincial or federal government whose department deals with these types of projects.

Do Computers Change How We Think?

Guy Saddy

"Early in the next millennium your right and left cuff links or earrings may   1
communicate with each other by low-orbiting satellites," writes Nicholas
Negroponte in his book *Being Digital*. "Schools will change to become more
like museums and playgrounds for children to assemble ideas and socialize
with other children all over the world. The digital planet will look and feel
like the head of a pin."

Such is the clear promise of the computer age, in the breathless prose of   2
Negroponte, founding director of the Massachusetts Institute of Technology
(MIT) Media Lab in Cambridge and a columnist for *Wired* magazine. Doubt
him, and you risk coming off as a technophobe or Luddite. Yet consider a
more sobering thought from the original information-age guru: "We shape our
tools," wrote Marshall McLuhan in 1964, "and thereafter our tools shape us."

As a tool of human thought and expression, the computer is clearly the
most earth-shaking technology to come down the pike since Gutenberg ushered
in the era of the printed book. As McLuhan recognized, the 15th century event
reshaped human culture. The fact that we could now convey our ideas via the
strict, linear logic of the page made way for a great flowering of logical argument and analytical thought. And that, of course, was the foundation for the
explosion of science and technology that continues to define our lives today.

Is the computer spurring another revolution with the same kind of   3
impact? Though we may not have a clear answer for some time, the question is already of pressing interest to a range of philosophers, psychologists,
and computer specialists. They see various indications that computers are
profoundly changing how we find, consume, and retrieve information; how
we organize and express our thoughts; how we define and solve problems.

The following two stories explore a sample of the most fascinating   4
issues. The common theme is that the computer is reshaping its users in
ways that may ultimately reshape all of us — how we think, how we live,
and who we are.

ARE COMPUTERS CHANGING HOW WE UNDERSTAND?

Sitting on my knee, Dylan expertly glides his computer mouse over its pad,   5
clicking away to direct the action on-screen. The scene before him ends as a

Tyrannosaurus rex moves in to tear huge chunks out of its prey. "Scary," comments Dylan, as he clicks again to exit his virtual world of prehistoric play. Looking up at me for approval, he says, "Good dob!" An understatement, surely, considering Dylan is just 2 years old.

6   Dylan is enjoying a multimedia CD-ROM, the ultimate confluence of sight, sound, and text. He's in the first generation to be raised on such graphic-heavy "edutainment" software. It's an exciting and seductive medium. But there's one problem: when we consume information via multimedia as opposed to reading it as printed text, we use our brains in an entirely different — and potentially dangerous — way.

7   That's the argument of Sherry Dingman, associate professor of psychology at Marist College in Poughkeepsie, New York. Dingman is a biopsychologist who studies brain laterality and its effects on information processing. In assessing multimedia's effect on people, she begins with a truth now widely accepted in neuroscience: the left hemisphere of the brain generally does most of our language processing (both speech and printed word), while the right side processes visual images. Multimedia tends to deliver most of its information in a barrage of visual formatting, with text as an incidental, rather than principal, element. "The kids don't read the text," says Dingman. "It's there at the bottom of the screen, but it's not being read." That means we tend to absorb and process multimedia content using the brain's right hemisphere.

8   The problem, however, is that the brain's right hemisphere does not filter information as critically as the left. "The right hemisphere doesn't do much higher-order linguistic processing," says Dingman. "It maybe understands words at about the level of a 6-year-old child, which means it's not very reflective." Not only does it process information in a holistic way, but it also is inclined to trust the veracity of that information too automatically, she argues. For thousands of years, humans have trusted their visual processing to help them do everything from hunting down dinner to avoiding oncoming chariots. "It's biological bias that we have, to believe what we see."

9   Essentially what this means is that information translated from print form to flashy multimedia will be consumed less critically. "The part of the brain that is able to say, 'Well, I know that's made up,' is over in the left temporal lobe, in the language-[processing] part of the brain," says Dingman. "I don't think the rest of the brain knows the difference [between real and imaginary]."

10   Dingman is greatly concerned about the proliferation of popular graphics-heavy multimedia games for children. Filtering graphic information through the uncritical right hemisphere, a child may grant the same credibility to a picture of

a real object, such as an airplane, as to a fantasy figure, such as a "live" dinosaur. "Kids don't distinguish between what's imaginary and what's not."

While Dingman is only beginning to research her theories, evidence from other studies suggests that neural wiring is quite malleable and open to environmental influences during a person's childhood years. Research done in 1990 at Radford University in Virginia suggests that up to age 21, areas of the brain associated with language abilities continue to develop. "Cognitive experience can. . . produce brain growth and, perhaps, alter the time course of cognitive development further," write study authors William Hudspeth and Karl Pribram. 11

With that in mind, Dingman worries that heavy use of multimedia may be building a generation of kids who are deficient in left-brain skills such as language processing. And that would represent a serious setback for human culture. "Language is the pinnacle of our species' ability to transmit ideas," she says. "We left the stage of thinking in pictures when we left the caves." 12

ARE COMPUTERS CHANGING HOW WE COMMUNICATE?

The icon of the electronic age sits on my desk like a plastic Buddha, imploring me to rub its stomach — or at least pound indelicately upon its keys. Slumped on my couch, I jot down the odd note on a yellow legal pad and collect my thoughts before committing them to paper. But the allure of my Macintosh proves too strong; I abandon pen and paper and opt instead to work on-screen. Does this automatically change how I will think and write? 13

You might assume that a computer word-processing program is merely a handier form of typewriter. Its editing functions, however, allow you to delete or move chunks of text with a few simple keystrokes. Many studies have shown that more editing makes us better writers, says Marv Westrom, coordinator of computing studies in the Faculty of Education at the University of British Columbia (UBC).

A 1990 study by Westrom and one of his graduate students, Richard Pearce, compared two groups of grade seven students: one with one year's experience using keyboards and word processors; the other with a minimum of three years. Study results showed that the more-experienced computer users were doing more editing at deeper levels — not just correcting typos, but working more on word choice and sentence structure. "Students with more word-processing experience exhibit an editing style that is characteristic of better writers," Pearce concluded. 14

Many other studies over the years, however, seem to cloud the issue. A 1988 experiment by researchers at Purdue University in West Lafayette, Indiana, compared the essay-writing styles of high school seniors when 15 using two different sets of tools: pen and paper, and a word-processing program that included text-editing features and helper prompts designed to guide users through various stages of essay writing. The results showed that the essayists on computer tended to write both longer sentences and more words overall — not surprising, since the program includes idea-generating prompts. Yet these longer sentences didn't indicate increased complexity of thought. And while the word-processing program contributed to an increased "maturity" in the essays of certain students, according to two Purdue faculty members who judged the essays, the overall quality of the handwritten essays and word-processed essays was virtually identical. Furthermore, the researchers observed that the students working on computers spent significantly more time at their essay-writing activity (and found that activity more "fun") than did the ones using pen and paper. But again, the increase in effort did not produce an increase in quality of the work produced.

16   Clifford Stoll isn't surprised by these results. He argues that word processing inspires people to write a lot of words quickly, then spend a lot of time editing. "Result: you need not write with any discipline," says Stoll. By contrast, when writing by hand or using a traditional typewriter, you know that making mistakes is costly, and therefore, you spend more time reflecting before you write. "Word processors do not make better writers. They make more writers. Our computers are termites, working against reflection and chewing away at the foundations of human culture."

Style and Structure

1.(a) Reread the first two introductory paragraphs. What do you suppose Negroponte means when he speaks of communicating cuff links or earrings?

(b) Identify any unfamiliar words or expressions in the first two paragraphs and research their meaning. From the writer's choice of words, who might you think his intended audience would be? Keep in mind that this article was originally published in a magazine that deals particularly with science and ecology issues.

(c) Saddy begins his essay with two quotations, one from Negroponte and the other from McLuhan. As a reader, do you consider one of these two sources, as Saddy presents them, to be more intelligible? Explain your response.

(d) Judging from Saddy's choice of quotations, how might you describe his attitude toward the computer and its impact on society's future? Explain.

2.   This essay, which is divided into three parts, originally contained more subsections on questions such as "Are computers changing how we remember?" and "Are computers changing how we solve problems?" How useful do you find the writer's technique of subdividing his essay with these question-titles? What might be the advantages or disadvantages of such a technique?

3.   Saddy introduces the second section of this essay with the image of two-year-old Dylan sitting on his knee and operating a computer. What does this image communicate to readers? Be prepared to offer several suggestions.

4.   To the uninitiated, the workings of the brain are difficult to comprehend. How successfully do you think Saddy manages to explain Dingman's theories on brain laterality and its effects on information processing" (Paragraph 8)?

5.   In the last third of his essay, Saddy discusses the computer's effects on thinking and writing and presents a summary of studies on the issue. Where does he place information on studies that are generally favourable regarding the computer's effects, as opposed to those that are negative? What does this placement suggest about Saddy's general attitude toward computers?

6.   For the portion of his essay on communication, Saddy begins with the image of a computer as a Buddha and ends with computers as termites. Compare the two images and discuss what the combination might suggest to readers.

Warm-up

1.   In the Style and Structure section, you saw how Saddy tailored his introduction to his intended reader. Assume that you are the author of this article and have decided to submit it to a magazine with a different readership. Work with a group of your classmates to create a profile for this new intended readership (perhaps, for example, college students, instructors looking for ideas on how to change their courses, or parents interested in learning how computer literacy will affect their children.)

Write a new introduction that is appropriate to your intended reader.

When finished, exchange your work with others in your group. How have their approaches differed from yours? What suggestions can you as a group make to help improve the effectiveness of the introductions?

Finally, exchange your introduction with one or two people who were writing for different readers. How effectively have they adapted to their readers? What suggestions can you offer that would help them?

2. Re-write a conclusion for this essay, making it appropriate to the intended reader you identified in Exercise 1. Exchange your work with others, to compare and critique as above.

Thinking and Writing

1. Work with the class as a whole to generate a list of 10 or 15 ways that computers are being used in education (e.g., to register students, to record marks, or to do research). Join with two or three of your classmates and, making sure no two groups choose alike, concentrate on the effects **one** of these uses will have. List the positive and negative effects of that use, examining the way work is done **and** how people involved think, feel and behave. Finally, based on your findings in these areas, identify ways that using computers will change the culture of schools.

   Write an essay to explain your findings to your classmates and the people who make decisions about computer use at your school. (Note: If the class intends to develop this theme further, select the best essay from those written by members of your group and present it to the rest of the class. Make notes on other presentations so you be prepared for Exercise 2.)

2. Someone once said technology, in itself, is neither good nor bad; but neither is it neutral. This is a variation on McLuhan's idea, "We shape our tools, and thereafter our tools shape us." Both emphasize Saddy's point that computers can have positive and negative effects.

   Write a cause and effect essay to discuss how using computers is having an impact on the culture of our schools. As you write, try to go beyond the superficial advantages or disadvantages (e.g., "We're lucky we can register from home through our modems.") to look at the more fundamental changes that may result (e.g., "We have no personal involvement with our school.")

   Audience: someone who gives direction to education either at the local or provincial level.

   Send a copy of your essay to the provincial government Minister who directs your educational system.

   Variation: Select some other aspect of technology and analyze the effects it has had on our culture. For example, you might wish to examine how the rapidly-evolving technology of the automobile has affected our sense of mobility or confidence; how microwave ovens have affected home life; or how medical technology has changed our attitudes toward health and longevity.

Writing To Be Read

Many hours of research, writing, and rewriting are frequently wasted simply because the writer has forgotten one cardinal rule of good writing: *Research into your topic must be accompanied by research into your reader.* Put another way, we do not write to communicate with ourselves; we write to communicate with others. Consequently, any insight we can get into the strengths, weaknesses, and prejudices of our readers may well improve the effectiveness of our writing.

The very worst thing a writer can do is to follow the misleading advice that it is somehow dishonest to employ a certain style, vocabulary, and format that you know is preferred by an instructor, on the grounds that it does not reflect your normal style — whatever that is. Surely our conversations reflect our *attention to audience* every day. Imagine some of the problems that would arise if we employed the same vocabulary, jokes, and tone of familiarity that we use with our friends in our conversations with teachers and employers. By all means write what you think you should write, but do not forget that your readers' knowledge of the topic, their preference for certain styles, formats, and vocabulary, and, in some cases, their attitudes must be judged, and the style varied accordingly.

"But how," you may ask, "can I hope to research my reader?" Obviously in some cases you cannot, and in those situations you would be best to adopt the middle road (employ generally accepted styles, formats, and vocabulary). On the other hand, most of your writing, both in school and at work, will be going to the same few people, so you should have little trouble following these three guidelines.

A. Pay careful attention to the instructions that precede the writing assignment.

No one in the business or academic world wants to read poor writing. In the workplace, supervisors generally have time to explain to new employees how they want reports, time sheets, and correspondence written. If you ask, some supervisors will provide you with examples of formats and styles peculiar to their company. They may even be willing to comment on the appropriate technical level of writing for various situations. Certainly instructors are willing to give students detailed information concerning format, documentation, style, and vocabulary requirements. Remember, if you are unclear on any of the above points — ask.

B. Seek the advice of more experienced employees or students.

If no one else is available to discuss your writing with you, you can always seek out a more experienced employee or student for advice. Most of us are genuinely flattered when someone approaches us for advice, and we are frequently more than willing to help.

C. Request an evaluation of your writing.

Evaluations need not be a threat; put them to work for you. In school, we get used to instructors evaluating our written work, but even here keen students can improve their chances for success. Ask the instructor to take ten minutes to go over your work in detail. Go prepared with a set of intelligent questions, not just complaints or pleas for a higher grade. Ask your instructor how the paper could be improved and if there are any elements missing. Supervisors in the workplace are not in the habit of evaluating your written work unless there is an obvious problem, such as poor spelling or incomprehensible sentences. In any case, it is a good idea for junior employees to request a few minutes of a supervisor's time to discuss their first few reports. Again, most people are pleasantly surprised to be asked for advice and will generally comply with any reasonable request.

If you are tempted to sit down and write before carefully considering your audience, please remember the Edsel. The Ford Motor Company spent millions to design, build, and market this luxury automobile, only to see it fail miserably in the marketplace. Eventually, it cost the company several hundred million dollars to learn that they had produced a well-engineered and -constructed automobile for which no appreciable market existed. You can avoid the same mistake for nothing.

Planning Your Written Communication

Whenever you talk to people, you use all kinds of nonverbal devices to clear up for your listener any ambiguities that may arise from imprecise communication. You make gestures with your hands, face, and body, you alter the tone of your voice, you watch for puzzled looks, and so on. If you want proof of just how much we all depend upon such devices to help convey our verbal messages, watch people talking on the telephone: everyone using the phone will still gesture, smile, and use body language as if the person being spoken to were present in the room.

When you turn to written communication, on the other hand, you no longer have such nonverbal devices to rely on, so you can no longer get away with the spontaneous and vague language you use in verbal communication. You must be much more precise in the words you choose, and must therefore give careful consideration to how the material is going to be presented to your reader.

Many people make the mistake of just sitting down and beginning to write. Yet charging ahead in this way is actually the hardest way to write effectively. The writer has to keep too many things in mind at one time, thinking ahead to what will come next, thinking back to what has gone before, trying to find just the right wording for the idea that is being dealt with right now, and making certain that the relationship of all of these words is complete and clear to a reader. In short, the sit-down-and-write technique almost guarantees failure. Once you have tried another approach to the task of writing, you will understand why most people who say they can't write are actually saying they cannot communicate effectively using the sit-down-and-write technique. Unfortunately, since these people are not aware of any other technique for writing, they make the mistake of giving up all hope of ever writing well.

As a matter of fact, there are a few easy steps you can take before you begin to write that will greatly improve the effectiveness of your expository writing. At first they will take a little extra effort, but after you have used them a few times, they will actually speed up the process of writing for you. Think, for example, how often you have had to waste time going back over what you have written to add some point that you left out when you used the sit-down-and-write approach. How often have you later discovered that you wandered away from the main point into some alluring but relatively unimportant side issue? How often have you wasted time putting down far more information than the situation called for? How often have you found that you have ended up putting ideas down in a piecemeal way that actually confused your reader? Thus, although many people who have never used a preliminary planning stage think that it will waste too much time, the steps outlined below will in fact *save* a great deal of time, worry, and confusion, while going a long way toward guaranteeing that your reader will understand your point exactly as you intended it.

Step 1: Decide on your subject and thesis.

In school, you are usually either assigned a specific **subject** or given a choice of predetermined subjects on which you are asked to write. This procedure corresponds far more closely to what will happen to you in the working world than you may think. Your employer may assign a report on a specific subject; a customer may present you with a specific problem to be solved; or your job itself may present a difficulty that can be overcome only by a written explanation to a superior. All these situations provide a subject on which you may write.

Whatever the source of your subject, the best way to proceed is first to define your **thesis** as precisely as possible. For example, jot down at the top of a piece of paper

Subject: office efficiency
Thesis: office efficiency and its positive relationship to
            employee morale

or

Subject: pollution
Thesis: cheaper, more efficient urban mass transit and how it
            will improve air quality in cities

Notice that the thesis reflects your angle, your interest in the broad topic at hand. Your thesis will form the basis of a **thesis statement** when you come to writing the essay (see p. 214).

Remember that at this stage of your planning you may not know all the implications of the problem or all the details of a process, so you may have to modify the thesis as your research proceeds. You may, for instance, define your thesis in the second example above still further by considering only Canadian cities or referring to only one specific type of urban transit. Still, you have a solid starting point.

Be careful not to choose a thesis that is too broad or too narrow for the situation or for the length of the report. Ask yourself: What thesis will reflect the needs of my reader? What thesis fits the context of the problem? If your employer asks for a report on how to improve office efficiency, a thesis such as "The History of Employment Practices and Their Effect Upon the Morale of the New Employee" will be far too general to suit the context — your employer wants a solution, not a history lesson.

In short: (i) determine the *appropriate* subject;
           (ii) determine the *appropriate* thesis.

Step 2: Explore the subject and the thesis.

a. If you are not certain of all the details involved in the subject, do research. Read and make notes on what you read. But remember to write down titles, authors, publishing information, and page numbers for your sources. You will need them later to give credit to your sources and to give authority to your opinion. Also, be sure to write on one side of the page only, to avoid confusion later.

b. Think about your subject and your thesis. Consider how the information that your research has turned up relates to them. Are you going to have to modify your original statements? Are you going off on a tangent with your present line of research?

c. Discuss your subject, your thesis, and your research materials with someone else. In the process of defining the material for this person, you will gain clearer insight into it yourself.

d. Complete your research.

These steps may at first sound as if they are meant to be used only for a major project on a subject that you do not know well. However, they hold just as well for small projects or familiar subjects. Even when you know the subject thoroughly, you need to think over the process, the situation, or whatever it is you are going to explain. What details are really involved? Are there any underlying factors that may not at first be visible? Is your approach too one-sided?

Discuss your ideas with someone else. By talking them over with another person, you will get a clearer concept of what the ideas really entail and the process you need to use in order for someone else to understand them.

Jot down your ideas as they come to you, in point form and at random. Put down everything that has any relationship at all to your subject and thesis. Often such a brainstorming session will bring to light all kinds of interesting insights.

Step 3: Select material from your collected data that is appropriate to your subject and thesis.

When your research has been completed, whether it is a list of random thoughts or a pile of extensive notes taken from outside reading, review the material that you have collected.

For each item or point, ask yourself whether it really does relate to your subject and thesis. If it does not, throw it away or scratch it from your list. If it does, jot down beside it in a word or two exactly how it relates to, explains, or illustrates your subject and thesis.

What you are doing in going through this step is ensuring that your finished product has **unity**.

Step 4: Group related points into clusters.

Go through the items that still remain in your collected research material and look for points that relate to the general subject and thesis in the same way. This should be a relatively simple process because you have already noted in a word or two how each point relates to the main idea.

If you are working from a revised list for a subject that you know well, you may find it easier when you first try this stage of planning to rewrite your list completely so that the clusters of related ideas are physically near each other.

With a little practice, you will soon find that simply writing the same number or letter beside related points will be adequate at this stage for such material.

If you are working with extensive research notes, now is the time to get out the scissors and cut out the various points that you have collected: you can then deal them into piles of related points in the same way that you would sort out the suits of a deck of cards. Remember, however, to note on each scrap of paper where the material came from, or you may find yourself doing a great deal of rereading so that you can give credit to your sources.

Whichever method you use for arranging your points into clusters, make certain that the points in any one grouping do not cover too wide a range of ideas. These clusters are going to form the basis for your paragraphs, and if a paragraph tries to cover too many points, the importance of each will be lost in the crowd. If you find that a cluster is becoming too broad in its range, divide it into two or three important subcategories.

Write a point form summary of the concept that binds each cluster of points together in their relationship to your subject and thesis.

Step 5: Choose an organizational approach that gives your ideas their strongest impact.

At this stage you must decide upon the order in which you are going to present your clusters or paragraphs to your reader. Usually your subject and material will suggest the most logical **organizational approach**. A report concerned with declining office morale might well suggest the chronological or time-sequenced organization. On the other hand, an essay on air pollution and urban mass transit might require a cause-and-effect organization. In addition, an attempt to convince someone to follow your proposed plan of action might call for an organizational structure in which you present your second-weakest argument first, followed by your weakest, and conclude with your strongest point.

There are other approaches that you might take as well. Generally, essays are organized in one of the following methods:

Keep in mind, however, that while most essays follow one overall approach, good writers combine elements of other approaches to give their ideas maximum effectiveness. For example, a writer choosing to discuss the effect of urban mass transit on a city's air quality might well, in order to really

process analysis	shows a sequence of steps or stages taken to produce a result
cause and effect	shows why and how a particular result has been achieved
compare/contrast	shows the similarities and/or differences of two or more ideas, objects, or processes
classification	identifies the categories contained within a topic and sorts data into these categories
argument	presents evidence to support a hypothesis and draws conclusions

(con't)	
example	illustrates a concept by giving one or more examples
narrative	illustrates a concept by telling a story
description	explains or illustrates by providing vivid details
definition	explains the unfamiliar by using a clear and detailed definition

set the scene for the reader, decide to begin with an extensive description of the city before mass transit was introduced. Depending on the projected reader-ship's familiarity with the subject, the writer might also decide that a working definition of urban mass transit is necessary. Both of these approaches are worked into an essay that is primarily organized to investigate cause and effect. Invariably, your purpose in writing and your readership's needs will determine the best approach, or approaches, to use.

The important thing to remember at this point in planning your written work is that this is the stage that is going to "make or break" the impact of your final product. A well-organized work will impress your points upon readers. A work that lacks organization, logical development, and, hence, **coherence** will at best cause readers to question your competence to tell them anything worthwhile; at worst, they will simply stop reading (an unfortunate event in the case of an employer, who may stop reading your work *permanently*).

Step 6: Within each cluster, arrange the points into an order that gives them their greatest effect.

Taking each cluster separately, examine each point you have included. Make certain that they do indeed have a direct relationship to the other ideas within that cluster and, by extension, to the overall thesis of your essay.

In deciding how to arrange these points, always place your binding idea first. This will become your **topic sentence**, setting out the main idea of the paragraph (see p. 217). Next, ask yourself the same questions that you asked when deciding upon the arrangement of the clusters themselves within the overall organization. Each paragraph thus becomes a mini-essay, with a logical, coherent organization to give ideas their most effective presentation.

Step 7: Begin to write.

By going through these stages or "steps" of planning, you will have saved yourself a great deal of anxiety, turmoil, and wasted time. You will have ensured that you stay on the topic when you come to the writing stage and that you present your material in an orderly fashion. You will also have helped to ensure that the rest of your task is easier, because now all you have to worry about is the actual wording of the paper and the creation of an appropriate introductory and concluding paragraph.

The Writing Stage
I. The introductory paragraph

A good opening paragraph, or **introduction**, serves three purposes in getting your message across to your reader: it focusses the reader's attention on your subject; it provides the reader with an idea of the specific stand you wish to take (in other words, your thesis), and it impresses and interests the reader by showing the importance of your subject.

A. Focussing the reader's attention
Many inexperienced writers make the mistake of beginning their written work simply by presenting the data they have gathered without first focussing their reader's attention on the general topic that this data is supposed to present or explore. The result is inevitably disastrous, for the writer has forgotten that although he may know the topic well enough to understand the significance of the data, the reader is probably coming to the topic for the first time. Attempting to read an essay that lacks a clearly defined **thesis statement** is like setting out on a journey without any idea of your destination: it is a frustrating experience that is more likely to arouse anger than provide knowledge.

If you have been following our steps of preliminary planning for your work, the construction of this thesis statement should be relatively easy, because all you really have to do is expand the idea that you jotted down as your thesis. (See Planning Your Written Communication, Step 1, p. 209.)

The placement of your thesis statement, however, is a matter of great concern. Consider the essay that aims to convince supervisors to buy a Merit X-2000 copier. The essay might be written in any one of the following circumstances:

 (i) managers know nothing about the Merit X-2000;

 (ii) managers have been briefed about the Merit X-2000 and are willing to hear arguments about its benefits;

(iii) managers are facing a tight budget and are openly hostile to the idea of a large purchase, unless it is absolutely crucial to the well-being of the firm.

Chances are very good that beginning the essay with the thesis statement "The Merit X-2000 copier would be the best purchase for our company" would not sit well with supervisors in situations (i) and (iii). The question "Who's going to read this, anyway?" is of great importance to the writer facing these situations.

Reader preparation is generally necessary before one introduces the thesis statement: the more likely the reader is to be resistant, the more preparation is necessary. For most situations, you will find it helpful to introduce your subject in the first paragraph, leading up to a thesis statement as the last sentence. The writer facing situation (i) would likely decide to prepare the reader with some information about the Merit X-2000 before setting out a thesis statement.

> On June 12, our printshop copier broke down for the fifth time in six months, causing a backlog of 200 unprocessed orders that sat until repairs could be made. In all, four days were lost before the orders could be sent out. Mike Mackinnon of the printshop suggests that the model presently in use is adequate for general use. It is not, however, capable of meeting the demand from each of six departments on an ongoing basis. A small but efficient copier would do much to keep business at the front desk moving smoothly. <u>My study suggests that the Merit X-2000 would be the most cost-efficient machine for our needs</u>.

Notice that the writer situates the reader, showing what the problem is and why the purchase of a copier is necessary, before actually suggesting which copier to buy. The thesis statement focusses the reader's attention, without giving a nasty surprise.

B. Providing the reader with a general idea of your approach

If an essay is like taking a journey and the thesis statement provides the reader with a map, the next few sentences of the introduction provide an idea of the roads to be taken. This information reveals the organizational approach, enabling the reader to grasp some idea of the scope of your essay before setting out in earnest. For example, the writer of the essay on the Merit X-2000 might continue into the second paragraph in the following manner:

> Compared to the other machines available to us, the Merit X-2000 will give the highest efficiency at the lowest initial, and operating, costs. The capacity of the machine is slightly larger than we need now, but with our proposed expansion next year we will quickly find additional need. Moreover, the service policy of the company would give us cheap and efficient maintenance.

In this way, the writer outlines the direction the rest of the essay will take. The reader will look for a compare/contrast of the Merit X-2000 with other machines on the basis of (a) costs, (b) capacity, and (c) maintenance.

As with the construction of your thesis statement, the construction of this section of your introduction should be relatively easy if you have been following our steps of preliminary planning: all that will be involved now will be the expansion of your organizational approach with the addition of the main points of your paper. Be sure, however, that the sentences that present your approach to your reader have a logical order, preferably an order that reflects in a general way the order in which you are going to present your data in the body of your essay.

C. Capturing the reader's interest

Whenever you are writing in the working world, your subject is most likely to be one that is important to you for one reason or another. If you are going to impress the importance of your subject upon your reader, you are going to have to make certain that your introduction arouses interest. This may not seem an easy or appropriate task in vocational writing, but it can be done fairly easily by the careful wording of the paragraph. Nothing is more boring, for example, than an introduction that begins "The topic that I am going to write about in this paper is. . . ." Although such a sentence may present your idea to the reader, the dryness of the presentation does nothing to encourage the reader to become involved with your ideas on any more than a very superficial level. Simply by providing a more stimulating wording, you can change your reader's attitude from bored perusal to interested exploration of an idea. The earlier example of the copier, for instance, invites the reader to become involved because it speaks to the self-interest of a manager who wants life to be problem-free and profitable. The sense of discovery will capture this reader's interest.

There are of course even more dramatic techniques that you can use, but you must be careful that they are appropriate for the situation for which you are writing. There is nothing wrong, for example, with starting off your introductory paragraph with a provocative quotation, question, statement, or other dramatic device to stimulate your reader's interest. The effectiveness of this technique can be appreciated by an examination of the following opening sentences:

This essay is going to deal with the topic of child beating.

Would you turn your head the other way and try to ignore a neighbour who was beating his child into insensibility? Of course you wouldn't. Yet with the present attitude of our society toward child beating in the community, that is precisely what we are all doing.

The personal involvement called for by the presentation in the second example will arouse far more interest and, it is hoped, action than will that in the first.

On the other hand, you must always be very careful that your attempt to capture interest does not distort the message you want to convey. You must still make certain that the introduction says precisely what you mean. Too often, inexperienced writers fall into the trap of melodrama or exaggeration and render their topic ridiculous rather than important. An opening statement such as "The beauty and symmetry of the Merit X-2000 put it in the ranks of Taj Mahal" would make your report more appropriate for a comedian than for an employer searching for machinery.

II. The body or development section

The **body** of your written communication is the section that carries the burden of your exploration of your topic. By organizing your material into a series of paragraphs that lead logically from your introduction to your conclusion, you are verifying and expanding on your observations in the introduction.

The writing of this section of your paper should be just as simple as the writing of your introduction was if you followed our preliminary planning process. You will have already collected the information that you want to convey and have arranged it in clusters that are going to form the basis of the paragraphs of this section. In fact, if you have followed Step 6 of our planning stage, you have even guaranteed that the writing of each paragraph is reduced to the problem of worrying about using just the right words to capture your exact meaning. Make certain that these words are grouped together in such a way as to make your readers hear your voice in their head, with all of the proper pauses and inflections; that is, make certain that you have used complete sentences and proper punctuation. See the two sections of this book that deal with these topics if you have any doubt at all about your abilities to do either.

III. The parts of the body: the paragraph

Every paragraph in the body or development section of your paper forms a complete unit of ideas that develops, explains, illustrates, or contrasts with one aspect of the thesis that you are presenting. In order to be complete, each paragraph needs a **topic sentence** that focusses your reader's attention on the aspect of the topic to be dealt with in this paragraph; since you have already noted the binding idea of each cluster of points as you went through the planning process and since each of these clusters is going to form the basis of a paragraph in the body of your paper, you simply have to expand this binding idea into a complete sentence to create the topic sentence for each paragraph. In other words, the topic sentence presents a generalized outline of the material to be dealt with in the paragraph.

The sentences that follow the topic sentence develop the aspect of the topic and approach introduced by that sentence. You have already ensured that these sentences will have a unified and logically developed impact upon your reader because you have eliminated unrelated points and arranged the remaining ones in Step 6 of that process. All that remains to be done is the expansion and/or combination of these points into complete sentences. As you write, of course, you can double check to make certain that the arrangement of the points you have chosen earlier is in fact the most effective. Ask yourself, "Do the sentences in this paragraph present the reader with a clear, logical sequence so that the real importance of my ideas is felt and understood?"

You will find **transitions** useful in helping the reader follow the flow of your ideas. Transitions are words or phrases that show the reader the connection between ideas, as illustrated below:

Relationship	Transition
result	therefore, thus, consequently
contrast	however, otherwise, on the other hand
example	for instance, for example, namely
addition	furthermore, moreover, besides
similarity	likewise, similarly
summary	in other words, in short
sequence	then, next, finally

The last sentence of each paragraph rounds the paragraph off by refocussing the reader's attention on the main idea that the other sentences of the paragraph were explaining, illustrating, and so on. Without this **concluding sentence**, you will leave your readers hanging in mid-air. They will either have to try to draw their own conclusions or go on to the next paragraph without really thinking about the importance of the points you have made. In either case, by omitting a concluding sentence, you undermine the impact of your idea.

From these recommendations, it should be quite clear that a one-sentence paragraph rarely does the job. Your reader will expect you to develop your thoughts. The one-sentence paragraph can, however, be used to isolate one idea you want to emphasize. But you do not want to overuse a technique that draws attention. In short, use the single-sentence paragraph sparingly, if at all.

Examine the structure of the preceding paragraph if you want an illustration of a well-designed paragraph: the topic sentence introduces the subject, and the concluding sentence summarizes and drives home the point. The following paragraph, on the other hand, shows effective use of a one-sentence paragraph.

Only when all three components — the topic sentence, body, and concluding sentence — are present in your paragraph will your idea appear complete to your reader.

IV. The concluding paragraph

Just as a paragraph will lose its impact upon the reader if you omit a concluding sentence, so too will the entire work lose much of its impact if you forget to end it with a **concluding paragraph**.

A concluding paragraph may do many things for your essay. For one thing, it may serve to refocus your reader's attention on the thesis by restating your original thesis statement in other words. A mere repetition of what you said in your introduction, however, is not going to do much to show off your ideas. The reader has been following your organized and expanded ideas throughout the essay and is now prepared for a somewhat fuller, more reflective look at the specific aspect of the subject you have chosen.

A conclusion can be used to perform many other duties as well. Many writers prefer to look toward the future, having satisfied themselves and their readers that all aspects of the thesis have been explored throughout the body of the essay. This technique is especially helpful because it shows readers something of the ongoing importance of the subject, while leaving them with something to think about after the essay is finished. As the reader continues the thinking process and remembers the essay, the writer's task is accomplished. No one, after all, wants to write forgettable essays!

The essay writer might use the conclusion to suggest ways of implementing the ideas raised in the essay, even to challenge readers to do so. Whatever the conclusion does, it provides a **clincher**, a sentence that (a) satisfies the reader that the essay is finished and (b) gives the reader something to remember. The conclusion does not, however, raise unrelated issues that will confuse the reader because they cannot be dealt with satisfactorily. A conclusion that leaves the reader on edge may work very well in a murder mystery, but it is highly unsatisfactory in expository prose.

With a little practice you will find that these procedures will become a natural part of your writing and actually speed up the process for you (to say nothing of simplifying the task by breaking it into smaller, more easily managed units). The steps become natural so easily because they really only reflect what your mind is trying to do with any idea when presenting it to a reader: they break the overall topic into its component parts, give these parts a logical order, and then put the parts back together again in a unified whole that is easily understood by your reader.

The first few times that you plan your writing according to our suggested planning stages, make certain you do not take on large topics. Narrower topics will be easier to manage at first and will give you the opportunity to go through the process more often.

Always remember that just going through the motions of planning will not accomplish anything: think the problems through as you go. Nor should you expect planning to remove all of your difficulties the first time that you use it, although it will remove many of the difficulties that you have experienced when using the sit-down-and-write technique. In any case, don't be discouraged: like any other art form, writing needs to be practised.

Finally, you will notice as you read through the essays in this book that the authors use a variety of approaches to constructing introductions, development paragraphs, and conclusions. These examples will no doubt give you a wealth of ideas to draw from, once you have mastered the foundations of expository writing provided in this section. Practise the basics according to the steps outlined above. Then, after you are more confident, explore some of the other formats — perhaps even invent a few of your own.

Fair Usage*

(*Note: This section is inspired especially by our daughter Alison, a student at University of Waterloo, Ontario. Alison is a skilful researcher but she says she has never felt comfortable with the mechanics of quoting her sources.)

"I heard Willis say that he would definitely run for the Student Executive Council." (Willis is indignant, knowing full well that he said no such thing and in fact has far too much work this term to consider taking on extra obligations.)

"I've noticed that eight out of ten women in this residence have long hair. I figure that if each buys a bottle of shampoo and conditioner every two weeks, at an average cost of six dollars plus taxes, that works out to a whopping $2070 going down the drain every month in this residence alone." (Overhearing this statement, Cheryl is furious. For one thing, her friend might have mentioned that Cheryl herself made those observations. For another, she's been misquoted; there are only 120 women in the whole residence and instinctively she knows the figures don't add up. She's annoyed when people bungle the facts.)

In our dealings with people we know, those who live and work with us, we are generally very careful about misquoting or misusing information they pass along. After all, we see them regularly and the consequences of dealing unfairly with them can be very grave. Friendships are broken, jobs are lost, feelings are hurt all round. In contrast, however, writers sometimes deal unfairly with sources of information they *cannot* see, those faceless researchers who publish in journals and reports and newspapers around the world every day. We should be as concerned about using those sources honestly and honorably as we are about quoting our friends and colleagues; otherwise, we can't claim to have a classy style of writing and, at the worst, we can be charged with plagiarism.

One novice writer, who claimed to have taken university courses in writing, attained a certain infamy when she published an article with the *Toronto Star* in which she lifted large passages from a book called *The Freedom Seekers* by Daniel Hill (Stoddart, 1981). Hill, it turned out, read *The Star* and of course recognized his own work. This flagrant example of plagiarism highlighted a serious problem for all editors and publishers, who must rely on the integrity of those who submit work for publication. One editor for *The Star* later noted that in an audience of 2 million, someone is bound to remember the original and complain. When the truth is known apologies and retractions must be made, to everyone's embarrassment. Imagine looking like a jerk to millions of readers!

Educators do not tolerate plagiarism. Every college and university has stern rules prohibiting the practice and severely penalizing anyone found to have submitted work that claims to be original but is not. Students can stay on the right side of academic law by observing the following:

- Find out exactly what constitutes plagiarism in your school and make up your mind to avoid it.
- Prepare assignments well ahead of time. Many plagiarized papers are the result of a last-minute panic, with the writer desperate to have something, almost anything, ready for submission at eight o'clock the next morning.
- Have confidence in your own writing ability. Too many people look at the work of published authors and become immediately convinced they could never write that well. Remember: professors are looking for competent, honest writing, not *The Decline and Fall of the Roman Empire*.
- Learn the value of thorough research, not just of individual creativity. Properly cited sources and a reference section of appropriate length never fail to impress readers. Be proud of the research that you do for

every project, but don't try to pad a bibliography with sources you have not used.

- Read research materials critically to determine their credibility and applicability to what you want to write. Broad-scale quoting betrays the writer's inability to understand, synthesize and evaluate information, all operations that separate students from mere fee-payers.

- Learn etiquette and style. To help you with the mechanics of fair usage, we have provided examples below. Be sure to refer to an accepted style guide such as that of the American Psychological Association or the Modern Language Association; your professor will indicate which method is preferred.

Original	Discreditable Usage	The Problem	Fair Usage
(a) "They're just part of the carnage in the blue-collar ranks as the Canadian economy restructures. While reams of newspaper columns have been devoted to white-collar losses, blue-collar workers have been hit far harder, without as much attention. More than 300,000 jobs were lost in manufacturing alone during the first three years of the decade, and nobody believes those jobs will be regained. " (See Schachter, page 62.)	These workers are part of the carnage in the ranks of blue-collar workers as our economy restructures. We see an abundance of articles on the plight of white-collar workers, but blue-collar workers have been hit far harder. More than 300,000 manufacturing jobs were lost between 1990 and 1993, and experts say they will never be regained.	This writer fails to acknowledge reliance on the information and style borrowed from writer Harvey Schachter. Some manipulation of words does not transform the original but maintains the outlook, the content, and in most cases the very wording Schachter uses. No source is given; no quotation marks are shown.	As Harvey Schachter points out in his article written for *Canadian Business*, the plight of blue-collar workers has received much less attention in the press than that of white-collar workers, in spite of the fact that many jobs in sectors such as manufacturing have been lost, probably forever (May, page 30).
(b) "Two-thirds of workers do manage to find work, either full- or part-time, within a year of being laid off,	Fortunately, according to Harvey Schachter, two-thirds of workers find new jobs within a year of being laid off.	Quoting out of context is the problem here. The writer ignores the fact that Schachter shows the workers' circum-	A study done for *Canadian Business* shows that, according to Statistics Canada two-thirds of workers find work

Original	Discreditable Usage	The Problem	Fair Usage
according to a study by Statistics Canada. But almost 25% of workers simply drop out of the work force. And for those who do manage to find jobs, layoffs and closures often strike again: 10% of laid-off workers in 1978–79 were laid off an average of six times in the following seven years." (See Schachter, p. 64.)		stances may be very different; that is, they find only part-time rather than full-time work. Nothing in the original suggests that Schachter feels the outlook is *fortunate*. The writer further ignores Schachter's reliance on Stats Canada and leaves the reader wondering who Schachter is and why his opinions should be held as creditable.	within a year. The news is not all positive, however: many workers drop out of the work force, replacement jobs may only be part-time, and lay-offs may hit again (Schachter, page 32).
(c) "[Paul Cloutier] is having to deal with an increasing number of formerly middle-class, male blue-collar workers who have been driven down into welfare." . . . "York University's Paul Grayson. . . found they 'tend to be downwardly mobile when displaced. They drift in and out of part-time work. It's a slippery slope, with life precarious occupationally.'". . . "Such desperation in male blue-collar ranks could be the breeding ground for political revenge." (See Schachter, pages 62, 64, and 65.	Schachter describes them as "formerly middle-class, male blue-collar workers driven down into welfare," as being "downwardly mobile" and desperate for "political revenge" (1995, pages 30–34).	Call this technique "cherry picking." Partial quotations are snatched from the breadth of the essay, ignoring both the context and the person who originally spoke or wrote the words used. Taken together they present a misleading view of what Schachter, and his resources, have to say on the issues. Moreover, on again-off again quotations splattered across the page are very annoying to the reader.	There *is* no way to correct cherry picking. It deceives the reader, it's unfair to research sources and it is just plain, bad writing. Don't do it. (Hint: If you want to estimate whether you've used too many quotations and risk annoying the reader, try reading your essay aloud, using the words "And I quote" and "end of quote" for each citation. How annoyed, as a reader, do *you* become?

Proofreading Your Composition

I. Sentence errors

People usually define the sentence by saying that it expresses a complete thought. However, don't "Wow," "Beautiful, man," and "Dumb" express complete thoughts? In one way, of course, such expressions are complete in themselves; indeed, they are often used in creative writing, where their context gives them appropriate significance. Nonetheless, for more formal situations calling for the clear, precise, and complete explanation of an idea to a reader, such expressions are not normally adequate. In short, good expository writing calls for the use of complete sentences, because the structure of sentences demands a clear definition of the ideas being presented to the reader; the sentences require that something (a *subject*) be carefully defined as *being* or *doing* something. A complete sentence, that is, demands a subject and a predicate.

Thus, if you read "The growling dog" you find yourself waiting for more information: What about the growling dog? Did it bite the writer? Did it turn tail and run? The fragment lacks an action (i.e., a verb or predicate) that would give you a complete idea about the dog.

If, on the other hand, you read "The growling dog stood across the body of his fallen master," you have a complete idea of the situation; you have read a sentence.

Although in informal writing occasional sentence fragments are not unacceptable and can be used quite effectively, most people use complete sentences in formal writing. In fact, *talking* in formal situations, such as job interviews, demands complete sentences, so writing them in similar circumstances is usually quite natural. Occasionally, however, you will find that in the effort to put words down on paper, you use incomplete sentences or run several sentences together into one: you must carefully reread everything that you write to make certain that in your haste you have not actually obscured your meaning by presenting your reader with ideas that are incomplete or that have been run together with others.

1. The sentence fragment

> My experience in sales management has taught me a number of important skills over the years. Organizing my time for one thing.

Read the second so-called sentence of the above example again, without rereading the first sentence. Obviously this "sentence" does not really tell the reader anything by itself, for it depends on the first sentence for its meaning. Such partial sentences are called **sentence fragments**.

Sentence fragments are usually created in only three situations:

a. You have isolated words in apposition to the last words in the previous sentence:

> Several machines will fit our present needs. Compton's Model XT-20, the Rainville 300, or the compact Watson 210.

The writer of this fragment tried to stress the number of machines available, but instead created a sentence fragment. The writer should have used the dash, as its purpose is to give dramatic impact (see, p. 250).

b. You have isolated a subordinate clause (used to expand upon the idea of the previous or following sentence):

> Our second production line will be out of service during July. Because of routine maintenance.

Such words as *when, if, since, as,* and *because* alter the meanings of the sections of a sentence that they introduce by making them subordinate, or secondary, in meaning to the main idea of a sentence:

> Our second production line will be out of service during July [main idea] because of routine maintenance [secondary or subordinate idea].

A subordinate idea always needs a main idea to expand upon: "Because of routine maintenance" means nothing by itself.

c. You have isolated verbal phrases containing a verb ending in "ing." Consider, for a moment, the following:

> having been there already
> being an example of professionalism
> doing what should have been done
> after having arrived in Hong Kong

Obviously none of these statements makes any sense: "ing" verbs depend upon other words for their meaning; used alone, as they are in these examples, they are meaningless. Yet how often in our rough drafts do we write such things as the following:

> We must never use verbs ending in "ing" as independent verbs. *The reason being that they depend on other words for their meaning.*

(If you didn't catch the problem with the second "sentence" the first time you read the example, reread it without looking at the first sentence.)

How to recognize sentence fragments

As you have seen in examining the examples given above, you subconsciously know already how to recognize a sentence fragment when you view it in isolation from the sentence that precedes it: it leaves you wanting more information so that you can form a complete idea. The way to recognize sentence fragments in your own revised drafts, then, is to isolate them from the rest of the work.

One approach you can try is to put the work away for a day or two; rereading a paper some time after you originally wrote it makes you more objective (i.e., it tends to place you in the situation of a reader coming upon a work for the first time); you will more easily recognize fragments. Reread your work aloud, making certain that you say what you have actually written. (Keep in mind that all too often we "see" with our minds; that is, we know what we meant to write and this knowledge causes us to think that we read things like complete sentences when indeed we have written only sentence fragments.)

If you still encounter difficulty identifying sentence fragments, there is a second approach that will help you to catch them: read the entire work over, sentence by sentence, *backward*. Almost every sentence fragment depends upon the sentence that precedes it to give meaning to its incomplete idea: hence, when you read your work backward, you encounter the fragment *before* you have read the sentence containing the idea to which it refers. This approach can effectively isolate the fragments and make them far easier to identify.

How to correct sentence fragments

Since the sentence fragment is not independent because it usually depends upon the sentence that precedes or follows it for its meaning, there are two methods for correcting fragments:

(i) Make the fragment independent by adding a subject or a verb; for example, change

> From that time on, he was a perfect citizen. *Doing what should have been done from the beginning.*

to

> From that time on, he was a perfect citizen. He did what should have been done from the beginning.

(ii) Incorporate the fragment into the preceding or following sentence; for example, change

> From that time on, he was a perfect citizen. *Doing what should have been done from the beginning.*

to

From that time on, he was a perfect citizen, doing what should
have been done from the beginning.

2. The comma splice

The **comma splice** is an error that occurs when a writer uses a comma to
replace the period at the end of a sentence. In almost every instance in which
such an error occurs, you will find that the comma has been used to replace a
period between two sentences that are very closely related in their meanings
(the second sentence may illustrate the point made in the first; add additional
information about the point made in the first; or give the effect of a cause that
was outlined in the first). Example:

We aren't that intelligent, our ideas and opinions are seldom our own.

Writers of comma splices try to create a certain effect but unfortunately
fall into a trap. They want to drive home a certain idea and subconsciously
realize that a period will bring the reader to a full stop, destroying the dramatic impact of the second point. Therefore, they mistakenly resort to the
comma. They should use the dash or semicolon instead (see A Short Guide
to Punctuation, p. 243).

How to recognize comma splices

The easiest way to spot comma splices is to listen to yourself carefully as you
read your written work *aloud*. Make certain that you read exactly what is written on the page (the mind has a strange way of fooling the eye into thinking
that it has seen something that it knows should be there but that, in fact, is not).
Most people, when they try to explain something with precision to someone
else, think in sentences; thus, you will find that when you encounter a comma
splice and read it aloud as it is punctuated (i.e., giving only the short pause that
is symbolized by the comma), the passage will not sound right; your mind will
recognize the confusion that the use of the comma can create. You will see the
point being made if you read the following "sentences" aloud:

I knew that I had made a mistake when she slapped my face,
it was all too obvious.
Whenever I came to call, no one seemed to be at home,
maybe they were giving me a hint.
Many recent films have tried to imitate *Star Wars*, not one has
succeeded.

In many cases the identification of comma splices is made much easier by
the fact that they very often occur just before adverbial connectives:

I had no warning about the test, *therefore*, I was not prepared.
A person who owns a small piece of land can save money, *for instance*, one might grow vegetables.

Some other **adverbial connectives** are

hence	however	thus
consequently	henceforth	moreover
nevertheless	otherwise	furthermore
on the other hand	namely	therefore
that is	for example	for instance

N.B.: Do not confuse adverbial connectives with **co-ordinate conjunctions** (*and, or, but, for, nor, so, yet*), which take commas.

I was late for work; *however*, I wasn't put on report.
I was late for work, *but* I was not put on report.

If you still have difficulty recognizing comma splices, you may have to use a special trick, which will take a little extra time, until you become better at finding them. As you proofread your revised draft, every time you encounter a comma reread the part of the sentence that comes before it to see if that part makes sense on its own. If it does, read the part of the sentence that comes after the comma to see if it makes sense on its own. If either part does not make sense on its own (i.e., is *not* a complete idea), the use of the comma is correct. If both parts do make sense on their own, look for the possibility of a comma splice. Examine the following examples:

Stereo-system enthusiasts will enjoy this magazine, it features articles on getting the most from your system. (*comma splice*)

Cutting corners in research is never advisable, but there are some shortcuts that will help you. (*correct*)

The second example shows two complete ideas joined with a comma and a co-ordinating conjunction. When no such conjunction joins complete ideas, as in the first example, a comma splice occurs.

How to correct comma splices

You can correct the comma splice by using any one of the following methods:

(i) Subordinate one of the ideas to the other, that is, one of the sentences to the other, by introducing a subordinate conjunction. For example, change

Environmentalists have become upset recently, there have been a number of serious oil spills. (*comma splice*)

to

Environmentalists have become upset recently because there have been a number of serious oil spills.

(ii) Join the two sentences with a co-ordinating conjunction.

Environmentalists have become upset recently, for there have been a number of serious oil spills.

(iii) Use a semicolon. It is designed to draw the reader's attention to the close connection of the ideas that precede and follow it, and thus gives impact to the second idea without creating a comma splice.

Environmentalists have become upset recently; there have been a number of serious oil spills.

Or, you may choose to vary the emphasis as follows:

There have been a number of serious oil spills lately; environmentalists have become upset.

(iv) A fourth possibility involves the use of the colon. In cases where your second idea amplifies or expands upon the first, you may choose this method of linking your ideas.

Oil spills have become a menace to coastal life: both waterfowl and fish stocks have been threatened.

3. The run-on sentence

The run-on sentence occurs when a writer uses no punctuation at all at the end of a sentence:

Environmentalists have become upset recently there have been a number of serious oil spills.

Actually, the run-on sentence is exactly the same error as the comma splice, except that here even the comma has been left out. The writer is trying to achieve the same effect as with the comma splice (i.e., to point out the connection between the ideas of two sentences by speeding the reader through to the second idea). If you find a run-on sentence in your own work, you should be able to use exactly the same methods outlined in the section on the comma splice to identify and correct it.

II. Agreement

1. Agreement: Subject and verb

The subject and the verb of any sentence must always have the same number (i.e., singular or plural).

Most of the time, we have no difficulty with subject/verb agreement, because our use of the language has so accustomed us to using correct agreement that errors immediately strike us as not sounding right. Few of us would have difficulty recognizing the problem in such sentences as "He go to the store" or "They goes to the store."

Occasionally, in more complex sentences or in constructions that we do not use frequently, we become confused or forget just what word is the subject of the verb, or what the number of the subject really is. The following section outlines the most common instances in which writers make errors in subject/verb agreement and suggests how they can be corrected and avoided.

Common problems of subject/verb agreement in number

Situation	Example of Error	Correct Form
(i) A group of words comes between the subject and the verb, one of which is a noun of a different number than the subject	One of the eggs are rotten. Life with all its trials and tribulations are hard to bear.	*One* of the eggs *is* rotten. *Life* with all its trials and tribulations *is* hard to bear.
(ii) The word *there* begins a sentence. In such expressions as *there is, there are, there was,* and *there were,* the number of the verb (e.g., *is* or *are*) is determined by the number of the noun that *follows* the verb (the real subject).	There is many cases of unnecessary surgery. There was times when I almost gave up.	There *are* many *cases* of unnecesssary surgery. There *were times* when I almost gave up.

Situation	Example of Error	Correct Form
(iii) A collective noun is the subject of the sentence. (Collective nouns are nouns that represent groups of people or things: e.g., *group, herd, crowd, jury, audience, class.*)	The class are late for the examination.	The *class is* late for the examination.
If the group is acting as a unified whole, use a *singular* verb.	The jury agree on the verdict.	The *jury agrees* on the verdict.
If the members of the group represented by the collective noun are not acting as a unified whole, use a *plural* verb.	The crowd disagrees on what to do.	The *crowd disagree* on what to do.
You can avoid the entire problem of awkward-sounding plural verbs in these circumstances by rewording the subject of the sentence.		
Remember: (a) When the members of the group agree, use the singular verb.		
(b) When the members of the group are not unified, *change the*	The herd are going off in all directions.	The *cows* are going off in all directions.

Situation	Example of Error	Correct Form
subject to a plural noun that identifies the members of the group.		The *members* of the herd *are* going off in all directions.
(iv) When the usual order of the sentence is reversed so that the subject follows the verb, make certain that you have the same number for the subject and the verb.	In the doorway was standing two gigantic police officers. What was I to do?	In the doorway *were* standing two gigantic police officers. What was I to do?
(v) Indefinite pronouns such as the following are *always singular* and therefore always have *singular* verbs: *one, each, every- body, no one, nobody, none, someone, somebody, either, neither, anyone, everyone.*		*Neither* of the men *is* able to do the job. *Someone* representing the colleges *is* to blame. *None* of the topics *is* interesting. *Each has* its proper place. *One* of the women who won the lottery *is* my aunt.
(vi) Two separate subjects of the same verb, joined by *and*, form a *plural* subject; they require a plural verb. An exception to the rule in situation (vi)		*My brother and I are* going to travel this summer. *Halifax and Quebec City have* citadels.

Situation	Example of Error	Correct Form
occurs in the following situations:		
(a) If the subjects joined by *and* refer to the same person, place, or thing, they take a singular verb		*My old comrade and close friend has* insisted that I stay with him and his wife. (*Comrade* and *friend* in this sentence refer to the same individual.)
(b) If the subjects joined by *and* are commonly considered to be singular (e.g., rock and roll, ham and eggs, Browning and Bowles Ltd.), they take a singular verb.		*Browning and Bowles is* the most prestigious insurance firm in Saskatoon.
(c) Although subjects joined by *and* generally take plural verbs, singular subjects linked by such expressions as *in the company of, assisted by,* or *as well as* always take singular verbs.		*My cousin,* assisted by a friend, *has* opened a used book store. (The real subject of this sentence, *cousin,* is singular and requires the singular form of the verb, *has.*)
(vii) Two subjects of the same verb, when joined by a *both... and* construction, always form a plural subject; they require a plural verb.		*Both* my father *and* I *are* going.

Situation	Example of Error	Correct Form
(viii) Two subjects of the same verb, when joined by *either... or*, *neither... nor*, or *not only... but also*, may take either a singular or a plural verb: if the subject *closer* to the verb is singular, use a singular verb.		Neither mother nor *Aunt Helen* is able to go.
		Neither the children nor *Aunt Helen is* able to go. (Note that even though *children* is plural, *Aunt Helen*, which is singular, is closer to the verb; therefore, the verb is singular.)
If the subject closer to the verb is plural, use a plural verb.		Either the instructor or the *answers* in the book *are* wrong. (Note that even though *the instructor* is singular, *answers*, which is a plural subject, is closer to the verb; therefore, the verb is plural.)
Remember: When in doubt, or when you get caught up in an awkward, confusing situation, take the easy way out: reword the sentence so that *either* comes before one subject *and* its verb, and *or* comes before the		Either *the textbooks are* wrong, or the *instructor is*.

Situation	Example of Error	Correct Form
second subject and another verb.		
(ix) *Who, which, that* (relative pronouns). When these words introduce a subordinate clause *and* act as the subject of the verb in that clause (e.g., "the man who was coming to dinner"), they always refer to a specific word used earlier in the sentence (e.g., in our example, to "man") and take their number from that word. Thus, if the word referred to is singular, use a singular verb after *who, which,* or *that*; if the word referred to is plural, use a plural verb.		The *stories* that *are* told about him are all lies. The *story* that *is* being told about him is a lie. The *person* who *is* telling the story is a liar. The *people* who *are* telling the story are liars. One of the *men* who *were* imprisoned was my uncle. (In this case, *who* refers to *men*, not to *one*; therefore, the verb directly following *who* is plural. The verb for *one* comes later in the sentence and is singular: *was*)

2. Agreement: Pronouns and antecedents

A pronoun always agrees in number (i.e., singular or plural) with the noun to which it refers.

The *men* said *they* were tired.

Most of the time, you will have no difficulty with pronoun/antecedent agreement, but there are four situations that might cause you confusion:

Situation	Example of Error	Correct Form
(i) Collective nouns (*crowd, jury, pack, group*, etc.) are considered singular if all the members of the collection are acting as a unified whole.	After the jury deliberated for six weeks, they reached a verdict.	After the *jury* deliberated for six weeks, *it* reached a verdict.
(ii) Collective nouns are considered *plural* if the members of the collection are *not* acting as a unified whole.	The jury still disagreed on whether it should ask for advice.	The *jury* still disagreed on whether *they* should ask for advice.
(iii) Indefinite pronouns (*one, each, everyone, either, neither*, etc.) are *always* singular.	Everyone did as they were told.	*Everyone* did as *he* or *she* was told. (But see Inclusive language, p. 241.)
(iv) Make certain that you know to which word the pronoun refers.	Neither of the boys knew what they wanted to do. (The word to which the pronoun refers is not *boys* but *neither*.)	*Neither* of the boys knew what *he* wanted to do.

3. Agreement: Possessive pronouns (my, your, his, her, its, our, their)

Just as a pronoun takes its number from the noun that it replaces, so too does the possessive pronoun.

Usually a writer has little difficulty in recognizing the appropriate number of the pronoun to use; we do it almost every time we speak:

> Where is Hilda's hat? It's with *her* coat.
> Here come the kids. Do they have *their* coats on?

A problem normally occurs only in the same four situations that we have encountered when discussing pronoun agreement:

Situation	Example of Error	Correct Form
(i) Collective nouns (*crowd, group, jury*, etc.) are considered singular if all the members of the collection are acting in a unified way.	The flock was sleeping quietly in their fold as the wolf crept closer.	The *flock* was sleeping quietly in *its* fold as the wolf crept closer.
(ii) Collective nouns are considered *plural* when the members of the collection are *not* acting in a unified manner.	The flock ran off in all directions as the wolf attacked its fold.	The *flock* ran off in all directions as the wolf attacked *their fold.*
(iii) Indefinite pronouns (*one, someone, somebody, everybody, each, either*, etc.) are *always* singular.	Each of the men did their homework.	*Each* of the men did *his* homework.
(iv) Make certain that in a complex sentence you know exactly to which word the pronoun refers.		Ms. Evans is one of those *instructors* who never forget *their* students' names. (Here, *who* refers to *instructors*, not to *Ms. Evans*.)

III. Pronoun reference

Pronouns are used to substitute for, or take the place of, nouns. Using them frees us from the boring and unwieldy repetition of nouns. Without pronouns, we would have to write the following, for example:

> Kathleen is a doctor. Kathleen lives in London, Ontario. Many patients feel that Kathleen is the best doctor that these patients have ever had.

Since we can use pronouns to substitute for specific nouns, however, we can avoid the rigidity and childishness that using them brings:

> Kathleen is a doctor *who* lives in London, Ontario. Many patients feel that *she* is the best doctor *they* have ever had.

When using pronouns, be careful to observe the following two rules:

(a) There must be a specific noun to which that pronoun refers.

(b) There must be only one noun to which the pronoun could possibly refer.

Look at the confusion that the lack of a specific noun to refer to causes in the following sentences:

> My uncle, an old college friend, and Dr. Peter Smith came for a visit yesterday. *He* is from Montreal.

This sentence causes confusion by not clearly defining which person the pronoun *he* refers to. In this case, the pronoun in the second sentence would have to be changed to a specific noun: e.g., "*Dr. Smith* is from Montreal."

> *They* don't know what they're doing in Ottawa.

To whom does the pronoun *they* refer: the cabinet? the civil service? members of Parliament? the Ottawa tourists? The sentence would have to be changed to replace the first *they* with a specific noun: e.g., "*Our members of Parliament* don't know what they're doing in Ottawa."

> Runaway inflation, increasing unemployment, and a mounting trade deficit are three major problems our country faces. *This* often causes people to turn to dictators.

The failure to have one specific noun to which the pronoun *this* refers causes the reader confusion. To convey a clear meaning, the second sentence would have to be changed — to read, for example, "*Such economic difficulties* often cause people to turn to dictators."

IV. Modifiers

Modifiers (i.e., words or groups of words that describe other words) attach themselves to the appropriate word closest to them in a sentence. Thus, unless you are very careful in placing modifiers, they may describe the wrong word and cause your reader to misunderstand your meaning, become confused, or end up laughing at what you intended to be a serious point.

Note how the change in the positioning of the following modifiers changes the meaning of the sentences:

He handed the book to the customer with the leather binding. [*This would be a rather strange-looking customer.*]

He handed the book with the leather binding to the customer.

She took a loaf of bread from the refrigerator that Aunt Bessie had made. [*Aunt Bessie, we must suppose, had a job in a factory that made refrigerators.*]

She took a loaf of bread that Aunt Bessie had made from the refrigerator.

I only asked for one ticket. [*I didn't demand, plead, or do anything other than ask.*]

I asked for only one ticket.

He lived in the house built by his great-grandfather for ten years. [*Great-grandfather either didn't want to take up permanent residence or was a very slow worker.*]

He lived for ten years in the house built by his great-grandfather.

Walking down the street, a courthouse came into view. [*An advance in bionics has apparently been made; courthouses are walking now.*]

Walking down the street, I saw a courthouse.

Such problems arise from the fact that *we* know precisely what we mean when we write the sentence, but we forget that *others* will not know what we mean unless we put our modifiers in exactly the right place. We know that Aunt Bessie never worked in a factory, so it doesn't occur to us that someone else could think that she did. We're just trying to get down on the paper that Aunt Bessie makes her own bread; doesn't everybody know that she does? The answer, of course, is no — not unless *you tell them.*

Make your modifiers say what you mean by placing them with the word that you want them to modify.

If modifiers are a problem in your writing, the easiest way to spot misplaced modifiers is either (a) to read your own work aloud, preferably a day or so after you wrote it, or (b) to have someone else read it aloud for you while you read to yourself over his or her shoulder. By putting yourself in the role of a stranger coming to the work for the first time, you will recognize the confusion or the change of meaning that results from "misplaced" modifiers.

Remember: Always ask yourself as you write and reread your work, "What will my reader take this passage to mean?"

V. Verb-tense consistency

Whenever you write, you must make certain that you always present the reader with one consistent point in time (that is, verb tense) from which to view your material. In the following example, the writer mistakenly presents two points of time (one present, one past):

> In *The Edible Woman*, Marion *intends* to marry Peter until she *discovers* he *is* trying to dominate her. When she *realized* what he *was* doing, she *refused* to marry him.

In the first sentence, the writer views the book as existing in the present tense, and thus presents the action taking place in the book as occurring right now. Confusion arises when the second sentence shifts to the past tense, perhaps because the writer read the book some time in the past or because the author wrote in the past tense. This writer should have determined in advance which point of time (verb tense) would be used throughout the essay.

Not all cases of changes in verb tense are as obvious as the example above.

> How many times have you had to hit the brakes because other drivers decide they want to gawk at a roadside emergency?

The immediacy of the situation has caused the writer to switch tenses. Nevertheless, the change strikes the reader as awkward and disturbing, and detracts from the importance of the argument. To take the reader through a complete and unified experience, the writer should correct the sentence to read as follows:

How many times have you had to hit the brakes because other drivers have decided they want to gawk at a roadside emergency?

VI. Inclusive language

What is inclusive language? Not surprisingly, inclusive language is the opposite of exclusive language, which is language that excludes women by emphasizing gender bias or stereotypes. Gender bias exists in our language for several reasons, but three are particularly obvious:

1. In the English language, there is no neutral pronoun for a nonspecified person or being. Therefore, "Everyone has driven *his* car to work this morning" is technically correct, even though "everyone" may include a number of women.

2. Traditional sayings have preserved many phrases that suggest gender bias. A writer may refer to a "gentleman's agreement," for instance, thus implying that only men make honourable contracts. Similarly, the reference to an "old wives' tale" may reflect an attitude that women have little else to occupy them than the spinning of incredible stories.

3. Some writers, wishing to show women in active roles in society, mistakenly give an undue emphasis to gender. Few women like to be referred to as "lady lawyers" or "janitresses"; most prefer simply "lawyers" or "caretakers."

The overriding concern of every writer should be *"Who's going to read this anyway?"* Is your reader likely to take offence at your choice of words, thereby missing the meaning of your entire message?

Manuals, textbooks, and similar materials are being rewritten using inclusive language because of the changes in our social attitudes toward gender. The following techniques will provide you with a handy guide to making your writing inclusive.

1. Substitute articles for pronouns.
   Not Everyone is expected to bring *his* own materials.
   But Everyone is expected to bring *the* necessary materials.

2. Combine sentences to avoid pronouns.
   Not The technician is responsible for supervising the process. He will arrange weekly meetings to assign tasks.
   But The technician is responsible for supervising the process, and will arrange weekly meetings to assign tasks.

3. Repeat nouns.

   Not The manager will be required to make frequent out-of-town trips. He will also make a full report upon return.

   But The manager will be required to make frequent out-of-town trips. The manager will also make a full report upon return.

4. Use plurals.

   Not Every student will prepare his own summary.

   But Students will prepare their own (individual) summary.

5. Use the passive voice.

   Not The manual provides the reader with a suitable background, and the instructor will give him more detailed information.

   But The manual provides the reader with a suitable background. More detailed information will be given by the instructor.

6. Avoid traditional expressions that preserve gender bias.

   Not in layman's terms
   But in easily understood language

   Not a weak sister
   But the weakest element

   Not mankind
   But all people

7. Avoid gender identifiers in professional titles.

   Not clergymen
   But the clergy

   Not policeman, police woman
   But police officer

   Not chairman
   But chairperson, the chair

Finally, try to avoid "he/she" except in isolated instances. For one thing, the expression is difficult to read out loud. Also, and more importantly, one must maintain consistency in the use of the pronouns throughout a paragraph, and the repetition of this awkward combination adds little grace to one's writing style. For example, consider the following paragraph:

There is a great deal the average student can do to preserve good relations with instructors. For one thing, he/she can simply attend classes. Furthermore, he/she can prepare questions to ask about his/her favourite element in the course, understanding that a teacher is kindly disposed to someone who shares an interest in the subject. Finally, he/she can remember to show simple signs of civility — a friendly "good morning" or "hi!" can do wonders.

A Short Guide to Punctuation

Many people are confused by punctuation because they mistakenly think they are dealing with some abstract, unknowable set of rules. In fact, nothing could be further from the truth.

Whenever you use punctuation in your written communication, all you are doing is trying to convey to your reader the structure of your meaning — which, when speaking, you supply by pauses, inflections, tone of voice, and so on. If you were talking to someone, the differences between the two following sentences would be immediately understood by your listener:

> John [pause] is the cause of the problem here [rise in voice to indicate a question]

and

> John is the cause of the problem here [no pauses, no change of tone]

When you are writing to someone, on the other hand, you use punctuation marks to make your meaning clear to your reader: if you intend the first meaning, you substitute a comma for the pause following "John" and a question mark for the rise in your voice at the end of the sentence; you do not use these punctuation marks if you intend the second meaning.

> John, is the cause of the problem here?
> John is the cause of the problem here.

Therefore, when you try to decide what punctuation to use in a passage, you are only thinking about how to represent on the page what you do all the time when you speak. For the most part, successful use of punctuation simply means conveying your meaning accurately by paying attention to how you would say the passage aloud, and translating that emphasis into a symbol.

In the following section, we summarize how each punctuation mark symbolizes a pause or an inflection. Refer to this guide if you encounter any situation in which you are in doubt about the correct punctuation symbol to use.

I. The comma (,)

The comma represents the short pauses that are used in speech to give emphasis or to maintain the clarity of an idea within the sentence.

There are basically eight situations in which you would pause in such a way when speaking and, hence, for which you should use the comma when writing.

1. In lists

When you speak, you pause between the *words* (or *groups of words*) in a *list* (or *series*):

> I went out to buy *margarine* [pause] *tobacco* [pause] and *coffee*.
> What walks *on four legs in the morning* [pause] *on two legs at noon* [pause] and *on three legs in the evening?*
> I believe *that he worked hard* [pause] *that he played hard* [pause] and *that he lived a good life.*

When you write the same sentence, you insert commas to represent these pauses:

> I went out to buy *margarine, tobacco,* and *coffee.*
> What walks *on four legs in the morning, on two legs at noon,* and *on three legs in the evening?*
> I believe *that he worked hard, that he played hard,* and *that he lived a good life.*

RULE #1: Insert commas between the words (or groups of words) in a list (or series).

2. Between adjectives in a series

When you use only one adjective to modify a noun, you do not pause between them when you speak; therefore, you should not use a comma when you write:

> the faithful friend

However, when two (or more) adjectives in a series describe the same noun, you naturally pause between the adjectives:

the faithful [pause] kind friend

When you write, this pause must be represented by a comma:

the faithful, kind friend

In the above example, the adjectives in the series modify the same noun, "friend," independently. In other words, they do not depend on or change each other's meaning. Thus, you could reverse the order of the adjectives without destroying the meaning of the passage:

the kind, faithful friend

If you encounter a situation in which reversing the order of the modifiers destroys the meaning of the passage, do *not* use commas between the modifiers; for example,

the very faithful friend

cannot be reversed to the "faithful very friend." In this case, "very" is modifying "faithful, not "friend." Therefore, you should not insert a comma between "very" and "faithful."

RULE #2: Insert commas between adjectives in a series when they (independently) modify the same noun.

3. Before the co-ordinating conjunctions *and, but, for, or, nor, so,* or *yet*

Whenever you orally connect two main ideas by using *and*, *but*, *for*, *or*, *nor*, *so*, or *yet*, you pause before you say this connecting word to draw attention to the transition between the two ideas. You should normally insert a comma to symbolize this pause when you write:

The thin woman ate her dinner, *and* the fat man ate his heart out.
He ended his speech, *for* he found that his audience had left.
She needed an ace, *but* she drew a two.

Do *not* use a comma before any of these connecting words when the subject of the second main idea is omitted because it is the same as the subject of the first:

She needed an ace *but* drew a two.

RULE #3: Insert a comma before the words *and, but, for, or, nor, so,* and *yet* when they join two main ideas that have separate subjects (i.e., when they act as co-ordinating conjunctions).

4. To set off nonessential information in a sentence

If you add information to a sentence that is not essential for your listener to understand the main idea of the sentence, you invariably pause before and after that added information. Commas are inserted when such passages are written to symbolize these pauses.

4A. Apposition

If a word or expression is placed beside another to give more information about that other word or expression, and if both have the same grammatical construction (e.g., both are nouns), the added word or expression is said to be *in apposition* to the other. Since words or expressions used in apposition do not add information essential to the understanding of the sentence, they are set off with pauses in speech, and with commas in writing:

> *A post-secondary institution*, the college deals with mature students.

> The college, *a post-secondary institution*, deals with mature students.

> Joanne found herself going to college, *a post-secondary institution*.

RULE #4A: Use commas to set off words or expressions used in apposition.

4B. Nonessential phrases and clauses

Clauses

If you use clauses beginning with *who*, *whom*, *which*, or *that* (i.e., relative clauses) to add information that is descriptive but not essential to your audience's understanding of the main idea of a sentence, represent the oral pauses with commas that set off the clause:

> Arlene, who won the hundred-yard dash, is my best friend.

Although the information in the *who* clause adds an interesting detail, it is not essential to the main idea of the sentence "Arlene is my best friend." Note how you would normally pause before "who" and after "dash" if you were saying this sentence to someone.

Consider, on the other hand, the following sentence:

> The athlete who won the hundred-yard dash is my best friend.

The *who* clause has become essential to the basic meaning of the main idea, because the athlete is not named or given any other form of identification; without the information in the *who* clause, the audience has no way of knowing which specific athlete is referred to. Note that if you were saying this sentence aloud, you would not pause before "who" or after "dash."

Phrases
The same rule applies to verbal phrases. When the phrase contains nonessential information, commas are used to set it off from the rest of the sentence (as pauses would if you were speaking):

> John, wearing a silly grin, wiped the cream pie from his face.

If the information contained in the phrase is essential to the main idea of the sentence, commas are *not* used (just as you would not pause when speaking):

> The boy wearing the red cap is my cousin.

RULE #4B: If a verbal phrase or a relative clause is vital to answering the question "which one or ones," then it is essential to the meaning of the sentence and does not require commas to set it off.

If a verbal phrase or a relative clause is not vital to answering the question "which one or ones," then it is nonessential and should be set off from the rest of the sentence by commas.

5. Interrupters
If you interrupt the natural flow of a sentence by inserting a word, phrase, or clause, you pause when you are speaking to set off or give emphasis to the interruption. In writing, this pause is represented by a comma. The interrupter can occur almost anywhere in the sentence and can take many forms, including a personal name. Notice how the interrupter (in italics) is set off by commas from the rest of the sentence in the following examples:

> I decided, *therefore*, to go.
> Charles, *no matter how much he tried*, simply could not pass a driver's test.
> Both partners in a marriage, *not just the wife*, should be responsible for doing housework.
> *No*, I refuse to get involved with that kind of nonsense.
> *Martha*, I have loved you madly all of my life.

RULE #5: Use commas to set off interrupters from the rest of the sentence.

6. To avoid confusion
If you listen carefully when you speak to someone, you will find that you make brief pauses in your speech simply to prevent your listener from confusing your meaning. Note, for example, how the pause alters the meaning in the following sentences:

> Have it ready for April Nelson.
> Have it ready for April [pause] Nelson.

These pauses are represented by commas whenever they are necessary to avoid confusion for your reader.

> Call me Gary when you arrive.
> Call me, Gary, when you arrive.

RULE #6: Use commas when necessary to avoid misunderstanding.

7. To set off dates and places

You use commas to symbolize the pauses that you normally make between the elements of dates and places.

> On October 13, 1812, the Americans attacked Queenston Heights, Ontario.
> I moved to 197 Clarence St., Brantford, Ontario, on April 12, 1979.

RULE #7: Use commas to set off dates and places.

8. After long introductory phrases and subordinate clauses

In speaking, whenever you begin a sentence with a subordinate clause ("If...," "When...," "After...," etc.), you pause at the end of that introductory element to allow your listeners to digest its meaning before you go on to the main idea of the sentence: for example,

> If you are going to be late [pause] please call to let us know.

When the introductory element is long, such a pause is particularly important because it prevents your listeners from becoming confused. It also allows them time to think about the meaning of the idea contained in the introductory element and to prepare to apply it to the idea coming next in the main clause of the sentence: for example,

> When you find that you have a large number of assignments
> due at the same time and only a few days to do them all
> (pause) you must be highly organized in your approach.

When you are writing, you should use a comma after such introductory clauses or phrases to take the place of these oral pauses (as has been done in this explanation). When you do, you help your reader to understand the meaning of both parts of the sentence.

As soon as you arrive, call us to let us know that you are safe.

Because my car would not start, I missed my first class.

Since I did not have enough money to buy my textbooks, I fell far behind the rest of the class.

Until a few years ago, greenhouse gardening was considered a rich person's hobby.

In the absence of a better alternative, we decided to return home.

RULE #8: Use a comma after an introductory element.

Note: Everyday speech patterns occasionally suggest commas where none should be placed. The most noticeable example of this error occurs when the subject of a sentence is separated from its logical completion. For example, a comma should not appear in this sentence: *The student who spends six hours a night on homework or studying is probably not using time wisely.* In spite of the long subject (everything that precedes *is*), no comma should be placed before the verb. Subjects and verbs logically belong together. Except when an interrupter is added, they should not be separated.

II. The dash (—)

Just as the comma is used to show a reader where we would pause in a sentence if we were speaking, so too is the dash. As long as you avoid excessive use of dashes, they can add variety to your punctuation.

You might at first think that such duplication is unnecessary, but the dash is used whenever we want to add a little extra dramatic effect to the pause:

I dashed forward to knock the gun from his hand — but I was too late.

History provides us with one overwhelming lesson — the silliness of the human race.

When you suddenly change the direction of the thought of a sentence, you might want to reflect the drama of that change by using a dash:

My father was a man of infinite kindness — but he died the cruelest of deaths.

You might want to replace the commas with dashes in order to give extra emphasis to explanatory phrases, words in apposition, and so on:

That young man — his own son — struck the old man.

You might also want to use the dash to give emphasis to the final words of a sentence when they sum up the preceding ideas:

> The backpack came complete with cooking equipment, sleeping bag, cook stove, and nylon tent — a complete outfit.

Most important, do not use commas to mark off an interrupter that forms a complete thought. Use a pair of dashes in such cases:

> Old Mark Hennessey — I'd almost forgotten him — turned up at the office yesterday.

III. The semicolon (;)

When you have two complete sentences that are closely connected in meaning, you can stress this connection by using the semicolon to replace the period:

> The perfect spot was down by the river; I knew that from the time I was a child.
> He's not a bad dog; he's got a mean temper, though.

Whenever a semicolon is used in such situations, it is only reflecting the type of pauses that are made in oral communication; someone speaking tries to draw the listener's attention to the connection between the ideas of the sentences by pausing slightly longer than for a comma but not as long as for a period. As a matter of fact, it is the misinterpretation of this shortened pause between two sentences that causes people to write comma splices and run-on sentences.

One of the most common difficulties that inexperienced writers encounter is the omission of the semicolon before transitional words other than conjunctions. You should be careful to use the semicolon between two complete sentences (main clauses), when the second sentence begins with one of the following adverbial connectives:

indeed	consequently	then
instead	henceforth	likewise
thus	furthermore	for instance
hence	nevertheless	that is
however	otherwise	for example
moreover	therefore	

Note that a comma is used to reflect the pause after such transitional words, except the very short ones ("then," "thus"):

> I was late; therefore, I had to do without breakfast.
> I know just how you feel; however, I still cannot agree.
> I did not have my car rust-proofed when I bought it; conse-
> quently, the car is now worthless.

Be careful *not* to use a semicolon in front of any of the adverbials listed above when they act as interrupters in the middle of a sentence (main clause):

> I know, however, just how you feel.

IV. The colon (:)

Although the colon does not reflect a unique type of oral pause, it is not diffi-cult to use because its purposes are so specialized.

1. To introduce a long list

If your list is relatively short and simple, try to incorporate it into your sentence and avoid the use of the colon:

> My greatest pleasures are a quiet lake, a snow-capped moun-
> tain, and the smell of pine trees.

If, on the other hand, your list is long and detailed, you should introduce it with a *complete sentence* and a colon:

> There are ten first-class dining rooms in Vancouver: . . . .
> My father would not allow me to have a motorcycle for the
> following reasons: . . . .
> Avoid situations such as the following: losing your passport,
> having your pocket picked, or missing your train.

But note that there is no colon when you *end* the introduction with *such as*:

> Avoid situations such as losing your passport, having your
> pocket picked, or missing your train.

2. To introduce a long quotation

If the quotation is relatively short, try to incorporate it into your sentence:

> "From each according to his ability, to each according to his
> need" was the basic doctrine of Marx and his followers.

If, on the other hand, the quotation is longer than one sentence, you should introduce it with a complete sentence and a colon:

In her book *Roughing It in the Bush*, Susanna Moodie described in unrestrained prose her joy on first seeing Quebec City: "Canadians, rejoice in your beautiful city! Rejoice and be worthy of her — for few, very few, of the sons of men can point to such a spot as Quebec...."

V. The question mark (?)

The question mark is used to convey to your reader the inflection (the rise in your voice) that you can use orally when you ask a direct question:

Are you going to the pub?

Remember that a quotation that contains a direct question is read with the same inflection as was used by the speaker quoted. Thus, we use a question mark within the quotation marks:

Marlene asked, "Are you going to the pub?"

However, when a sentence contains an *indirect question*, you do *not* raise your voice and hence do *not* use the question mark.

Marlene asked if I was going to the pub.

VI. The exclamation mark (!)

An exclamation mark is used only to point out to the reader the emphasis you would place on a statement that expresses surprise, shock, or some other sudden emotion. Be careful not to overuse it.

Get out of the way!

VII. Quotation marks (" ")

Quotation marks are another instance of punctuation marks that do not reflect a distinct pause or other change in your speech patterns. Once again, however, the very specialized function of quotation marks makes their correct use relatively easy.

1. Direct quotations

Use quotation marks to enclose the exact words that someone has spoken or written:

The old-timer asked, "Who was that masked man?"

"Who," the old-timer asked, "was that masked man?"

Do *not* use quotation marks around *indirect* quotations.

The old-timer asked who the masked man was.

2. Extended quotations

If the passage that you are quoting is longer than *five* lines, you should use a completely different technique to show your reader that you are giving an exact quotation. For the entire passage quoted, indent approximately 15 cm from the left and right margins, single-space the entire passage, and *do not* use quotation marks.

The following article, printed on July 1, 1867, illustrates the enthusiasm of the founders of our nation:

> Upon the occasion of the birth of this great nation, stretching from sea to sea, from the temperate climes of the South to the frigid climes of the Arctic waste. . . .

3. The position of other punctuation when used with quotation marks

(i) Place periods and commas *inside* quotation marks:

"Come here," he shouted.

The reply came back, "Never."

(ii) Place colons and semicolons after the closing quotation mark.

The police officer shouted, "Hands up"; however, the burglar fled.

(iii) When you use question marks and exclamation points with quotation marks, observe the following rules:

(a) If the question or exclamation is found *only* within the quotation, the question or exclamation mark goes *inside* the quotation marks.

"Why are you so late?" John demanded.

Mary replied, "What's it to you?"

(b) If the question or exclamation takes in the entire sentence, the question or exclamation mark goes *outside* the quotation marks.

Did John say, "I am leaving for Saskatoon tomorrow"?

VIII. Punctuation of titles

1. Whenever you refer to the titles of any of the following, use quotation marks around the title:

    (a) a chapter of a book (e.g., "The Advance of Democracy" in *A History of the Modern World*);

    (b) an article from a newspaper or magazine (e.g., "Motherhood Alone: A Choice and a Struggle" in *The Globe and Mail*);

    (c) an entry from an encyclopedia (e.g., "Shakespeare" in *Encyclopedia Britannica*);

    (d) a single episode from a TV series or a single song from a record album (e.g., "Arrival" from the TV series *The Prisoner*);

    (e) the title of a short story or a poem (e.g., "Daffodils" from *The Norton Anthology*).

2. Whenever you refer to the titles of longer works, such as books, plays, films, newspapers, magazines, and encyclopedias, *underline the title* to indicate that it would be italicized in print, as in the examples above.

IX. The apostrophe (')

1. To denote possession

The concept of possession often presents difficulties for inexperienced writers, because the apostrophe itself is not heard when we speak. In fact, the failure to use the apostrophe for possession is perhaps the most common error in writing.

The concept of possession itself, however, is not difficult to learn, and, with a little practice in identifying specific examples of possession in your work, you should be able to avoid misusing or omitting the apostrophe.

"Possession" simply means that you are showing that one thing belongs to another (e.g., "John's hat" means "the hat belonging to John").

You should not have too much difficulty with the idea of possession when it applies to a person owning something (e.g., John's hat), but the problem becomes a little more difficult when you approach the idea that things and abstract ideas can "possess" characteristics or other things:

> The colour of (or belonging to) a rock is the *rock's colour*.
> The troubles of (or belonging to) life are life's *troubles*.

You may have to be careful not to go to the other extreme of placing an apostrophe after all words that end in *s*. If you are in doubt, apply the "belonging to" test:

Reverse the order of the words (e.g., from "The country's borders" to "The borders — the country") and insert the words
"belonging to" between them (e.g., "The borders belonging to
the country").

If the meaning of the words remains the same, you know that you have a
case of possession and should use the apostrophe.

The rules by which you determine the position of the apostrophe in the
possessing word are the following:

(i) If the "possessing word" ends in any letter other than *s*, add *'s*:

John*'s* hat
the hors*e's* stall
wome*n's* coats
the ma*n's* shirts

(Note that both singular and plural words ending in a letter other than *s*
take an added *'s*).

(ii) If the possessing word is plural and ends in *s*, add only the apostrophe:

horses' stalls
dogs' lives

(iii) If the possessing word ends in *s* or an *s*-sound, pronunciation is the key
to forming the possessive:

the class*'s* opinion
Joyce*'s* new car
Mr. Jone*s'* address
Jesu*s'* followers

(iv) If two or more people (or things) possess the same thing, only the last
noun is given the apostrophe:

Fred and Joan's car [they jointly own the car]

(v) If two or more people (or things) possess two of the same things, both
receive apostrophes (and note that "car" becomes plural).

Fred's and Joan's cars

2. In contractions

When one or more letters are left out of a word, the apostrophe replaces the
omitted letter or letters.

Don't [Do not] do that.
Let's [Let us] go.
I couldn't [could not] do that.
I'll [I shall] go.

A word of warning is in order. Sometimes people confuse contracted words with possessive pronouns. *Remember:*

You're [You are] doing well.
but
Your coat has been stolen.

It's [It is] not too late.
but
Its fur was matted.

They're [They are] coming over later.
but
Their jobs were boring.

Who's [Who is] coming to dinner?
but
Whose lipstick is on your collar?

3. Plural forms of letters, figures, and signs

Styles of writing change over time. It was once fashionable to write plurals of letters or figures with an apostrophe.

Watch your P's and Q's.
All of the 6's and 12's go in this column.

However, the more modern style is to simplify writing by doing away with any punctuation that can be omitted without causing confusion. No confusion arises if the examples given are simplified.

Watch your Ps and Qs.
All of the 6s and 12s go in this column.

If there is any possibility of confusion, however, the apostrophe must be used.

SIN's are recorded next to the surnames.
I hadn't considered the expense of c.o.d.'s.

Commonly Confused Words

There are a number of words that are often mistakenly interchanged or confused by people when they speak and write. Sometimes the mistake can bring a ridiculous meaning to the sentence that completely destroys the seriousness of the message that the writer intended the reader to receive.

"They found his body in the middle of the dessert" brings up an image in the reader's mind of a hulking detective found dead in a giant bowl of jello — a good scene from a Woody Allen movie, perhaps, but definitely not the tragic *desert* scene that the writer intended to depict.

The following section is intended to give you a quick reference to check the most commonly confused words whenever you have the slightest doubt about whether you have used the right word or not.

It is a good idea to read this entire section over a few times even if you have no doubts. All too often, people assume that they know the correct word or the correct form of a word when in fact they have been making an error for years.

ACCEPT — EXCEPT

ACCEPT — means to receive something or to agree with something:

> I accepted the certificate from the Dean.
> I accept that concept.

EXCEPT — means "other than" or "but":

> Everyone except Joan had to rewrite the test.

ACCESS — EXCESS

ACCESS — means "coming toward" or "a way to approach something," or "permission to approach something":

> I had access to the library.
> The only access to the mansion was through a guarded gate.

EXCESS — means "an extreme," "too much":

> His head felt like a race course for the Austrian cavalry because he had drunk to excess the night before.
> We have had an excess of rain during the last month.

ALSO

"Also" is not confused with any other word, but it is commonly overused and abused. It is always best to try to find another word to replace "also."

AFFECT — EFFECT

AFFECT — means to cause change or to influence something:

> Smoking affects your breathing.

EFFECT — as a *verb*, means to result in or to produce a result:

> The prime minister was unable to effect his legislation.

> — as a *noun*, means the result of something:

> Troubled breathing is the effect of excessive smoking.

Note: "Effect" is most commonly used as a noun. Except in a few obsolete or technical cases, "affect" is *not* used as a noun.

ALREADY — ALL READY

ALREADY — means "previously":

> We were already there.

ALL READY — means that everyone or everything is prepared to do something:

> We were all ready to go.
> I was all ready to go.

AMONG — BETWEEN

AMONG — means to be in the midst of more than two things, or to divide something for more than two people:

> The five of you will have to decide among yourselves.

BETWEEN — means to be located or to happen so as to separate two things; or to divide something for two people:

> I was caught between the devil and the deep blue sea.
> I divided the last of the wine between my girlfriend and her brother.

AMOUNT — NUMBER

AMOUNT — means the quantity of something:

> The amount of snow that fell last night was incredible.

NUMBER — means a collection of persons or things:

> A number of people came to our house on Christmas Eve.

Note: Errors usually occur in the use of these words when a writer confuses a collection (i.e., a group of people or things) with a quantity, and puts down, for example, "The amount of people who favour abortion is changing."

The correct wording recognizes that the people involved are individuals gathered into a collection, not a lump of undifferentiated flesh: "The number of people. "

ARE — OUR

ARE — is a form of the verb "to be":

We are going to the store.

OUR — is the possessive form of the pronoun "we":

Our house burned down.

The confusion of these two words results from the pronunciation of "our" in some Canadian dialects. If you are in any doubt about whether you have made the error when you reread your paper, see whether you can reword the phrase to read " belonging to us"; if you can, use "our."

A WHILE — A LOT

No one confuses these expressions, but they certainly are overused. Both are colloquial phrases and are not appropriate in many formal situations in expository writing. *Avoid* them if at all possible.

CAN — MAY

CAN — means "to be able":

A cheetah can run at 130 km per hour.

MAY — means "to have permission":

May I go to the washroom? (The only time you should ask, "Can I go to the washroom?" is after being treated by a doctor for bowel problems.)

CHOICE — CHOOSE — CHOSE

CHOICE — is a *noun* that means "selection," or "choosing," or "option":

What choice did I have?

CHOOSE — is a verb that means "to select." The "oo" is pronounced the same as the "oo" in "tool":

Choose the right tool for the job.

CHOSE — is a verb, the *past* tense of the verb to choose. The "o" in "chose" is pronounced the same way as the "o" in "elope":

They chose to elope.

COARSE — COURSE

COARSE — means "rough":

This sweater is made of coarse wool.

COURSE — means a plan of action or direction:

No course will guarantee you a passing grade.
The golf course is a good place to meet people.

DESERT — DESSERT

DESERT — as a *noun*, means "a place where there is little rainfall":

Cacti grow in the desert.

DESERT — as a *verb*, means "to abandon":

He deserted his family.

DESSERT — refers to those delicious, fattening goodies at the end of a meal:

No more dessert for me, thanks. I'm obese already.

DEVICE — DEVISE

DEVICE — (the "-ice" is pronounced the same as the frozen substance, ice) as a *noun*, means "a tool, a scheme, an invention," etc:

That device will never fly, Orville.

Devise — (the "-ise" is pronounced the same as the "-ies" in "lies") means "to invent, to plot, to contrive":

You had better devise some good lies to account for the pies.

EMIGRATE — IMMIGRATE

EMIGRATE — means "to leave" a country:

He emigrated from Canada to avoid paying his taxes.

IMMIGRATE — means "to come" to a country:

He immigrated to Canada to find a better life.

EMINENT — IMMINENT — EMANATE

EMINENT — means "important, distinguished":

> She is an eminent lawyer.

IMMINENT — means "about to happen":

> From the darkness of the clouds we knew a storm was imminent.

EMANATE — means "to originate from, to come from a source":

> Light emanates from the sun.

FEWER — LESS

FEWER — is used to refer to a collection of things that can be counted:

> Fewer people watch the late movie than watch *The National*.

LESS — is used to refer to the amount of a material or thing:

> Less time was lost when a stoplight replaced the stop sign.

Remember: Fewer people ski when there is less snow than usual.

I — ME

I — is the subjective form of the first person pronoun:

> When I forgot the punchline, I became the joke.

ME — is the objective form of the first person pronoun:

> When he hit me with the pie, the joke was on me.

ITS — IT'S

ITS — is the possessive form of the pronoun *it*.

Remember: none of the personal possessive pronouns (*my, your, his, her, our, their*) uses an apostrophe; therefore, *its* is no exception:

> Its tail drooped between its legs.

IT'S — is the contracted form of "it is":

> It's about time for supper, isn't it?

Remember: Only if you can substitute "it is" should you use an apostrophe.

KNOW — NO

KNOW — means "to be aware of":

I know how to do trigonometry.

No — means "not in any way":

"No, no," she cried, "you must not give up."

LATER — LATTER

LATER — means "subsequently." The *a* in later is pronounced the same way as the *a* in "play:"

Stephanie can come out to play later.

LATTER — means "the last-mentioned thing of two things mentioned." The *a* sound of latter is pronounced the same way as the *a* sound in "ladder."

John and Bert helped us elope. The latter brought the ladder.

LAY — LIE

LAY — in the *present* tense, means "to put something somewhere":

Lay the book on the table.

LIE — means to assume a horizontal position, as opposed to placing something else in a horizontal position:

Lie down, please; it's time to go to sleep.

The problem: the past tense of the verb "to lie" is "lay":

John lay in bed thinking, "Shall I just lie here and hope that I laid the book on the table?"

Remember: You lie down each night.
You lay something down on a table.
You lay in bed last night.
You laid your coat down yesterday.
(There is no such word as "layed.")

LESS — LEAST

LESS — the comparative form of "little," it means "not so large," etc. "Less" is often used with adjectives and adverbs to create a "negative" comparative:

likely . . . less likely
beautiful . . . less beautiful
sure . . . less sure

LEAST — the superlative form of "little," it means "smallest in size, quantity," etc. "Least" is often used with adjectives and adverbs to create a kind of "negative superlative":

certain . . . least certain
costly . . . least costly

Do not make the mistake of thinking that adding an "-er" or "-est" suffix to the end of a word accompanied by "less" or "least" adds emphasis: it simply reduces your phrase to nonsense. *Never* write such things as "least likeliest" or "less fiercer."

LETS — LET'S

LETS — means "allows":

She always lets him go early.

LET'S — is the contracted form of "let us":

Let's go to the show.

Remember: Only if you can substitute "let us" should you use the apostrophe.

LIKE — AS — AS IF — AS THOUGH

LIKE — usually a preposition introducing a prepositional phrase, which *never* contains an independent verb; normally compares *things* or *people*:

I wish I were like him.
He was out like a light.

AS — usually a conjunction introducing a subordinate clause (containing a subject and a verb); normally compares *states* or *actions*:

I cook as my mother does.

not

I cook like my mother does.

Note: If you are unsure whether to use "like" or "as," look for a following verb. If there is one — or if one is *understood* — use "as."

In the following sentence, the final verb, *has*, is understood: *I'd be very happy to have the same salary as Joan.* Thus, *as* is correct. This would not be the case if no verb was understood, as seen in this sentence: *I'd be happy to have a salary like Joan's.*

You will often find that when your first impulse was to use "like" as a conjunction, the words you really wanted were "as if" or "as though."

He lay there as if he were dead.

LOOSE — LOSE — LOSS

LOOSE — (the *s* is pronounced in the same way as the *s* in "moose") as an adjective, means "not tight," and as a verb, means "to untie":

> Who let the moose loose?
> Is the skin of a moose loose?

LOSE — (the *s* is pronounced in the same way as the *s* in "blues") means "to mislay":

> I just can't lose the February blues.

LOSS — (rhymes with "toss") means "something lost":

> The loss of the toss meant the end of the game.

The confusion between these words simply results from not knowing which spelling goes with which sounds: remember one and you have them all.

MORE — MOST — -ER — -EST

MORE — is the comparative form of "much"; it means "greater in quantity or quality":

> I have had more to drink than I should.
> More haste makes more waste.

"More" is often used together with an adjective or adverb to create a "comparative" form for that word:

> likely . . . more likely
> certain . . . more certain

MOST — is the superlative form of much; it means "greatest in quantity or quality":

> I love you most of all.
> She had the most money of all of us.

"Most" is often used together with an adjective or an adverb to create a "superlative" form for that word:

> certain . . . most certain
> quickly . . . most quickly

-ER — is a suffix added to the end of many adjectives and adverbs to create the comparative forms of those words:

> great . . . greater
> large . . . larger
> late . . . later

-EST — is a suffix added to the end of many adjectives and adverbs to create the superlative forms of those words:

> sure . . . surest
> full . . . fullest
> late . . . latest

People are often confused over which of these alternatives to use when they want to create comparatives and superlatives, but there is a relatively simple guideline to use that regularly works: *If the word that you want to make into a comparative or superlative form has* three or more *syllables, use* more *or* most:

> su-per-cil-i-ous . . . most supercilious
> ri-dic-u-lous . . . most ridiculous

(Any dictionary will give you the number of syllables in a word by breaking the word into its component syllables as we have done here.)

Never use both "-er" or "-est" and "more" or "most" with the same word: never write "most fiercest," "more faster," etc.

PASSED — PAST

PASSED — is the past tense of the verb "to pass"; it means "went by":

> We passed the bus.

PAST — means that something happened earlier:

> That's all in the past, now.

PERSECUTE — PROSECUTE

PERSECUTE — means "to oppress, to harass, to cause someone trouble":

> Hitler persecuted the Jews.

PROSECUTE — means "to put on trial, to try to prove charges against someone in court":

> Trespassers will be prosecuted.
> Of course, you could always try to persecute trespassers, but you would probably be prosecuted for doing so.

PERSONAL — PERSONNEL

PERSONAL — means "private":

> These are my personal belongings.

PERSONNEL — means "the staff that works for a firm, college," etc.:

> The personnel in the store are a pain.
> The personnel office is upstairs.

PRACTISE — PRACTICE

PRACTISE — is the *verb*, and means "to do, to do repeatedly in order to learn a skill," etc.:

> He must have practised in order to do so well.

PRACTICE — is the *noun*, and means "a custom, a repetition of a skill in order to learn it well," etc.:

> It is a good practice to check all buttons and zippers.
> Make it a practice not to practise your drums after midnight.

PRINCIPAL — PRINCIPLE

PRINCIPAL — as an *adjective*, means "the most important":

> The principal cause of lung cancer is smoking.

PRINCIPAL — as a *noun*, means "the person in charge of a school":

> The principal is your pal.

PRINCIPLE — is used only as a *noun*; it means "fundamental truth or rule of conduct":

> This is the main principle behind our action: all people are created equal.

STATIONARY — STATIONERY

STATIONARY — means "standing still":

> The bus remained stationary.

STATIONERY — means "paper for writing":

> Good stationery makes writing easier.

THEIR — THERE — THEY'RE

THEIR — is the possessive form of "they":

> They forgot their heir when they left their money to charity.

THERE — is an adverb, used in such constructions as "here and there," "over there," and "there are "

THEY'RE — is the contracted form of "they are..."

TO — TOO — TWO
TO — is used as a preposition: "to the store," "to town," etc.
    — is part of an infinitive: "to go," "to run," "to fall," etc.
TOO — is an adverb. It means (1) "likewise or also" and (2) "more than enough":

    I, too, had had too much to drink.

TWO — is a number:

    I'll take two minutes.

WERE — WE'RE — WHERE
WERE — is the plural form of the past tense of the verb "to be":

    We were later than we thought.

WE'RE — is the contracted form of "we are":

    We're in hot water now.

WHERE — is used to ask about the location of someone or something:

    Where on earth are you dragging me now, Rover?

Make certain that you know where to use "were" and where to use "we're" (know which spelling goes with which sound).

WEATHER — WHETHER
WEATHER — refers to the state of the atmosphere:

    We have been having rainy weather lately.

WHETHER — is used in such constructions as "Whether you're ready or not, I'm going."
Note: the word *wether* does exist, but it means "a castrated ram."

WHO — WHOM
WHO — is the subjective form of the pronoun:

    Who is coming to the party?

WHOM — is the objective form of the pronoun:

    Whom do you prefer?

WHO'S — WHOSE

Who's — is the contracted form of "who is":

> Who's going to Pub night?

Whose — is the possessive form of the pronoun "who":

> Whose hat is this?

Remember: None of the possessive forms of pronouns uses an apostrophe: *my, your, his, her, its, our, their,* and *whose.*

WORSE — WORST

Worse — is used to compare two possibilities:

> His condition is worse than it was yesterday.

Worst — is used to consider more than two options:

> Of all those lazy bums, he is the worst.

YOUR — YOU'RE

Your — is the possessive form of "you":

> Here's your hat; what's your hurry?

You're — is the contracted form of "you are":

> You're the cream in my coffee.

Spelling

One spelling mistake can mean your letter of application finds its way into the garbage. One spelling mistake can mean your boss doubts the validity of your whole report. One spelling mistake can make you the laughing stock in a customer complaints department. If you are working in law enforcement, one spelling mistake can mean your case is thrown out of court.

So what can you do to make sure such problems do not creep into your work?

You could find a book of spelling rules and try to memorize them. But there are hundreds of spelling rules. And there are even more exceptions to each of them!

You could ask one or two people to check your finished work for spelling. And take the chance they are better spellers than you! (Besides, they may not be there when you are working on that one absolutely crucial document.)

You could hire a good copy editor. But they are expensive.

Many people have come to depend on the spell checkers included in word processors. But they cannot tell the difference between "accept" and "except" or "it's" and "its": if the spell checker finds a word in its dictionary that matches the one you typed, it assumes you meant to use that word.

To make matters even worse, most errors in spelling occur in situations not covered by the rules. Sometimes the way you pronounce a word causes you to misspell it (e.g. "could of" instead of "could have" or "prejudist" for "prejudiced"). Other times you find, to your great embarassment, that you have simply been using an incorrect spelling for years.

Thus when it comes to spelling there is no alternative: you have to use a dictionary — frequently, painstakingly, and thoroughly.

But there are some skills you can develop that make the process a little easier:

1. Save one last reading of your work to do nothing other than check for spelling. Don't waste too much time checking for spelling during the earlier drafts.

2. Read each word separately and make sure your eye scans the whole word. Most spelling mistakes occur in the last part of the word because people quit looking at the individual letters after they recognise what the word is.

    One technique used by professionals is to cover the entire page except for the line you are working on. Advance word by word, line by line. Some even run a pencil under each word, letter by letter, to help them concentrate on the job.

3. Don't let yourself be side-tracked into reading for the meaning of a phrase, sentence or paragraph. When you do, your mind stops looking at the ends of words. If you find you are reading for meaning, stop; go back to the last word you remember looking at individually for its spelling.

4. Never assume that a word is spelled the way it sounds.

5. Pay special attention to words that have prefixes (as "<u>mis</u>spell") or suffixes (such as "edit<u>ed</u>").

6. Watch out for words that come from other languages (like "omnibus," "minuscule," "kindergarten," "karioke," or "manoeuvre").

7. Be careful with the spelling of place names ("St. Cath<u>a</u>rines," "St. John's," and so on).

8. If you have the <u>slightest</u> doubt about a word, check it in the dictionary.

9. When you do look up a word in the dictionary, be sure to read the definition accompanying it: make sure you have the right word ("accept," not "except," or "busing," not "bussing," for example).

10. Be patient. Thorough proofreading takes time.

Index

Reader Reply Card

We are interested in your reaction to *Class Act: Readings for Canadian Writers* by Gary Webb and Donna Kerrigan. You can help us to improve this text in future editions by completing this questionnaire.

1. What was your reason for using this book?

   ❑ university course ❑ college course ❑ continuing-education course
   ❑ personal interest ❑ professional ❑ other (please specify)

2. If you are a student, please identify your school and the course in which you used this book.

   _____

3. Which chapters or parts of this book did you use? Which did you omit?

   _____

4. What did you like best about this book? What did you like least?

   _____

5. Please identify any topics you think should be added to future editions.

   _____

6. Please add any comments or suggestions.

   _____

7. Please give your reaction to the usefulness of the reading exercises listed by title and author in order of their appearance in the text, rating each essay from 1 (liked least) to 5 (liked best).

Title/Author	Rating	Didn't Use	Title/Author	Rating	Didn't Use
Monster Threatening... (Suzuki)	____	____	Is Plea-Bargaining...? (Adler)	____	____
Roller Coaster... (Sandell)	____	____	There's a Trickster... (Taylor)	____	____
Crime Rate's Down... (Carey)	____	____	How Jane* is... (Klein)	____	____
Baby, It's Yours (Hunter)	____	____	Teen Runaways... (Weagant)	____	____
Repeat... (Rabkin)	____	____	Turning Down... (Roseman)	____	____
How Dumbed...? (Gordon)	____	____	Peace at Any Price... (Byfield)	____	____
An Alternative... (Heaton et al.)	____	____	Fashionable Ideas (Estabrook)	____	____
Why Men Are Mad... (Maynard)	____	____	Policewomen... (Brouse)	____	____
Power and Control... (Goodwin)	____	____	So You Want to...? (Cornell)	____	____
The Dispossessed (Schachter)	____	____	Respect... (Gottlieb)	____	____
Muscling In... (Reynolds)	____	____	Second Opinion (Shapiro)	____	____
Autophobia (Vanagas)	____	____	Stop the Music (Headlam)	____	____
Living and Dying... (Koehn)	____	____	Integrated Sports... (Rider)	____	____
Math's Multiple... (Finlayson)	____	____	Crowd Control (Colapinto)	____	____
Let the Punishment... (Brickman)	____	____	Saying Goodbye (Cameron)	____	____
Judy (Muhlstock)	____	____	The Making of... (Mohs)	____	____
Deliberate Strangers (Angus)	____	____	Do Computers Change... (Saddy)	____	____
Education for One... (Costello)	____	____			

(fold here and tape shut)

0116870399-M8Z4X6-BR01

Heather McWhinney
Director of Product Development
HARCOURT BRACE & COMPANY, CANADA
55 HORNER AVENUE
TORONTO, ONTARIO
M8Z 9Z9